Wakefield Press

OUR FATHERS

TWENTY-SIX EVERYDAY HEROES

EDITED BY JUDY MACPHERSON KENT
AND ANDREW COLLETT

Wakefield Press
1 The Parade West
Kent Town
South Australia 5067
www.wakefieldpress.com.au

First published 2014

Cover designed by Liz Nicholson, designBITE
Edited by Charlotte Michalanney, Wakefield Press
Photographs compiled by Bryan Charlton
Text designed and typeset by Wakefield Press
Printed in Australia by Lane Print and Post

National Library of Australia Cataloguing-in-Publication entry

Title:	Our fathers: twenty-six everyday heroes / edited by Judy Macpherson Kent and Andrew Collett.
ISBN:	978 1 74305 313 3 (paperback).
Subjects:	Linden Park Primary School (Linden Park, S. Aust.) – History. Fathers – Australia – Biography. Linden Park (S. Aust.) – History. Australia – Social life and customs – 1922–1945. Australia – Social life and customs – 1945–1965. Australia – History – 1922–1945. Australia – History – 1945–1965.
Other Authors/ Contributors:	Kent, Judy Macpherson, editor. Collett, Andrew, editor.
Dewey Number:	920.710994

Contents

Introduction

The idea for this book came from the 50-year reunion of our 1962 Linden Park Primary School Year Seven class, which was held in September 2012.

Linden Park Primary School started in 1950. It was established to cater for the burgeoning new suburbs of St Georges, Beaumont, Glen Osmond and Hazelwood Park, which had been created or expanded by the post-World War Two baby boom and European migration.

These new suburbs were almost entirely populated by young married couples establishing their families after the war. In the main, the houses were funded by war service loans, which offered housing finance to ex-servicemen at 3.75% interest. Thus St Georges was known as 'Mortgage Hill' with, some say, Beaumont called 'Second Mortgage Hill'.

Into this emerging and youthfully optimistic environment Linden Park Primary School was born, contrasting with the surrounding pre-war schools in Glen Osmond, Marryatville, Rose Park and Highgate, which were seen as less progressive.

No other school was within walking distance of Linden Park Primary at a time when most families had no car, so the authors of this book grew up both playing and going to school with their neighbours. Five members of our Year Seven class lived in my street.

Linden Park's enthusiastic beginning was steered by an excellent principal, or 'Master of Method' as he later became, Ray Sexton. The school grew quickly and within the first five years 'temporary' weatherboard buildings were added, which were still there 30 years later. Linden Park quickly established itself as a successful school; such that by the time we entered year three in 1958 it had become a demonstration school designated to train prospective teachers.

As a student who went to Linden Park from 1956 to 1962, I had no idea of the richness and diversity of our fathers' backgrounds or, of course, the place they occupied in postwar South Australian history. However, while talking to classmates over a wine or three at the reunion, it became clear that many of them had great stories about their fathers – and very different ones at that.

As a student I had assumed that at Linden Park we were largely a homogenous group – the only migrants in our school were those few kids who turned up speaking a different language. As these stories show, not only did our fathers come from very different places, they also had very different experiences and journeys getting there. For example, Frank Frolich came from Hungary, Leo Adler from Austria, Danni Leoni from Italy, Stan Joyner from England via New Zealand, Bill Cramond from Scotland and Pearce Perkin from New Zealand. From across Australia, Harold McConville came from Sydney and my father, George Collett, from Perth. Within South Australia, Gordon came from Maitland, Gréham Laycock from Port Augusta, Donald Wake and Colin Dyster from Buckleboo, and Bill Corey from Tarlee.

Having planted their roots in and around Linden Park, few of our fathers ever left. They were married and wanted to create normal lives for themselves and their families after surviving the depredations of the Depression and World War Two. Because our fathers continued to live around Linden Park, most of us stayed at Linden Park Primary School until we completed Year Seven and had to move on to local secondary schools.

So many friendships developed between us. These friendships were easily strong enough to prompt a 50-year reunion. The event was conceived by a small group of us who worked together over a year to track down as many of our classmates as we could. After countless phone calls, Google searches and record checks, 89 of 120 were located. Seven had died. Of the remaining 82, 62 attended a joyous reunion in the Beaumont Bowling Club on 7 September 2012 and a barbecue at the school the following day. For all who came, the experience was profound – friendships were rebuilt and memories revived. The classrooms and desks had also clearly shrunk in the time since we had last used them.

In conversations with Rick Frolich, George Adler and Rob McConville in particular, it became apparent to me for the first time that they had most unusual and heroic stories to tell about their fathers. Hence the idea emerged of compiling a book that would capture and celebrate these extraordinary stories.

Judy Macpherson Kent and I floated the idea of this book with our old classmates and the response has been extraordinary, as have the stories that have emerged and the insights provided into the sociology of our new community. We have been overwhelmed by the fact that 25 of our fellow students have responded so positively and generously in providing their fathers' stories.

Every story provided has been included in this volume. Each is a significant piece of the jigsaw that comprises the background to our generation, who are proud to be called 'baby boomers'.

These stories depict a very different world before the Depression and World War Two and chronicle the remarkable upbringings of those one generation above us. Given that our fathers' stories now reach back four generations from our grandchildren, they span a period of momentous social upheaval followed by the comparative stability of Linden Park life. Our fathers' lives were so dramatically different from ours that it is very important to recognise their critical role in providing us with stability and aspirations well beyond theirs.

What we started with was chronicling our heroes. What we realised was that although many performed heroic acts, many others were ordinary men doing their best to raise their families and give them a better future.

This volume does not tell the equally important stories of our mothers – only because it was the stories of our fathers that were mainly told at the reunion and I wanted to keep faith with that.

There is a similar volume of remarkable stories of our mothers still to be written.

The small steering committee that brought this book to fruition worked with great purpose and good humour. Without Dave Brecht, Di Corey Skull, Rick Frolich and Bryan Charlton, the task would have been very much harder. Without the drive and fastidious editing of Judy Macpherson Kent it would not have happened at all.

We hope you enjoy *Our Fathers*.

Andrew Collett AM

Immigration

Francis John FROLICH
(1913–1985)

by Richard Frolich

It was very early morning on 13 March 1932, the heavy mist still sitting firmly on the huge and fast flowing Danube River in Budapest. My father was rowing in an eight for the Budapest Rowing Club and the crew were off for a ten-kilometre practice row – one they did twice every day.

Dad was 18, and the recognition that he had finally been accepted into the elite university men's eight weighed heavily on his shoulders. The next International University Games were to be hosted in Budapest in 1935, and every crew member knew they had to operate as a cohesive unit of eight, but also work hard to consolidate a place in the side to represent their homeland, Hungary.

My dad was a little more ambitious. He hadn't been rowing long enough to get into the upcoming 1932 Olympics, so with every stroke of the blade he pictured his crew winning in 1935, putting him into contention for the 1936 Olympic Games – the next he would be eligible for.

Budapest was a very sophisticated city in the 1920s and 30s. Its customs, food, hundreds of wineries, and beautiful buildings positioned either side of the mighty Danube made it a small but welcoming playground to the rich and famous residents of Eastern Europe. As handsome as Clark Gable, my father was having a fantastic life. He was a medical student, an elite sportsman, and the son of a doctor … what more could anyone ask for?

Three years of hard training earned him a seat in the eight for the 1935 Budapest University Games. Regrettably they did not win, but their hometown advantage rewarded the crew with third place. The crew selection for the 1936 Olympics was to take place shortly after, and sure enough Francis John Frolich made it into the squad. Somewhere between 1933 and 1936 Frank would be relegated to a four crew for the Olympics. I never really found out why, but my subsequent research in Budapest in 2005 revealed that it may have been to do with equally assertive peer competition for Berlin. Every rower wanted a birth in the first eight.

My emotional assessment of Frank's positioning in the four might have more to do with his Catholic-Jewish background. His father was Jewish, so while not purely Jewish in the traditional sense, I believe he harboured deep-seated anxiety about going to Berlin considering the Nazis and their planned elimination of the Jewish culture from Germany. This was well documented in Europe by 1935, and newsreels showed the worst treatment of humanity in that very country adjacent to Hungary to which Frank aspired to row.

Frank did march onto the Berlin stadium in 1936 with the Hungarian team, representing his country. Unfortunately his four did not make the finals and he returned to Budapest a disappointed man. He was also very anxious after what he witnessed in Berlin; the affirmation of the storm clouds hanging over Europe heralding the threat of German power. Due to his rowing commitments and, I suspect, his good life as a student in those years, he did not complete his studies in medicine. Instead he commenced work in a glove factory in Budapest.

In the late 30s, Tom Playford, South Australia's esteemed premier, was busy scouring Europe for expert technicians in manufacturing. Playford wanted to build a manufacturing dynamo state to meet the demands of a growing Australia, and to diversify from the already rich pickings that the wool and grain industries were bestowing on South Australia.

Frank applied for migration to Australia to escape the impending doom. His application was accepted by a willing South Australian government keen to invest in diversified industry. So, the now 25-year-old Frank boarded the last cruise liner to leave Europe for Australia in August 1939, three weeks before Hitler marched into Poland.

There are many photos of that eventful journey, as people with their cameras had by then started to chronicle everyday activity with great enthusiasm. There are memorable photos of daily parties on the ship, including the customary dress-up to pay tribute to Neptune as they all crossed the equator. For this handsome sportsman, life must have been very exciting, albeit his heavy heart at leaving behind his mother and friends in Europe.

The sophistication of Budapest was quickly lost to Frank when he arrived in Adelaide. There were no coffee and cake shops, there were no restaurants, and there were no European dry goods available for cooking. It was a culinary desert. He didn't overly complain about his shock at lamb and beef roasts, Yorkshire pudding, crumbed chops, and the like, but he knew that his days of fine food, wine and coffee were over. I should point out that this shock resulted in him never eating those foods again after about 1955.

Frank applied himself to his work diligently, setting up Adelaide's largest government-sponsored glove manufacturing business at Prospect. The business flourished, and soon needed additional expertise. He was able to encourage the government to sponsor a worker in the Budapest glove factory to come to Australia to be his lead designer and pattern maker.

Whilst a luxury in the 40s, gloves were considered an essential part of a woman's wardrobe, so the business became a safe landing space for Frank as he began to explore what little culture existed in Adelaide. His looks and charm enabled him to meet many interesting people. Immigrants in South Australia were quite a novelty pre-50s and so fellow immigrants of Hungarian-Jewish background, together with an interesting band of tennis playing, horse riding, and rowing 'Aussies', became Frank's comrades.

He met Greta Ellman Dempster in 1945, the daughter of John Dempster, Adelaide conductor of the Philharmonic Choir, the organist at St Peters Cathedral, and a music teacher at Presbyterian Girls' College and Walford Anglican School for Girls. They married in 1947. The photo of their marriage is quite remarkable, because the fashion of the day was all about Clark Gable and Elizabeth Taylor. They were a very attractive couple forming the image of two Hollywood stars as they exited their wedding church through a tunnel made by oarsmen, acting as a guard of honour while holding their boat blades above Frank and Greta's heads.

By this stage, Frank had, with his experience in Hungary, joined the Torrens Rowing Club, and during the 40s rowed for South Australia at Kings Cup level from 1943 to 1948. By 1949, having given up rowing at 35, he maintained his connection by becoming coach of the Prince Alfred College first eight, a role he held until 1954.

In 1950 the first of his children – that is me, Richard, the author of this story – was born. Two years later a second son, John, was born. As Frank's competitive nature continued, he sought solace and interest in playing bridge, concentrating his spare time on the game particularly when his work in rowing declined after 20 years.

Contemporaneously, Japan had started to become a manufacturing dynamo in its re-build after World War Two. This resulted in many consumer products being produced less expensively in Japan than Australia, and one by one, whole industries started rationalising or closing. Gloves were one of the products affected, and by 1952, Frank was forced to close the factory after 12 successful years of operation, and re-commence work as a fashion agent. He took with him his lead cutter, Anne, as his business partner in the agency as she had been such a strong part of his glove making successes. Anne was also my godmother, and very much a part of our family.

The 50s for Frank were both joyous and hard work. He now had a wife and children, had built two houses to accommodate the family's growing needs, had a difficult business to grow, and had his card playing skills to hone, as he asserted himself into another competitive sphere. By the mid-50s, Frank had a diversified group of friends, who all loved his sense of humour, his legendary parties, and his beautiful wife, who, as an accomplished musician like her father, was the personification of the liberated woman Germaine Greer so formidably espoused in her book in 1970. My mother had already been teaching music four days a week at Presbyterian Girls' College, Walford and then St Peter's Girls School when it opened, had been cooking beautiful Hungarian-influenced meals for her family every night, and was able to meet all the social obligations that their busy life bestowed upon them.

1960 was the next big highlight year in Frank's life. He and his bridge partner, Ron McIntosh, won the Australian Bridge doubles championship. It was an incredible achievement for Frank, and was a defining moment for him 20 years after arriving on Australia's shores. More importantly, the recognition helped his confidence and self-esteem. Mild discrimination permeated Australia, acceptance and understanding of other cultures by the Australian majority was still a generation away, and so many immigrants in those years worked very hard to achieve and make a mark in their new country.

Some had more courage than others. In 1955 I remember Frank entertaining Joe Brenda, another Hungarian immigrant, who was setting up the Katies chain of stores around Australia at the time. He'd come to our home to invite Frank to be his partner in South Australia, an offer that my father turned down. Katies went on to become the first multiple store chain in the fashion industry and was sold in the 80s for millions.

Another younger peer of my father's was Hungarian Frank Lowy and his business partner John Saunders, the founders of Westfield

Corporation. They listed on the Sydney stock exchange in 1960, the same year as Frank's bridge victory. These and so many other successful Hungarians both inspired Frank and highlighted his conservative and not-so-confident approach to life.

So to this end, my father never quite achieved in commercial and security terms the dreams I'm sure he dreamt. But he did raise his two boys to have a decent work ethic, and through osmosis, learn that risk-taking was just a part of life, and to win or lose was simply another experience lesson.

Frank died in 1985. It was a shock to learn that my father had collapsed in Grenfell Street from a fatal heart attack. I was 35 and he was 72, and it was too early to lose my father. His ashes were interred at St Matthews Church, Marryatville, South Australia. Over the years, this became problematic for me. How could a person of Catholic-Jewish descent be buried in a Church of England church? It had come about through my great grandfather who was the pastor at St Matthews from 1900 to 1930.

By 1999, the year my mother died, my brother wanted to spread her ashes on the edge of the water at Moana Beach. This where she was at her happiest, watching us boys surf all day during summer holidays. She'd pack a lunch for our voracious appetites. She'd meet our eclectic group of surfing buddies. It just made sense. So we did it.

Having now lost my mother, I was asking the question as to why Frank's ashes shouldn't be taken back to Hungary and spread in the Danube, where he enjoyed his exciting teenage years and climb to Olympic success. I shared this frustration with a artist Marion Borghelt in Sydney in 2003. She and her husband Leo, who had become a very influential mentor in my emerging life with art benefaction, offered to participate with me on this journey. But, more importantly, Marion decided that Frank's ashes had to be delivered first class.

After a long dinner, she concluded that the ashes should be in a glove, and then dispersed into the Danube. That evening was illuminating, and set in motion an exciting two-year plan. There was a minor detail. As it turned out, Frank's ashes had been interred into soil immediately in front of his walled plaque at the church. This meant I would have to dig for his ashes. What pastor in his right mind would allow this?

Well, after negotiations of an interesting nature, he agreed. One 42-degree day in February 2005, I started digging. Bucket after bucket revealed small quantities of ash and carbon. I took these buckets home and sifted them down to the purest of ash I could get. This was about 300 grams. Then there was another minor detail: how would I get these ashes through the borders I was about to face in Singapore, London, Venice and Budapest? So my creative side kicked in, and I rolled Dad up into small Glad sandwich bags, into the shape of no. 3 corona size cigars. I figured the X-ray technicians at airport security would 'see' them as cigars.

We arrived in Venice in June 2005 for the Biennale. Leo and Marion summonsed us for drinks at their hotel on the Dusadoro one warm evening. Out came the champagne. Marion then presented me with a beautifully wrapped box. I opened it, and inside, were two beautiful hand-made pigskin gloves, just like those Frank used to manufacture 40 years earlier. In the neck of each glove, Marion had sewn and glued an ebony 'trapdoor', through which the ashes could be poured, then closed and clip locked. This was a very emotional experience for me, and shortly afterwards we flew to Budapest.

On the windy Sunday morning of 19 June 2005, we walked to edge of the mighty Danube, said a little prayer and cast one glove filled with Frank Frolich's ashes into the choppy water. To our delight we were able to see it float gracefully downstream, until finally sinking. My wishes had come true.

What happened to the other glove? I gave it to my son, in case he has equally romantic aspirations for his father's ashes.

It has now been 28 years since Frank's passing, and 14 years since my mother's. What does this mean? Well at 62 I see their world then with more clarity today. I look back at the absolute good fortune of my being a teenager in a middle-class family in the 60s, enjoying the huge cultural shift, which moved like tectonic plates. I know that for my father this was very difficult to comprehend.

I look back on my father's achievements, and have great clarity now as to how they have shaped me as a person – my work ethic, my decency, my honesty, and my integrity. I also look back with fondness at how his tastes shaped my understanding and appreciation of food, wine, and a zest for life.

But more than anything, he subliminally shaped two very important things for me. His conservatism helped me to take more risks, and his upbringing of me shaped how I raised my own children and in later years, through circumstance, my two godchildren.

So thanks Dad.

I miss you.

I miss you more the older I become, and wish you were still here to share in my achievements.

Richard Frolich

Richard ('Rick') Frolich was born 2 July 1950. He lived at St Georges with his family for 20 years, attending Linden Park Primary School until 1961, then Prince Alfred College from 1962–1967. Rick was a very involved student at PAC, finishing with representation in the school athletics team, the Cadet Corp as an officer, the lifesaving team and winning a school literature prize. After matriculating, he studied accounting and marketing at the SAIT, and joined Myers as a trainee in 1969. He enjoyed a retail career with Myers, then Harris Scarfe until 1977.

Rick started a retail consultancy in 1978, which evolved into a specialist strategic marketing business over the next 15 years. Married in 1983 to Jan, Rick has two children, Jonothon who works in New York and Danielle who is a director of the family company in Adelaide.

In 1992, Rick joined with Jan his wife in Tynte Street Flowers as a partner. Together they have grown the business into Adelaide's largest fresh flower retailer and digital marketer.

Rick has been heavily involved in the visual arts community for many years, being retired treasurer and a director of the Melbourne Art Foundation, a retired Venice Biennale Council member, a board member of the Sydney Biennale, and the founding chair of the Contemporary Collectors benefactor group at the Art Gallery of South Australia.

Danny LEONI
(1921–2004)

by David Leoni

Danny Leoni was born in the small village of Ronchis, near Udine in north-east Italy. He was the eldest of three children born to Luigi and Maria. He had a happy childhood until he was six when his father left Italy for Australia to build a better life for his family. He was a bright student at school and he and his friends would kick an inflated animal bladder around as a soccer ball as there was no sports equipment. Dad wrote to Mussolini and told him about his poor school that he attended and that there were no balls to play with. Some time later a soccer ball and a letter from Mussolini arrived at the school much to his delight. Dad left school at 13 to earn a living to support his family.

Dad left Italy in 1938 at the age of 17 because there was talk of war in Europe. He was to join his father in Adelaide and work together to earn enough money to bring out the rest of the family. He sailed to Adelaide via the Suez Canal on the SS *Ormonde* in 27 days.

He and his father travelled to Hahndorf to work on a farm and lived in a barn. This is where Dad's first cooking experiences started. They ate rabbits nearly every meal and he would cook them in many different ways. When the war broke out his father was sent to Kangaroo Island to work and Dad was left to fend for himself. He was only 18, had no family support and spoke very little English.

While working in Hahndorf he would make extra money by collecting stray golf balls at the local course and selling them back to the golfers. One day he noticed a man sitting on a stool, painting. The man called Dad over and it turned out to be Hans Heysen, painting a blue gum. Hans Heysen offered Dad a job at his place as a gardener and would often talk to him and teach him English. The Heysens treated Dad really well and invited him to attend their social gatherings. He had a very good baritone voice and they invited him to sing for their friends at their gatherings.

He really enjoyed his time with the Heysens but he found work in Adelaide at Gibbs making pies and pasties. During the war all the young, non-naturalised Italian men were sent to camps at Loveday. Because Dad was working at Gibbs the authorities thought he was a chef so he was sent to cook for about 120 men. This is where his love of cooking really started and he would create a variety of dishes for the men.

Dad met his wife Gemma at this time and they were married after he received a permit from the police. Unfortunately the authorities wouldn't let his dad return from Kangaroo Island for the wedding. After the war Dad lived with his in-laws at Crafers and worked as a stonemason. In 1947 he had saved enough money to buy a small business in Gouger Street. He set up the first continental store in Adelaide and it was a huge success. 'New Australians' heard about Leoni's Fine Foods, a shop where you could buy oil in bulk, coffee, imported cheese and pasta. Olive oil at the time was sold in small bottles at the chemist. Mum and Dad lived above the shop and this is where I was born and spent my early childhood. In 1951 Dad brought out his mother, sisters and brothers-in-law from Italy. His dad joined them and we all lived upstairs together in three rooms. Also at this time, Dad helped set up the Juventus Soccer Club and was their first goalkeeper.

In the early 50s Dad's parents and sisters moved to homes in Klemzig. In 1955 we moved to a 'real' house that my grandfather built at 13 Fifeshire Avenue, St Georges. Dad would have liked to have been a chef but couldn't find the time with such a thriving business and four children to raise. Dad's passion for food was evident and he was asked to compere a cooking program on TV but he declined the offer because he felt his strong Italian accent would be a problem.

Dad befriended Don Dunstan and cooked for him and his friends on many occasions. He asked Dad if he sold wine but Dad said he didn't have a liquor licence. Don advised him to apply for a full licence and after 12 months battling in court Dad got the first full liquor licence in South Australia.

Dad was a successful businessman and stayed in the food industry throughout his working life. He enjoyed his retirement years cooking wonderful meals for his family and friends. He loved spending time at his holiday house at Carrickalinga, which he called '*La Dolce Vita*'. Translated it means 'The sweet life' and this sums up what Dad had here in Australia.

I'm really proud of my dad and admire him for what he achieved. He endured great hardship and loneliness, but he was a survivor, and I'm glad I've been able to share some stories from his life. I find it amazing that he achieved so much in such a short amount of time.

David Leoni

I was born on 19 May 1950 in Adelaide to Gemma and Danny Leoni and lived in the rooms above my parent's shop at 80 Gouger Street (now Lamberto Travel). We moved to 13 Fifeshire Avenue after my grandfather built our house and I attended Linden Park Primary with my sisters Sandra and Nadia, and my brother Mark. I remember friends coming to my house to play tennis and cricket against the back wall, play in the tree house in our olive tree and build billy carts to test on our steep street. I started secondary school at St Ignatius College but finished at Rostrevor College. I really enjoyed sport and played tennis for Beaumont as well as football and soccer for the school. I attended Bedford Park Teacher's College (Sturt CAE) and my first teaching appointment was Risdon Park Primary School in Port Pirie. I really enjoyed my time there and played football and cricket for the small country community of Wandearah. I transferred to Murray Bridge in 1978 and taught at Fraser Park, then Jervois, Tailem Bend and finally at Murray Bridge Primary until I retired in 2007. I married Jill in 1984 and have three step children, three beautiful grandchildren and one very beautiful great grandson. I'm enjoying my retirement, doing relief teaching, driving school buses, driving tour buses at Monarto Zoo, travelling and trying to reduce my golf handicap.

William Alexander CRAMOND

(1920–2004)

by Anne Cramond Sutcliffe

On 2 October 1920, my father was born in Aberdeen in north-east Scotland. His parents were William (Bill) and May Cramond; she was the daughter of a tailor and came from a family of seven daughters and one son, while he was the son of a gamekeeper and had one sister.

The family was not well off, but they were able to send him and his brother Tom, born five years later, to Robert Gordon's College. This school, founded by a rich Aberdonian merchant who had spent much of his life in Poland, opened with 14 pupils in 1750. I'm afraid that Dad did not enjoy his time there very much at all. In fact, playing sport was the only thing that made his time there bearable. He excelled in rugby, and would often say that he could have played for Scotland had he not had polio in his early 20s. He also loved gymnastics. His father didn't help matters much either; my mother recently told me the story of my grandfather marching off to remonstrate with a teacher who had marked an essay of Dad's as 'very good' but had missed two spelling errors. Clearly it wasn't very good at all!

As my grandfather came from the country, it was to the country that they all went for summer holidays. Dad and Tom loved the times they spent at Annie Mack's cottage at Monymusk – their great affection for this place lasted all their lives. When my brother and I were young, we spent summer holidays with his parents in Aberdeen and my other grandmother in Embo (in Sutherland). I remember my father driving my grandparents and us on the annual pilgrimage to all their important places.

One of these was Bennachie, a small hill in undulating country – you would have thought it the greatest mountain on earth if the reverence they had for it was any measure. One of my memories is of Grandpa, Dad, my brother Stephen and me climbing the hill, eating blaeberries on the way, and, near the top, scrambling over a pile of stones that Grandpa said was the remains of a Pictish fort. Dad's brother died soon after Dad, and because of the meaning of Bennachie for the brothers, my aunt suggested that some of Dad's ashes be scattered there, with those of my uncle. So that's what happened.

Because of his love of the country, Dad, on finally escaping from school, decided to study agricultural science and was thinking of taking up forestry. However, in 1940, soon after the beginning of World War Two, he enlisted in the army, and his life took a completely different direction.

Originally, Dad served with the Royal Scots, but he ended up with the tenth Gurkha Rifles in India. India was another passion – he always maintained his contact with the Gurkhas, and accumulated many mementos of the regiment and of India itself. When we stopped in what was then Ceylon during our passage here in 1961, even we as children were aware that Dad was drinking in the smells and sounds of a country and people that reminded him so much of India. For us, India also meant that Mum made curries occasionally – the hotter the better!

It was in India that Dad contracted polio. He told me that he realised that he had polio when, after a couple of days of feeling vaguely unwell, he fell out of bed as he was trying to get up. This was the beginning of an illness, which initially confined him to hospital for a year and went on to affect every aspect of his life. His right leg was paralysed, and his right hand and some facial muscles were also affected. And of course he had the immense difficulty of coming to terms with being disabled instead of a good-looking, physically fit young man.

After recovering, he was invited by his commanding officer to stay at his home in Market Drayton (in England) while he recuperated. When he left hospital, he was told that he would never be able to walk properly again – that he successfully met this challenge was the first indication I had of his determination and courage, as I was much older before I understood the psychological aspects of his disability. He decided that he would walk, and eventually he did. And sport at Robert Gordon's proved very useful – he found that having learnt how to fall in gymnastics helped him cope with the many falls he had while teaching himself to walk again. He ended up throwing his paralysed leg forward from his hip and did it so well that no one would have known of his disability until he was very old, when he needed a caliper. He also had to learn how to eat politely again, as paralysis of part of his lips meant that food would inadvertently spill out until he mastered this too. I don't think that I ever knew how much he continued to suffer as a result of this illness, particularly when he developed post-polio syndrome later in his life.

He certainly didn't let his disability stop him doing anything – he used to play tennis, football and cricket with us – admittedly he couldn't run much but that wasn't a problem for any of us. And he loved walking – on family walks he would be striding ahead as if there were no one else there, while we struggled to keep up! Occasionally he and I went for a long walk. There are two that I particularly remember – one soon after we arrived in Adelaide, when I proudly took him walking in the hills near Belair where I'd originally been with a friend. She and I had taken such important supplies as condensed milk in a tube, and he was good enough to pretend that he liked that too! The other was a walk in the rain one winter evening – we both liked walking in the rain, and we discussed the important things in life, at least those important to me as a 17-year-old. I'm sure he didn't talk about anything that was important to him.

It was clear that he could no longer pursue a career in agriculture or the army (which he had also enjoyed), and his experiences while seriously ill led him to study medicine. During his studies, he found time to take a leading role in student productions; while I was looking through some of his papers I found the front page of the 29 March 1945 edition of *Aberdeen Bon-Accord and Northern Pictorial* which was devoted to the students' revue, complete with a photo of Dad as the comic turn. He also managed to meet my mother, whom he eventually married on 19 July 1949.

After graduating, he spent a year in general practice in Clackmannan (in central Scotland), which brought home to him the importance of the way that feelings influenced illness. This, together with his observation while he was ill that nurses had more understanding of feelings than doctors, influenced him to learn more. And so he began his career as a psychiatrist.

As a result, until I was 15, I lived nearly all my life in the grounds of mental hospitals. This was something that made me distinctly odd to my school friends. My earliest memories of our home are of a cottage in the grounds of Kingseat Hospital in the countryside near Aberdeen, where Dad was one of the psychiatrists.

I think that Dad must have always been ambitious, as next stop was Woodilee Hospital near Glasgow, where he was the superintendent. This was where he obtained much of the experience that helped him when he began working in Adelaide, but from our point of view it was a terrific place to be a child. The house was enormous and we often got lost when we first arrived – but what potential for imaginative, exciting games! And the grounds (yes, grounds) were equally huge – we could easily spend the whole day outside playing, only coming in for sustenance. This was also in the country, which meant we had a bit of walking and bus travel to and from school.

Because Dad lived and worked in the same place, in a way he

was always at work, and I don't really remember him doing very much with us. But I do remember his love of driving – we were always going out for a run, especially if someone was staying with us. One of Dad's specialities was an inability to decide on a good picnic spot – when one was hopefully pointed out, he would always say that there would be something better later on, and at least once we got home without having had our lunch. And of course, in sunny Scotland it was often raining, so we would have our picnic sitting in the car in the pouring rain. It's amazing what you need to invent in rainy climates – I don't know if you can still buy them, but we put our sandwiches on a little tray that hooked over the back of the front seat of the car.

On our frequent trips he would take us to visit old castles and abbeys, as well as other historical places, so that we ended up with a good knowledge of the popular history of Scotland. In those days, there was no such thing as Occupational Health and Safety, and the ruins we visited had no niceties such as safety rails, so we were free to run up and down disintegrating staircases and battlements, pretending to be Sir Lancelot come to rescue a fair maid. I must admit it was a bit of a shock to come to Australia and find that there was nothing old – I did miss the castles.

I sometimes wonder if we fuelled his competitive spirit on these trips, as we would often egg him on to pass the car in front – I thought it was great fun sailing past! Later on, of course, he took me out while I was learning to drive – he was very patient, I must say. I always remember driving into the hills and putting my foot down for a while (those were the days when learner drivers had fewer restrictions) until he gently reminded me that I'd had my fun, and that this was now forbidden.

But I'm getting ahead of myself. One day in 1961, Mum and Dad summoned us to a meeting (that's what it felt like, anyway). They were next to a National Geographic globe of the world, and we were told that we were going to be moving again, this time a long way away. We were asked to point to where on the globe we thought it might be. Neither of us guessed that it would be so far. And yet we had connections here, as Tom, Dad's brother, spent some of the war at Jervis Bay in New South Wales, and one of Dad's cousins emigrated to Dubbo when he was 16.

One of the reasons that they decided to come to Australia was that they felt they could offer us a far better future here. And, since India, Dad had always liked hot weather, so that settled it! He came out to be the director of Mental Health for South Australia, and we lived on Greenhill Road in the grounds of Parkside Mental Hospital. Almost immediately, he set about trying to improve mental health services, starting with taking down the bluestone wall that partly enclosed the hospital grounds; other improvements on the list were giving the patients decent clothes to wear, increasing the numbers of social workers and occupational therapists, and improving the training of medical and nursing staff. We think that the wall coming down was the biggest single factor in changing in the way that South Australians view mental illness.

Where should we go to school? We had to start soon after we arrived, and Mum and Dad asked their new acquaintances for help. It seemed to boil down to a choice between Rose Park and Linden Park, and the latter was chosen, although it was further away, because it was said to be the better school. I don't think we ever rode our bikes to school, but I remember catching the bus, and the excitement whenever the trolley pole came off when it was going around the roundabout at the intersection of Portrush and Greenhill roads. Then the conductor would have to get out and use a trolley boom to reattach the bus to the electrical supply.

It wasn't long before I had two psychiatrists as parents, thus adding to my peculiarities from the point of view of my peers – Mum decided to go back to work, and to take up child psychiatry. Eventually Dad became Professor of Mental Health at Adelaide University – I recently discovered that among his students was my sister-in-law! She is not alone in saying that he taught an important subject well.

His contribution to education and psychiatry continued back in Scotland, because after I finished my science degree in 1970, my brother and parents left to live in Edinburgh. But my father's itchy feet kept everyone moving, and after setting up a new medical school at Leicester University, in 1974 he became Principal and Vice-Chancellor of Stirling University in Scotland. Eventually they decided to return to Australia, ending up back in Adelaide after a brief sojourn in Sydney. My brother had returned separately, so once more the four of us were in the same city.

While they were living in the United Kingdom, I visited them a couple of times. The first time was winter 1972, and Dad took us to a really special rugby match in which the Barbarians were playing. I knew nothing of rugby, a state of affairs that has persisted, but Dad did his best to explain it all, and I certainly was very touched that he wanted to share his special sport with me.

During the second trip, once again in winter, they were living in Stirling. As this is not far from Aberdeen, especially if you've become used to the Australian concept of distance, Dad decided that we would go to see my Aunt Teena, his mother's sister. One thing about his aunts was that you felt they were your aunts too, not great-aunts at all – I don't know how they managed this. Anyway, we set off and eventually got to a point where there was a choice of direction. The way Dad favoured had a sign stating that the road was closed, but he dismissed this as it had stopped snowing some time ago and obviously the sign should have been removed. So off we went up the hill and it wasn't long before we came upon a queue of cars that were stuck. Here the limitations of an automatic car became evident as we got stuck in turn. I got out (in my good clothes!) and tried to push, with no success – Dad ended up reversing down the hill and we continued to Aberdeen by the other route. On the way it was clear that we would be late home and that Mum would be worried, and incandescent if she found out what had happened, so we agreed that we wouldn't tell her anything about our little adventure. Better not to fan flames!

Dad continued to be a teacher, administrator and clinician, and never really seemed to retire – people were always asking him to undertake tasks for which his skills made him admirably suited. In fact, this is the source of an amazing link with Linden Park School, this time through Dad rather than me. In the mid-1990s he was the chair of a State Mental Health Committee and Andrew Collett (whose father is the subject of a chapter of this book) was a member of the committee. They got on very well together.

I think I became closer to him in the last 20 years of his life – before this, we had had a difficult period where we were quite antagonistic. It was hard to sort this out, but he was able to analyse and accept his part in it, and eventually tell me the reasons for his behaviour. For this, I admired him tremendously, as I think that many parents would not have recognised their part in the problem. From then on, we used to have regular lunches that were special for us both, and I have always been glad that I could enjoy with my father an adult relationship, which incorporated friendship.

He had an excellent sense of humour, which ran to clever puns – it must be a family trait, as his father, brother and son also excelled at this (although my brother's sense of humour is blacker). It was always fun to listen to pun upon pun from them, punctuated by groans from the rest of us as we realised what had been said! We had to get used to being teased very early on. Something else that he shared with his father and brother was a love of crosswords – and not the easy ones either. I must have tried to mimic them, as I remember getting crossword puzzle books and working my way through them, and even making up my own, but it was not something that I continued to enjoy.

An unexpected talent of his I discovered by accident – I had always assumed that the way things looked in their houses was due to my mother's taste. However, I was wrong – it was a joint effort – I found out that Dad gave a lot of thought to the way a room appeared from different angles and its overall effect.

My parents, particularly after we moved to Adelaide, always seemed to be doing something with friends, and I suppose must have found it hard to juggle this with demanding careers and children, just as we do. Despite all the moving that they did, they remained in contact with friends that they'd made in each place, and even now people first met years ago in the United Kingdom are still turning up to see my mother. Dad used to enjoy going out to lunch with friends – occasions to talk and share food and wine was a feature of his retirement. And I know from reading many letters that have been kept how much his friends valued his qualities. He was an extremely generous host both with his time and with hospitality.

Among his interests were music, theatre and walking. The latter was the most difficult for him as he got older, but he kept walking to town and back from his North Adelaide home for as long as he could. And there was always music in the house – I remember hearing classical music from their records as well as on the radio, particularly programs such as 'Singers of Renown' with John Carger. They also attended many concerts such as the Musica Viva series. But their tastes also ran to Gershwin and Bill Haley and the Comets.

Because of his work and his disability, Dad wasn't able to do as much with us when we were children, as other fathers seemed to. Looking back, I feel that what we shared most was a passion for reading and buying books. When I was young, I loved exploring their bookshelves, and I would read all sorts of books; we ended up sharing many tastes, particularly history, thrillers and the novels of Anthony Trollope.

Education is very important to the Scots and both he and my mother encouraged me to do well at school – it was assumed by all of us that I would go to university. The only difficulty with that was that I chose science rather than arts or medicine, something that neither of them ever really understood. But I think that, apart from the love that they both gave me, almost the most important thing that I absorbed from them is an insight into psychology.

I sometimes wonder what he would have been like if he had not had polio – I think that this, and the experiences emerging from this illness, perhaps particularly developed characteristics such as patience, stoicism, courage and determination. Then his decision to become a psychiatrist, and the knowledge of people that came from this, gave depth to his kindness, integrity and wisdom.

His abilities have been recognised in many ways, for example, he was awarded an OBE for his work at Woodilee Hospital, an honorary doctorate from Stirling University to acknowledge the importance of his period as Vice-Chancellor and Principal, and he was an Emeritus Professor of Flinders University. But I think that we all thought that the award of Officer of the Order of Australia was important because it showed the esteem in which he was held by his adopted country.

I'm pleased to be able to acknowledge here that my father made a difference to the world he lived in, for example, to mental health in South Australia, and to Stirling University in Scotland.

He died from pneumonia on 7 June 2004. A great friend of his once said to him that his car registration VFG had been given to him because he was a very fine gentleman – I think he was.

Anne Cramond Sutcliffe

Anne was born in Aberdeen, Scotland and emigrated with her family to Adelaide in 1961. After attending Linden Park Demonstration School and Presbyterian Girls' College, she obtained a BSc and BPharm. Most of her work was in hospital pharmacies and she is now an editor in a small publishing company involved in providing information about drugs to health care professionals. This satisfactorily brings together her love of science and of English. She has been divorced and has since remarried.

Leo ADLER (1906–1987)

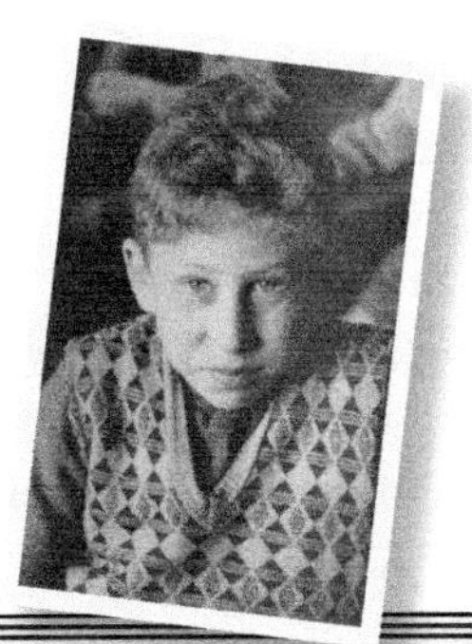

by George Adler

Leo Adler, my father, was born into a world where Jews in Europe were persecuted or at best tolerated. This ongoing anti-Semitism would see him flee Nazi Austria for Australia.

On 31 December 1906 his mother Bertha gave birth to him in the small village of Yablonitz in what was then Monrovia and part of the greater Austro-Hungarian Empire. His father, Rudolf, registered the birth as being the 1 of January 1908 to postpone compulsory national service by a calendar year.

When Leo was still a toddler his, parents, with his new born brother Walter, moved to Laa An Der Thaya on the Austrian side of the border with Czechoslovakia so that Rudolf could take up the post of overseer of a large farming complex.

My memories of Dad's life in Laa are jumbled, out of sequence and not necessarily accurate as I was very young when he enthralled me with stories of his past. These stories, all told in German, captivated my young mind with vivid images of his early life. I will in turn tell you of some of them.

Rudolf, Dad's father, was a *Feldwebel* (sergeant major) in the Austrian Army assigned to the Russian Front from 1914 to the end of the war. Father fondly told me of his dad's visits home during those tumultuous years. How proud he was of his dad mounted on his horse with sabre at his side. How his father had remained non-combatant, refusing promotion so he didn't have to kill. Instead he was in charge of a horse hospital behind the front lines. The pleasure he had as he out-witted a Prussian officer who was obnoxious by giving him a mount that would throw him.

My father's eyes would light up as he told this story. Rudolf selected a replacement mount for this Prussian, which would buck as soon as the reins were held tight. True to Prussian Cavalry protocol the officer mounted, pulled the reins taught and subsequently landed on the ground. Not to be beaten, the officer regained his feet and composure to repeat the sequence. After numerous encounters with the ground the officer then complained to Rudolf that the horse was bad. Rudolf then summoned children who wandered the camp for scraps of food to mount the steed. They held the reins loosely and none were bucked off. The Prussian, somewhat embarrassed, remounted the horse only to encounter the ground a few seconds later. The story went that the Prussian didn't give up till he was stretchered away to hospital.

Father also recalled Rudolf telling him of regularly sharing food and sitting around the table with Russian prisoners of war. He said he felt no animosity towards them nor did most of the Austrian troops he was with. My father also told of how, after the war ended, Rudolf was in charge a detachment of troops on the border where they lived and of the regular exchanges of rifle and machine-gun fire from one side to the other. He recalled how he and his brother at around the age of ten would wriggle up beside the soldiers during these fire fights to collect the hot cartridge cases as they were ejected from their Mausers. He continues to tell how he and his brother got the hiding of their life when their mother found out about these dangerous adventures.

He went on to explain that as he progressed from child to

teenager then to young man, there was a small group of friends who stayed together regardless of their religious affiliations. In particular there were two Catholic girls who made up the mixed group of Jews and non-Jews. They didn't care about the anti-Semitic taunts of being Jew friendly that they were subjected to, they were all just mates. One of them whom I met when she was 90-years-old told me how it was custom that when the girls and boys stripped husks off corn any boy who found pink corn had to be kissed by the girls. She went on to say how my father dyed the corn pink and so attained the extra kisses.

Another story was how he and his mates carried a wind-up gramophone through the streets of Laa in the wee small hours disturbing the quiet village to have shoes and abuse hurled at them, only stopping when chased by the local police. How when his German Shepard, Luxal, stole three fat geese from mother's larder he had used the last of his money to buy three scrawny replacements and how his mother could not understand how the geese could have shrunk but how he had got away with the rouse.

Dad went on to explain how he had fallen in love with Gretel, one of the two Catholic girls in their group and how happy the two of them were when together. Sadly by then the Nazi movement was gaining strength and he and his brother were in regular fights with the Nazi youth. Most Jews just took the beatings but father proudly told how he and his brother took on their antagonists even though out-numbered. He related how this probably saved his life when he was eventually jailed during the roundup of Jews in 1938.

In 1938 he and his brother were jailed in the Laa police lock up for the crime of being a Jew. They were forced to pick up dog droppings with their fingers and do other humiliating tasks between the beatings from their Nazi former schoolmates. Father was beaten with such ferocity by one group that he subsequently lost most of his hearing. He would probably have been beaten to death except for the intervention of some of the Nazis they had fought who said: 'Go easy on them, they are not like normal Jews who are weak but they are more like us and fight back.'

The Adler family must have had a conference before this to draw up contingency plans to flee the Nazis as they had applied to immigrate to Australia. Unlike many other Jews who fled to Poland or France they decided to go long distance as did most of the extended family. Australia was picked for two reasons. Firstly it was one of the very few countries that accepted Jewish refugees and the other was that Rudolf spoke with many German soldiers who had fought the Australians on the Western Front. They had told him that they were the best troops that they had ever fought against and Rudolf said that 'any country that could produce such a fine soldier must be good to live in' (quite a compliment from the enemy).

In 1938 Nazi Austria the plan to exterminate Jews had not yet come into effect and so, if Jews could pay two hundred pounds each, which was a small fortune in those days, and were prepared to sign a declaration on how well they had been treated by the Nazi regime, they could immigrate. This was still conditional that they forfeit all their land and valuables. Luck was on their side as an unknown Egyptian Jew paid the ransom. They were subsequently released and travelled by ship to Australia.

Dad told me of his anguish at leaving those he loved not knowing whether he would ever see them again. His brother and he decided that on arrival in Australia they would put every penny they earned into buying their parents freedom even though they longed to bring out the girls that they had wanted to marry. He explained with a tear in his eye that his parents faced death at the hands of the Nazis but their Catholic girlfriends did not.

They arrived in Australia penniless and set about raising the funds necessary to gain their parents' freedom. Soon after they had landed, Australia was at war with Germany. Both brothers tried to enlist to fight Nazis but were turned away as Australia didn't trust refugees not to be spies.

Dad soon had work in a factory working on war production. He proved innovative, having a modification he had invented adopted so that the hurricane lamp would be less prone to blowing out in windy conditions and developing a method to collect excess solder so it could be reused. As a result he was promoted to supervisor with the extra responsibility of ensuring the plant would be destroyed should the enemy invade. Failure to do so had an automatic jail sentence of six months. The funny part was that another law stated that all enemy aliens, as he was classified, had to head for the hills as soon as invasion was imminent. The penalty for failing to comply was six months mandatory imprisonment. He was so pleased that the invasion never happened.

By 1940 the brothers had raised sufficient funds to buy their parents' freedom and again luck was with the family. Rudolf and Bertha left Laa to be released across the border into still neutral Italy by no other Nazi than Adolf Eichmann. Even though the Nazis were gathering Jews and had started the extermination camps they liked the ransom money more than the lives of two old Jews. Rudolf and Bertha had just rounded the Cape of Good Hope when Italy joined the Axis. But for those few days their fate would have been sealed and their lives ended in Auschwitz.

The family was reunited in Adelaide with all members pooling their meagre resources. Slowly they gained sufficient funds to put a down payment on an old blue stone villa in Melbourne Street, North Adelaide. They lived in a few rooms and sublet the rest gaining funds to help pay the mortgage.

After the war had ended they went into business with the son of the local synagogue's cantor, running a small electrical appliance repair business on Magill Road, Norwood. They had no previous experience in this field but proved resourceful and successful. Sadly their partner was in the till and rather than embarrass the old cantor with a police action, the brothers suggested he leave the business forthwith without the need to repay what he had stolen. The family was again in business for themselves.

Soon the brothers started to expand their business, hiring a trained electrician to do small house wiring jobs. A new switch here, a light fitting there. It was small-scale work but I remember how proudly he spoke about this. As the soldiers returned from the war and were demobilised houses needed to be built and the brothers saw an opportunity to expand as electrical contractors. They contacted several large home builders and for a change being Jewish was not a hindrance but a help. One of the builders was a Christadelphian who were by faith Jew friendly. He gladly gave them the chance to submit quotes for wiring homes. They won the contract, hired electricians and expanded their business.

Father, now in his 40s wanted to marry, to raise a family and to have a normal life in his adopted country. To that end he advertised in the Jewish paper in Melbourne. My mother, also a refugee from Austria, replied and in 1948 they married. It was a marriage of two lonely souls with little in common bar lives destroyed by war. Mother had come from a wealthy family with servants, was previously married into Austrian Catholic nobility and titled, and father came from a poor rural town where they had to toil hard for everything they had. She also had two children, the youngest whom she told father about, and the eldest who she kept secret until after the marriage. I was born in 1950.

In 1952 the family had pooled sufficient funds to gain a loan to buy an old boarding house on the Esplanade at Glenelg. My parents and my younger brother moved in, transforming the boarding house to a bed and breakfast. Mother did most of the cooking, cleaning and supervising staff whilst father dealt with the electrical business. Being just down from Jetty Road the business prospered as Glenelg at that time was a hive of activity with little space on the beach during summer.

Over the years both businesses prospered. By pooling family resources the Adler clan bought more properties, supported each other and grew the electrical business into the largest electrical contractors in South Australia. Electro-Help as the business was called wired a large percentage of new homes in Salisbury and Elizabeth, expanded into Canberra, Alice Springs and for a while in Melbourne. The brothers were an awesome team with great business acumen.

In 1956 my parents purchased a half acre property in Beaumont, a then near rural suburb at that time. Father loved the farm next door, the orchard at the back and the majestic eucalypts that were plentiful in our street. He loved nature but sadly his extreme deafness meant he never got to hear the myriad of birds that chorused every day.

In 1964 his brother died of a massive heart attack, probably brought on by his three-packets-a-day smoking habit. This left Dad devastated, both at the loss of his dear brother, but now at the fact he also had to take on his brother's task of negotiating contracts as well as continuing in his own role of supervising the work force. This was not an easy task, due to his deafness. He battled on for a few years before closing the business. I was too young to take over and he was by then too old and too hearing impaired. Instead of selling his business as he could have, he called in his two foremen – one from Adelaide and the other Canberra – and gave them the Adelaide and Canberra businesses respectively, with all the tools, contracts etc. He told me that he viewed them like extended family. He had taken them on as apprentices, seen them graduate, marry and have children, and he wanted to see them successful. He said it was good to give without expectation of return.

Father was always very generous. He gave to ex-workers funds for operations and other needs knowing they would never repay the debt. He also gave to the United Israel Appeal when Israel was fighting for its survival as well as to many other charities. He always reminded me that had it not been for the unknown Jew in Egypt who had bought his freedom without even knowing him we would not be in the 'Luck Country'. Leo loved Australia with a passion. He loved the outdoors, its rugged nature and its liberty. He instilled in me a sense of justice, duty and the need to fight for the freedoms we take for granted. He said to stand up for the oppressed, not to allow rights to be withdrawn and to help those even if you don't agree with or like them. He pointed out how the Nazis had got away with what they did because the average citizen did nothing to stop them.

Dad loved and cherished Australia's freedoms and would not accept oppression from any quarter. I was with him and his brother as they drove up Anzac Highway around 1960 when they were pulled up by a motorcycle cop for supposedly not giving a stop hand signal at an intersection. This was at a time when cars had just been fitted with brake lights and indicators, and signals with the hand were not required with vehicles fitted with the new technology. Uncle, who was the driver, explained this to the officer who sarcastically asked 'How do you know that the lights were working?' Uncle who had the vehicle serviced the previous day knew they were and explained this. The patrolman refused to accept this and said he would book them with the offence regardless. The officer then mounted his motorcycle and left the kerb without a hand signal, which was illegal. Uncle, on father's instigation, sounded his horn and pulled the officer over. Father questioned the officer as to the law regarding leaving the kerb and noted that the motorcycle was not fitted with indicators. He took down the officer's badge number and said they would report him for breaking the law. They then drove straight to the police headquarters, insisted on seeing an inspector, and reported the incident. The brother's charge was dropped and the patrol officer reprimanded. I asked Dad why he did what he did and he replied: 'Son in this country we have rights. In Nazi Austria we had to kowtow but in Australia we don't and we won't.'

My father gladly took a step back when I joined the family business to be my advisor. He had taught me well and our family prospered but that is more my story than his. Dad was not an overly religious Jew but was very proud of our heritage. He passed on to me that we came from the tribe of Benjamin, that we were directly related to Sigmund Freud's partner, Alfred Adler and that we also had a black sheep in the family who had assassinated a politician in the Austrian government. More notably his father, Victor Adler, had started the first socialist newspaper in Vienna (it still exists today). He was proud of the fact that even though the family had lost everything three times in his lifetime, they had prevailed.

He was proud of his grandfather Samuel who was best mates with the local Catholic priest and how at sermon his friend would often say: 'If only you were as good as my Jewish friend Samuel.'

He was also proud that his father, Rudolf, was a generous man who gave food and money to the poor of Laa regardless of their faith. When I visited Gretel, his old girlfriend in Laa just before she died, she confirmed this generosity to me.

Dad left me with a love of life and this country. He did, however, leave me with the thought that no Jew is ever truly secure in the world. History had proven this over the centuries. His own family had fought for Austria, he had lost an uncle on the Eastern Front, his father was a decorated ex-serviceman and yet when anti-Semitism raised its head they were treated as filth. He told me to love this country but be prepared to flee if you have to. Be prepared to leave everything behind but your loved ones and be adaptable. Don't be too proud to take any job or to live humbly. Try in life to gain as many skills as you can so if you need to flee or if economic circumstances change you can survive. I have taken his teachings on board and they have patterned much of my life.

Sadly in later life he suffered from dementia and in the European way of life, my wife Cilla and I cared for him at our home till he died 11 January 1987. His last years with us were extremely difficult and have clouded my memory of him. He has, however, left me a legacy of knowledge, moral fortitude, duty and a great love of Australia.

George Adler

George Adler, baby boomer, was born 13 August 1950 to Leo and Trudy Adler. He attended Linden Park Demonstration School and later Norwood High. Having completed his Bachelor of Business he worked for two years for the State Public Service Board as a research officer and later conducting all the state government's induction courses. He left the public service to develop the family business and was successful in his career. As well as managing Glenelg Holiday Flats, a 130-guest establishment, George successfully bought and sold properties. He volunteered with the CFS for over 45 years and as an ambulance officer with St John for 18 years. He has been happily married to his soul mate Cilla since 1977, and has two boys. Having taken early retirement at the age of 55 he spends his time with Cilla boating, fishing and exploring the world.

Walter Stanley JOYNER

(1914–2003)

by Steve Joyner

Dad, known as 'Stan', was born in Stonehouse, Gloucestershire, England in 1914. His parents were John Henry and Helena Emily Sarah Joyner. Dad's father worked in the local engineering works and like many found it tough providing for a growing family. Dad was the youngest of four brothers. The Joyner family all originated from Gloucestershire with the first records of James Joyner, born about 1653, who married a Sarah Hornedge in 1674. By pure chance my first child was named Sarah. I had no prior knowledge of my dad's mother's names as I never met my grandparents on Dad's side, or knew of the original 'Sarah' connection in the family history. Dad was chuffed and quite emotional when he found out that his first granddaughter was named Sarah.

Dad grew up at 3 Verney Road, Stonehouse, and recalled it as a real home in all the best senses of the word. Despite many trials and tribulations they had some very happy times and were a home-loving family. Along with his brothers John, who became a pharmacist and ran the Boots Chemist Shop in Rugeley, and George, who became a teacher and moved to Bristol, they were all involved in the church choir. Dad's other brother, Frederick, died of tuberculosis in 1936 at the age of 24. Dad's father died in 1943, followed by his mother in 1954. Dad attended the local Stonehouse Council School. He then obtained a scholarship to go to Marling School in nearby Stroud and later regarded this as 'the most important event to shape my life outside my home indoctrination'. Leaving home in 1932, at just under 18, he secured a student apprenticeship with Ericsson Telephones at Beeston, Nottingham and completed his electrical engineer's diploma at Nottingham Polytechnic College.

The course was over three years and involved one day at the college and four-and-a-half days at the factory from 7.30 am to 5.00 pm, including Saturday mornings, plus evening subjects at the college. Dad joined the Institute of Electrical Engineers (IEE) in 1935 as a student member and was later to become a fellow in 1958. He stayed a member until 2001 after setting up and serving on the Retired Engineers Group SA Branch of IEE.

At the time Dad had very little money indeed and his attitude towards spending and recreational indulgences stayed with him for the rest of his life. For instance, he stated he never smoked or drank in those days. Well whilst I never saw him smoke he did have the odd gin and tonic and enjoyed a good glass of wine or bubbly, but in very limited quantities, as I remember when growing up in the 60s and beyond.

In 1935, when on a job installing a telephone intercom system at Weston's Toy Wholesalers in Sheffield he noticed 'a very attractive assistant was Della Greenwood to whom I became very attracted who would eventually become my wife'. A long distance courtship ensued, as they were only to see each other at weekends on Sunday rail excursions, as Dad was living in Nottingham and later had taken a job at RCA Photophone based in London.

The tempo of international politics was increasing in parallel with Dad's desire to marry and they had originally fixed their wedding date for 3rd September 1939. Life was pretty hectic in

London at the time and the evacuation of children to the country had started and civilian train travel restrictions were being talked about so they decided to advance their wedding. They got married on Sunday 27 August 1939 at St Timothy's Church in Slinn Street, Sheffield, just a few days prior to the outbreak of World War Two. After the wedding they caught the evening train to London and to their first house together at 51 Alicia Avenue, Harrow. No honeymoon and back to work the next day.

During Dad's time in London (1937–39) he would spend his recreational time exploring the West End and history of London. As he was based on the Embankment he frequently went to the Houses of Commons. He undertook further studies and did the Chartered Institute of Secretaries exams in Accountancy, which he noted would later stand him in good stead when he held managerial roles.

In January 1940 Dad started work with Telecommunications Research Establishment (TRE). Initially Dad thought he would have to relocate to Dundee in Scotland as TRE had moved there from Suffolk on the Thames Estuary at the outbreak of war. Dad was lucky to be posted locally, at a smaller civilian unit, at Stanmore. Dad recorded that he went to every radar station from Orkney (islands at top of Scotland) to the Isle of Wight. He also noted that it was a most interesting and vivid experience that he would never forget. Dad mentioned that Della would often go with him on his travels to assist in navigation as all signposts had been taken down as an anti-invasion measure.

Later they were to move to Malvern with TRE. In September 1941 the whole of TRE was moved in three weeks (some 3000 persons) to Malvern Boys College, which had been closed to receive them. Dad recorded that they later found out that Intelligence had suspected that the Germans intended a full-scale commando-type raid on TRE at the next full moon. It did not of course actually take place. Dad was involved with the secret RAF-TRE at Malvern, United Kingdom, where the ground mapping radar was developed.

In early 1942 he joined the TRE team that developed the OBOE, a precision bombing targeting system, which was used in the bombing raids on Germany. In 1945 Dad managed to 'hitch a ride' in a Mosquito aircraft and flew over a 'bombed' Dresden, Germany, to see first-hand the effect of the 'successful' bombing that was assisted by the newly developed targeting system. Dad later confided to Mum that this vision of total destruction did play on him and like many others questioned the futility and brutality of war. I actually have some of the original RAF aerial photos taken at the time showing the devastation of a number of German towns. Dad left England in 1946 to take up a post with TRE in New Zealand on the Canterbury Project, a radar experimental program with ground and airborne radar both on ships and aircraft.

Initially Dad came out on his own by ship, the SS *Ruahine* in May 1946 via the Panama Canal. I have two handwritten letters from 5th and 28th May 1946, each some 17 pages long that Dad sent to Mum back in England while he was on the journey. Dad wrote in extraordinary detail about the ship, the daily happenings, the size of cabins and all sorts of tips and advice to Mum on what to expect when she was on board her ship. Remembering this was the first ship journey either had taken. It would take around six weeks to complete the journey. Also it was the first time they had been apart since they got married. Dad wrote in detail of how he was missing Mum and his young son and how he was looking forward to being together in New Zealand. I recall I counted some 15 kisses on the bottom of each letter. They were truly in love. Mum and my older brother Peter (born 1943), came out on a later ship, the *Akaroa*, which also went via the Panama Canal. Dad's advice on ports of call and shopping spots would have undoubtedly been useful to Mum.

In 1948 Dad joined the New Zealand Civil Aviation Department as Chief Radio Engineer and worked on upgrading/establishing the radar/radio transmitter network around the region. Just for the record, I was born in Wellington, New Zealand, in February 1950, so that makes me a Kiwi of sorts. The family moved to Melbourne in late 1950. Dad's notes show that he, and presumably the rest of the family, arrived by boat, the *Dominion Monarch*. Dad had taken up a job with Department of Civil Aviation (Australia). Here he was involved in the planning of communication and navigational aid systems to meet the post-war introduction of air traffic control on Australian airways.

My recollections and memories of my dad pretty well start when I am about three or four. By this time Dad had purchased a new dark blue Vanguard car and a Bondwood caravan. Our caravan holidays to Lakes Entrance, Victoria, are still vivid, with my brother and me in our bunks and Mum and Dad squeezed into the converted dining table/bed at the front of the van. Dad seemed to always be carrying me over the hot summer sand. I must have had a low threshold for pain.

In May 1956 the family moved to England for a short time, returning to Australia in November that year to settle in Adelaide. Whilst Dad flew there and back the rest of the family took the more leisurely option of going by ship. I remember that just prior to leaving Melbourne Dad sold the Vanguard to our neighbour, Carl Lungren. I can still see Dad counting out the money on the piano in the lounge room.

We all went to England as Dad had to go to sort out his new job he had secured with De Havilland Aircraft Company to develop a Woomera Trials Unit that would be based at Salisbury, South Australia. Subsequently Dad took up the role of general manager of Hawker Siddely Dynamics Australia 1959 also based at Salisbury.

During this period of the late 50s and through the 60s Dad was involved with various rocket testing and space launches at Woomera including Blue Streak, Black Knight and Black Arrow. Dad was also involved with the maintenance and operations services of the Space Tracking Satellite Dish at Tidbinbilla in the Australian Capital Territory that was utilised by NASA and the ELDO Tracking Station at Gove in the Northern Territory.

In 1957 Dad had purchased land at 45 Hay Road, Linden Park, and our new house was built (Bruce Retallick was the builder and A.C. & C.C. Adcock were the agents), so I didn't have far to go to get to school.

I recall that Friday night was a 'special treat night' as Dad always bought home a chocolate for each of the family. A Mars Bar one time, or a Violet Crumble the next.

Despite that fact that Dad travelled overseas extensively, up to three times a year at the peak, he always seemed to be around for us. If we weren't playing French cricket in the driveway we were making things out of wood together, like my first boat. I also recall Dad making trunk calls to England many a night and always asking for a 'call back price'. No emails or STD calls in those days.

Because of Dad's work we were fortunate, as a family, to be able to travel to England a couple of times during this period. At that time I was fascinated with medieval history and airplanes, and Dad was glad to oblige by taking me to see the armoury collections in some of the castles in England and the Tower of London and to the Farnborough Airshow on one occasion.

Dad was always willing to please me. On one return trip to Australia – I must have been about 12 – we detoured via the United States, stopping off in Hawaii. I insisted Dad take me surfing at Waikiki Beach, so he dutifully hired a Malibu board and together we paddled out to the surf. We only managed to catch one wave that knocked us off the board. Dad lost his false teeth and I nearly drowned, only to be plucked from the water by a large Hawaiian surfer who suggested we should have stayed on the beach.

Dad always made sure we had a family holiday each year, which ensured we had some good, and at times, memorable adventures. These included many road trips to Queensland, or back to Victoria to see old friends. One trip saw us attempting to camp on the beach at Rapid Bay. On the first night, the dog pulled the tent down and ran away, resulting in it becoming the first and last camping trip Dad ever took us on. It didn't, however, deter me from later camping and caravanning.

Dad would regularly take me, with my brother, to the Par 3 Golf Course at North Adelaide. We all had great fun attempting to be the next Arnold Palmer. After golf Dad would always drive home, via the AMSCOL shop in Pulteney Street in the city, and buy us all an ice-cream and a bottle of Coca-Cola, a big treat back then.

He was not a sportsman, having never played sport at school, and did lack some coordination skills. This was probably best illustrated by his attempts at waterskiing. Dad was about 50 when he had his first ski. After many attempts and tumbles, he finally managed to get up, but never progressed past double skis.

This was an era of great memories as Dad bought a ski boat and built a holiday home at Riverglades on the River Murray near Murray Bridge. Dad always had a steady stream of visitors from England, and some from France, who were involved in the Woomera rocket launches. Dad was a generous and sociable man and he would have them up the river learning to ski. This involvement with waterskiing would continue in my adult life with my own family and friends.

Dad left the space/defence industry for a few years and became general manager of the small contacts division with Fricker Brothers, a major Adelaide construction company in its day.

It wasn't long, however, before he was drawn back to his passion when, in 1973, he took up a role with De Havilland Dynamics that necessitated a move to Canberra. He then became the manager at the Canberra office for British Aerospace Australia. During this period Dad was involved in the IKARA – anti submarine weapon, that was being sold to the Brazilians. Dad nearly had one final move to São Paulo, Brazil, because of this work, but cold Canberra was to be home until he retired in 1979.

By this time my brother had a medical practice at Mannum, South Australia, and Dad decided to settle there and actually built a new house next to the golf course. Dad intentionally built a large house with plenty of bedrooms, family areas and a pool. This was to ensure that there was always plenty of room for the family to visit and stay. Dad was always busy establishing the gardens and was 'obsessed' with having the clearest, best filtered swimming pool water in Mannum, a pretty mean feat considering how muddy the River Murray water was. He did achieve this. Dad had always been able to float on his back for long periods and seemed to 'doze off', which impressed me no end when I was a child. Dad was still able to perform this skill in his new pool.

Dad took up golf in retirement and was a regular winner of his age group, probably because he was the only and oldest in his category. It at least gave him physical exercise.

Grandchildren had started to arrive, firstly with my brother's three boys and later my two girls. Dad had a new lease on life as he welcomed the next generation. He was always listening to the boys and, as they grew, was often in deep conversation about all sorts of topics and often about the importance of education and careers.

Retirement for Dad seemed to keep him as busy as ever. He became a councillor in 1983 and also chaired the local branch of the National Trust and for some 16 years was involved with the restoration program of the PS *Marion*.

Dad certainly had an interesting life and satisfying professional career. He was not afraid to chase an opportunity even if it meant leaving family and friends and moving to the other side of the world. He died in Mannum, South Australia on 10 July 2003, when he was 88.

Reflecting on what I got from my dad and what I carry with me to this day is varied. There is undoubtedly a continued strong sense of family unity and participation. Also instilled is the need to take up opportunities to advance yourself, particularly in your working life, and to not be afraid to change direction and try something new if certain work becomes unfulfilling. This has certainly featured in parts of my life. The support of a great partner (wife) is immeasurable in all aspects of your life and I count myself fortunate in this regard. Finally to always have some fun along the way, something I try hard to fulfil.

Steve Joyner

Steve was born in Wellington, New Zealand, in 1950. He came to Adelaide with his parents and brother in 1956. He lived at 45 Hay Road, Linden Park, and attended Linden Park Primary School, then went onto King's College (now Pembroke). At school he was a keen rower and was a team member of the King's first eight that won the Head of the River in 1967.

He commenced his professional career in the commercial real estate industry, working predominately in the leasing field with such companies as Jones Lang LaSalle, Knight Frank and Colliers International, and now works in an independent property consultancy firm in Adelaide.

Steve has been married to Lea for some 34 years and lives at Norwood. He has two daughters, Sarah and Amy, plus four grand-children, Sophia, Elsie, Oscar and Jake. He enjoys family and friends and always looks forward to that next holiday or caravan trip.

Harry Pearce PERKIN

(1919–)

by Greg Perkin

Pearce, as my dad is called, was born in Leeston 40 km south of Christchurch, New Zealand, and came to Adelaide as a five-year-old lad. The fact that he was born at all is like so many, the result of fate and coincidence.

My grandfather Francis Henry (Harry) Perkin was born in Devon, England, and as a young lad of ten lost his father to tuberculosis and at 15 was left an orphan. My grandfather and his younger brother were apprenticed to their uncle as butchers to earn their keep. It was while rowing out meat supplies to ships in Plymouth Harbour that my grandfather dreamed of the exotic places that all these ships were visiting. At the age of 21 he followed his dreams and sailed to New Zealand were he worked to earn his fortune so that he could return to England and buy a farm. World War One stirred his patriotic fervour and he enlisted in the New Zealand Expeditionary Forces and was soon back in Europe. He spent time in the trenches on the Western Front at Passchendaele, Ypres and in the Battle of the Somme. He was gassed at Passchendaele, possibly by the British; such is the stupidity of war. He was repatriated to England and while in Cornwall reconnected with my grandmother whom he had known before heading for New Zealand. They married in 1918 in Twyardreath Cornwall, the home of my grandmother, but only after Harry had promised his new mother-in-law that he would return to England in five years' time. They were soon heading to New Zealand via the United States of America, which they crossed in a stagecoach.

Dad's birth soon after arrival in New Zealand was difficult; gran was not a young woman by this time and it was doubtful whether both would live. Those doubts have been well and truly trumped with Gran living to her 99th year and Dad still alive at 93! The result of these difficulties at birth meant that he was an only child.

In 1924, when Dad was five, his father Harry had amassed a small fortune and, in line with his promise to his mother-in-law, the family home in Christchurch and all their goods and chattels were sold ready for the return home to England. News then came that mother-in law had died and the family, having sold all of their possessions, decided to move to Adelaide where Harry's younger siblings brothers Sam and Bill, and sister Win, were living. Before long the tough times of the depression were upon them and both of Harry's brothers borrowed money from the hard-working and frugal Harry. Harry's generosity saw his fortune frittered away and he returned to earning a living operating what we now call delis.

Harry Pearce Perkin was called 'Pearce' as a result of his Uncle Pearce Paynter's tragic death on Armistice Day in Salonika, Greece. As a British soldier he had apparently stuck his head above the parapet to talk to the German enemy on hearing the war had ended. It would seem the Germans had not yet heard the news or perhaps they had heard it and learned they had lost! Whatever the reason, Pearce Paynter was shot dead. His name is immortalised on the church gate in Twyardreath where his sister was married. Their forebears were allegedly the local aristocracy called Treffry of Place House in Fowey, Cornwall, who trace their ancestry to Edward I of England and allegedly King Arthur. I am still to confirm this connection. Stories say my grandmother's family lost Place House to another branch of the Treffry family over a bet for a pint of beer! My brothers and I relate to this.

One of the stoic female members of this family is recorded pouring molten lead onto the heads of the marauding French who attacked Place House and the village of Fowey while men of the house and village were away pirating boats in the English Channel, and attacking villages in France.

From the swashbuckling days of yore to North Croydon it's a long way, but it was here that Pearce lived and went to school, first at Thebarton Primary School then completing his schooling at Croydon Technical High School. The family home had a verdant vegetable garden with a chooks at the end of the yard. Yes 'chooks'! I still feel really peeved at Mrs Brooks in year 4 who advised that chooks did not exist; according to her they were either chickens or fowls. Well not at *my* grandfather's place; he had CHOOKS, because he told me so. I vividly remember Grandpa and his mate Curley sitting in his garden shed going over their wartime stories and life in general. This is my first recollection of what mateship was all about. I still have the army issue knife and canteen that were the focus of their stares during long periods of silence and reflection.

From high school Pearce found odd jobs before gaining a position in the spare parts division of United Motors, handling spares for Vauxhalls and Pontiacs. While working here he trained as a draftsman and won a position as a civilian in the Engineering Services Branch of the Australian Army at Keswick, undertaking architectural drafting. It was in this workplace that he met my mother. He was an avid tennis player and played tennis with the Woodville Methodist Church and attended dances at this same venue.

When World War Two broke out, Dad enlisted in the Army and was posted as a sapper with the 6th Division Royal Australian Engineers who were due to head to Darwin to see off the Japanese. His drafting prowess, however, was recognised and he was transferred to the RAAF and posted to Melbourne to draft designs for the manufacture of Catalina and Kingfisher aircraft. Dad had wanted to be a pilot but someone in the hierarchy considered that colour blindness was an impediment to such a calling and Dad, who is colour blind, stayed grounded for the war. This myth about colour blindness has since been dispelled.

After the war, Dad returned to Adelaide, married Mum and worked as a draftsman for Dean Berry and Gilbert Architects before working for a builder where he learned how to dig and lay footings. My earliest memory of Dad's work is from when I attended a lecture he provided for draftsmen at the Technical Correspondence School where he was involved in designing courses for students. In 1956 he moved to ETSA as head of its building and design team, where he worked for 24 years before retiring in 1980.

Dad was always very frugal with his money, lessons learned through the depression, and he had saved enough to own his own car. As a very young child I remember travelling to Melbourne in the car with a camper trailer. The thrill of camping and travelling has remained with me. The first years of family life began in two rooms at the back of Dad's parent's home in Tait Street, North Croydon. During these times Dad would leave work in the city and travel to the block in Highfield Avenue, St Georges, to build the family home. He had bought the block in 1950 for 420 pounds. Building supplies were scarce and trained labour was expensive so Dad did it himself. He dug footings, poured concrete, built all the kitchen furniture and tiled the bathroom. My older sister Dianne does not remember Dad during these times as he was always at work, whether earning a living or building a house.

In 1952 when I was two-and-a-half we moved to our castle at 52 Highfield Avenue. We still regularly visited my grandparent's house and stayed during school holidays and even more so when they moved to Cooper Place, Hazelwood Park, in 1957. In view of my grandfather's many years in New Zealand we would sit around the piano and sing songs in Maori and hear stories of Cornwall and Devon. In a strange sense it was a multicultural upbringing with stories of life in Cornwall, Devon and New Zealand. That could be one reason I moved to New Zealand in the mid-70s and love exploring the villages and lanes of Cornwall and Devon.

Dad's pattern for living was set by this period. He spent most of his free time building – adding rooms as my two brothers Kym and Bruce joined the family or building a garage or pouring a path or changing a wall. As the eldest boy I had the key role of head labourer and dog's body, spending weekends handing tools and waiting and watching in case my help was needed. I obviously learned a lot from this experience having since built additions to my house in Tusmore, knocked down an old cottage by hand and developed two town houses in the city. I am now also renovating my house in Port Augusta.

In his younger years Dad was a keen cyclist. I remember the racing bike with nickel front forks that was parked in the back veranda. I cannot actually remember seeing Dad ride it but I was warned not to touch it. Unfortunately I had riding in my blood and even though I could not sit on the bike I found a way of riding the bike by squeezing under the cross bar. I think Dad suspected I was riding the bike but in any event the bike was soon sold as times were tough when two brothers joined our one-income family.

Another string to Dad's bow was his musical prowess. He played a range of instruments including the violin, oboe, clarinet, piano accordion and piano. I remember seeing him perform in the Adelaide Town Hall on at least one occasion but unfortunately I did not inherit these skills. He still gets great pleasure listening to classical music. I was amazed as a young child to watch Dad build the cabinet and connect together all of the components and create a radiogram so that he could listen to classical records. I boasted about this in the schoolyard but was not believed because the common view of the boys was that radiograms had to be bought at a shop and could not be made in a back shed! I guess I just filed away their attitude with that of Mrs Brooks' view on chooks.

When ETSA moved its offices to Greenhill Road in Glenside Dad took the opportunity to save petrol costs and get some exercise by walking to and from work. I suspect this regular exercise helped keep him fit and healthy but it also meant that when Dad arrived home at about 5.15 pm he was hungry. Our family was therefore having tea when other children in the neighbourhood were out and about. It made for a long period after tea to do homework and 'do the dishes'. It was while doing the dishes that my sister and I listened to the wireless and were introduced to pop music. I distinctly remember Bob Dylan singing 'Like a Rolling Stone' while I was deftly swishing the tea towel in the early 60s.

Family life followed a standard pattern as four children being raised on one income provided minimal opportunities for out of the ordinary experiences. We did go on holidays, caravanning and camping in the Flinders Ranges and Grampians and once even made it to the snowfields in Victoria. It was great that when we kids were off my parents hands they were able to afford to travel overseas and visit familiar places from the stories around the fire of Cornwall, Devon and New Zealand.

When it was time for me to choose a career I focused on the built environment, mainly because of my experiences as a young boy helping with building projects. It seemed to me that building cities would be an extension of the building experience I had as a lad and accordingly studied town planning as a first degree. My parents were relieved that I had made a solid career choice rather than following a Henry Lawson-inspired fantasy of becoming a shearer.

Like all parents I know, mine were keen to see their children improve the family's lot. All of us attended university and completed post-graduate studies. I know Dad really wanted to be an architect but did not have the opportunity to study at university. I am sure he gained satisfaction in his children having those chances as a result of his frugality and support. I know Dad is proud of what I have achieved and should know that his dogged commitment to the protestant ethic has rubbed off on me and ensured that if it could be done it would be done. The other mantra that I have inherited is that if you can do it yourself, do it. His protestant faith has not made the same impact on me – rather the reverse and I cannot comment on how our politics compare. Despite ongoing chiding by my brothers and me, we still do not know with any certainty whether Dad backs the blue, red or green team. For all the things in common that hold families together, it is the things you don't share that make family a stronger force.

I am thankful for the lessons in self-reliance and self-control that my dad continues to display. I am lucky enough to be able to be a bit more self-indulgent than he could be but I am mindful that such would not be the case if I had not made the most of the grounding and lessons that he provided.

Greg Perkin

At Linden Park Primary School Greg was more usually known as Pegory Gherkin, or the boy with the patch on his glasses. As a result he developed a keen sense of humour, which has proved to be a great asset for his career working with elected members and ratepayers. Greg initially qualified as a town planner and worked in Australia and New Zealand, including a project in Vietnam. Mid-career he added qualifications in management, administration and project management and an MBA, and stepped up to the role of chief executive officer in local government. In the last five years he has combined his range of qualifications and experiences to take a City Making approach in building a harmonious community and sustainable economy for Port Augusta. Greg has been married to Raelene for 40 years with three daughters Kylie, Rebecca and Emily who also attended Linden Park Primary School. In his spare time Greg enjoys bike riding, camping and kayaking (including on Coopers Creek!) as well as visiting his three grandsons Max, Harlowe and Phoenix in country New South Wales.

Legacy of War

Harold McCONVILLE (1919–2003)

by Robin McConville

My dad was born in 1919 at Dapto (near Wollongong, New South Wales) the middle of three children. His father had been the shipping agent for the Illawarra Steamship Navigation Company at Bermagui on the far south coast, close to Eden and the Victorian border. At that time, the coastal railway line south from Sydney only went as far as Nowra, near Jervis Bay, and the road south of Nowra was not much more than a track.

The Illawarra Steamship Navigation Company provided a more comfortable and reliable alternative to the road route, moving goods and people from ports on the New South Wales south coast to and from Sydney. It was known as the 'Pig and Whistle' line. Bermagui was (and still is) a quiet little town that gained an international reputation in the 1930s as a popular game fishing destination. The American author Zane Grey was a frequent visitor and wrote a book about his experiences there. At some stage my grandparents moved further up the coast to Dapto and had a small farm there.

Soon after Dad was born my grandparents moved to Sydney. Dad grew up in Abbotsford, a Sydney suburb on the Parramatta River about halfway between Parramatta and Sydney. My grandparent's house, a bungalow named 'Bermagui', still stands more or less in its original form today.

In 1935, Dad started work as a junior for Meggitt Limited, a company based in Sydney that was founded in the 1860s. It traded in linseed oil and linseed meal, at a starting salary of £1 per week. During the Depression he must have been very fortunate to have a job at all. In 1942 after the Japanese attack on Pearl Harbor, Dad signed up with the RAAF.

I always knew my dad had been in the RAAF. A lot of the kids I went to school with had fathers who were involved in World War Two in some way or another, as were some of the teachers. I think one of the Year Seven teachers was involved with radar, which sounded particularly interesting, but that could be a bit of rusty memory. Once a year the school used to commemorate Anzac Day and we used to salute the flag at weekly assemblies. Some kids' dads went to the Anzac Day march and then on to unit reunions. My dad had some medals, but he didn't join the march – at least not that I recall. In our garage were two large trunks that contained a couple of heavy wool uniforms (my mum was in the services too) that smelled of mothballs and in the house were photo albums full of colour postcards and black and white photos of snow in Canada, villages and churches in England, places I'd never seen and people I never knew anything about. There was also a little plywood tag with a big blue number stencilled on it with a piece of kitchen string at each corner that went around in a loop. It was my dad's POW number that he had to wear around his neck. He'd been shot down over Germany. I didn't think what Dad did was exceptional. I just assumed every kid's dad did something like it, just an episode straight out of 'Ripping Yarns'.

I was in my 20s, living at home in my parent's house out on the edge of Sydney. I mean really out on the edge. I had a full-time job and was studying part-time for a degree. The round trip each day, work – lectures – home, was, I recall, about 70 miles. My brother had gone overseas (to the United Kingdom) and my mum had gone away, ostensibly to visit her sisters in England, but no doubt to make sure my brother wasn't hanging out with hippies, or worse. Dad had a similar commute to me, so although we were in the same house, we didn't see a lot of each other. It was possibly a Friday or Saturday night and there was one of those 1950s black and white war movies on TV, with secret agents being parachuted into France (or somewhere else in Europe) with the scene where the pilot turns around to address everyone behind: 'We're nearing the DZ (drop zone) now. Get ready everyone.'

Curiously, my dad had joined me to watch the movie, which was odd because had didn't watch much TV and it was rather late. When the pilot addressed his 'special' passengers, Dad said, 'You know, it was never like that!' Then he told me how it worked.

Dad was a Halifax pilot in RAF 644 squadron, which was not under Bomber Command, but came under Fighter Command as a Special Duties squadron attached to SOE (Special Operations Executive). SOE was what I like to think of as 'the export division of MI5'; MI5 used to look after internal matters (espionage) in the United Kingdom, MI6 used to 'export' the same affirmative policy overseas (James Bond's lot) and MI9 carried out the special air services operations.

A Halifax was a four-engined bomber, which looked somewhat like the more famous Lancaster, but did not have quite the same performance in regard to speed and operating height. Nevertheless, it was a powerful aircraft and there was a role for it. There are very few of them left, certainly none flying.

According to my dad, prior to a flight the navigator would get a separate briefing from the pilot and crew. The navigator alone would know the destination of the aircraft, the rest of the crew wouldn't. The aircraft would be prepared and the crew (plus navigator) would board and take their places. Then a car (a black Humber) would arrive and someone (the cargo) would be placed aboard. The crew never knew, or had direct contact with, their passenger. If the mission was 'scrubbed' (cancelled), the aircraft would stay on the ground (or return) with the crew at their stations until the car arrived and the passenger (or passengers) were taken off. On these special operations, the aircraft operated on their own with no fighter escort, at low level and in the dark. If the aircraft was shot down, or crashed, there was very little information that any surviving crew could reveal.

Dad was 20 when the war broke out in 1939. I think he was more worried about the Japanese, when they attacked Pearl Harbour in December 1941 than he was about Germans on the other side of the world. Anyhow, shortly after the Japanese attack, Dad joined up with the RAAF. His initial duties included sentry duty, protecting the flying boat base at Rose Bay in Sydney Harbour.

In September 1942 Dad was posted to EFTS (Elementary Flying Training School) Temora, New South Wales, where he got training in DH 82s (Tiger Moths). Temora is about half way between Griffith and Yass. It's an impressive town that, in its day, was the centre of a prosperous wool and wheat production. There is now an air museum there, which is well worth visiting. There were 2500 World War Two pilots that received their initial training at Temora.

Between November 1942 and January 1943, Dad was packed onto a troop ship and sent to Canada. Because of hostilities in the Pacific, the convoy (if indeed it was a convoy) took the long way round, steaming to South America, then north past Easter Island into San Francisco, then on to Vancouver, Canada. Passing Easter Island had an interesting effect on Dad. After the war he developed an interest in Thor Heyerdahl and the Kon-Tiki expedition, which had set out to show that people from South America could have settled in Polynesia.

From Vancouver, Dad boarded a steam train for the trip over the Rockies, via Jasper and Edmonton, then on to Brandon (population 17,000 in 1941) Manitoba, a town about 100km west of Winnipeg in the middle of the Canadian prairies. It gets very cold in Brandon. During winter it can get down to 40 below whether that's Centigrade or Fahrenheit, it doesn't really matter. I flew past

Winnipeg some years ago and, like Temora, the land is as flat as the proverbial billiard table. A Canadian told me that his son had moved out to the prairies and when his dog ran away from home he could still see it from the front porch three days later!

Dad had been posted to No 12 SFTS (Service Flying Training School) where he arrived some time before 27 January 1943 with 60 hours flying time, departing in May for the United Kingdom with 219 hours.

Although the terrain in Manitoba was very flat and there were no hard-centred clouds (hills) to fly into, casualty rates (fatal accidents) during training at training establishments were very high. The SFTS program anticipated and accepted up to 16 per cent, which approached eventual casualty rates encountered on wartime combat missions. Inexperience no doubt was a significant contributory cause.

'Join the navy and see the world' was the recruitment claim for the Senior Service, i.e. the navy. The air force couldn't have been far behind. In late July 1943, Dad arrived in Lulsgate Bottom, Somerset, England (now Bristol airport) taking a couple of months to get there, passing through Toronto, Niagara Falls, Quebec and across the North Atlantic by ship.

At Lulsgate Bottom, Dad received training in an Airspeed Oxford, a twin-engined trainer and was then posted to Tilstock in the Midlands where he had time in twin-engined Armstrong Whitworth Whitleys, and four-engined Short Stirlings. The Stirlings were a big aircraft and I remember Dad telling me that he didn't like flying them because they had a pronounced swing, or tendency to veer severely to one side, during takeoff. They were a big airplane.

Dad left Tilstock with 454 hours of airtime, arriving at RAF 644 Squadron, Tarrant Rushton, Dorset, England, inland from Bournemouth on the English Channel coast in April 1944. RAF Tarrant Rushton was constructed between 1943 and 1944 by demolishing and levelling the two villages of Tarrant and Rushton, then building an airfield over the top of the site. It was on elevated ground, above the level of prying eyes, and was miles from any town or civilisation of any significance. Home once to 3000 men, the base has been decommissioned and has since been returned to farmland. It was built as a centre of glider operations and support for the Normandy landings and later was extensively used during the Berlin airlift. Because of its involvement in glider operations, 644 squadron developed skills in airborne refuelling and after the war evolved to become an RAF airborne tanker unit. The present village near the site now has a population of just over 100. During the war there was only one pub in the area, and it had a dirt floor.

At Tarrant Rushton, Dad got his training on Halifaxes and it is not until April 1944 that his logbook lists his first operational flight. The logbook then goes on to list another 27 operational flights; 18 to France, four to Holland, four to Norway and two to Germany. Interspersed with the operational flights are numerous non-operational flight entries. The Norway flights took between ten and 12 hours each. Withstanding ten hours flying at night in sub-zero temperatures flying an aircraft without pressurisation, heating or sound-proofing with a 13 foot propeller about six feet away can only be a feat of endurance. For the month of May 1944, before the D-Day landings, Dad did 23 flights and one operational flight. Once they got the training, the RAF sure kept their crews busy. By March 1945, Dad's airtime had totalled 889 hours. The operational flights in the logbook included dropping containers to people on the ground, dropping jeeps, paratroops, dispersing 'Window' (aluminium strips designed to interfere with enemy radar) and towing gliders.

On 24 March 1945, Dad was on his 28th operational trip, taking part in Operation Varsity, the Allied crossing of the Rhine River, which involved the dropping of two divisions by parachute and in gliders behind enemy lines to secure a foothold on the opposite side of the river. What happened next is contained in a letter that Dad later wrote to his parents back home in Sydney. I'll let Dad tell the story (verbatim):

Aust. 422630
F/O H. McConville
R.A.A.F. Base P.O. London, England

Dear Mum and Dad

This is an account of my prison life and how I had the misfortune to be there. I am commencing this in a prison camp in Germany a day after our liberation, mainly to fill in time and also because it may be of some interest to you.

On 24th March we took off from one of England's mammoth dromes soon after seven a.m. We were on our 28th trip and the fifth as a glider tug. The object of the 'lift' was an airborne crossing of the Rhine around Weisel. Everything went well till an oil filter burst in the port inner engine and I had to 'feather' it and continue on three. The aircraft handled very well but the speed was reduced and by the time we reached the Rhine, I believe we were last in the stream.

About 10.45 am we crossed the Rhine and were then over enemy territory. The real release point was less than ten miles past the river but the area was full of enemy light flack guns and we were hit numerous times by machine gun fire without suffering any apparent damage. We released our glider at the specified point and turned back for base. As we turned there was a terrific thud directly below me in the wireless operators compartment. Fortunately Ken was not there and was sitting beside me in the second pilot's seat. In a few seconds the plane was on fire, one in the wireless operator's compartment and another in the fuselage around the oxygen bottles. The crew attempted to extinguish them but reported them out of control. It was evident that nearly all the crew would be burnt before we reached the Rhine and those remaining in a safe position would have their escape cut off by fire so I told everyone to bail out.*

The jump was carried out very quickly and everyone got out of the plane. I went last and received slight burns on the hand and neck. The plane continued a short distance and then blew up. All the crew considered themselves extremely lucky to be out of it. I imagine the oxygen bottles burst to cause the explosion.

I pulled my ripcord rather quickly than the text book method but it opened smoothly and didn't jolt. It was a very pleasant sensation and quite peaceful for a while. As I moved slowly down someone on the ground commenced shooting at me and I tried to manoeuvre the 'chute around. I noticed then that it was only clipped in one catch and not two. That didn't seem to make any difference. Fortunately the shots all missed and very soon I neared the ground. The ground came up very quickly and once again doing the unorthodox I hit the ground without any jar.

Before I could release my chute two Germans were beside me with automatic guns. They were terribly excited and were evidently cursing me. I gathered also they wanted my revolver which I was carrying inside my tunic. They took off my mae west, tunic, collar and tie to search me and threw the lot away and forced me to double march ahead of them with my hands up. Red came down in the same field before me and shared the same fate except that his captors returned his tunic. These men belonged to a German Paratroop Regiment who were now fighting as infantry due to the lack of planes in the Luftwaffe. They handed Red & I (sic) over to some men on a Jeep and they took us to several first aid posts where my hand and neck were dressed. None of the others were injured but at that stage I had only seen Red.*

After a very short attempt to interrogate us they gave it up and we were sent back to a barn a few miles from the front line. Our morale was very high as we considered the Allies would overrun the place in a day at the outside. Here we spent slightly longer than a day and left on the Sunday afternoon much to our disappointment. During our stay we had spent several hours talking with our guards through a German soldier aged seventeen who had lived in America till he was twelve. We learnt from them they fully expected to lose the war and that they would desert at the first opportunity some of the prisoners attempt to persuade them to surrender immediately but they said they were afraid of their officers and of what would happen to their relatives. Most of these boys were under twenty and were the best I have met of this sheep-like people. Many of the boys had once belonged to the Luftwaffe as aircrew and were terribly disappointed at their transfer to the Army.

Our move was only to have been a few miles but as we neared the other town the Allies began shelling it and several landed within a few hundred yards of us. The guards then handed us over to some official and he and the Volkstruum (German Homeguard) took us some eight hours travelling that night. We spent half the time walking and half in a huge motor truck. On this journey we saw how short of fuel the Germans were and the terrible situation of the transport. In fact during my whole stay in Germany, I have never seen a thing to impress me, everything is old and worn out. The cities are wrecked and very few small towns even have not been bombed. People are still carrying on the war because no one will tell them to stop and Germans never think for themselves.

That night, Sunday, we stayed in another barn which was serving as a collection centre. They didn't give us any food and in the first forty eight hours of capture I had a thin slice of sausage and some black bread. We were thoroughly searched again on Monday morning and as usual the vultures took everything of value from us. I forgot to mention our wrist watches were stolen within a few minutes of our capture.

At nightfall the Home Guard commenced to march about a hundred of us off after giving us barley soup. We moved eastward the whole time and that night we covered 40 kilometres or 25 miles. It took us 12 hours but we had the satisfaction that the guards were more tired than us. We walked through several cities, some still with fires from the bombing and without a single building intact. Once the guard had to use a compass to get through, the roads being indistinguishable from the buildings. At seven in the morning we reached our objective a small town some 23 kilometres from Munster. Already they had a large batch of prisoners from the same offensive and we were delighted to find Jock, Ray and Bob amongst them. What happened to Ken, I don't know yet but hope he managed to reach our own lines.

This place was slightly better organised and as usual we were searched. The 'hangers on' taking even articles of clothing this time. We spent Monday night 26th sleeping in a hay loft there and all day Tuesday, our only rations being a daily bowl of soup and black bread.

On Tuesday we moved off again. As usual at night the Germans are so afraid of the Allied Airforce that all transport and movement is done at night near the front. Red and I were separated from the others and put with a party of twenty officers. Fifty of us were herded then into a goods truck and for three days we lived like sheep with barely enough room to sit down let alone lie down. Water was another problem and as usual the Huns didn't bother to give us any. We complained but they would do nothing for us.

The trip was a nightmare but uneventful and we were even pleased to reach the prison at Falingbostel. Things were organised here but very crowded, it wasn't an officers camp but thirty six of us shared one room and were better off than the men. Beds or bunks were three deep and that gave us enough room in the centre. Food consisted of 1 loaf of black bread between seven, 1 bowl of soup, 4 potatoes, a little margarine and sugar each day. We received a half Red Cross parcel each week and with this managed to live fairly comfortably for a week. The camp contained some of every race in Europe and had some 15,000 prisoners. The Russians received shocking treatment and were starving. Russia is not a member of the International Red Cross and they do not receive parcels. We couldn't give them any of ours as we felt hungry and weak ourselves. Not once during my 23 days as a prisoner did I finish a meal without still feeling empty.

*For a week we remained in this compound and each day heard the news of the Allied advance. Apparently someone had a radio in the camp. Then on Saturday just as the Allies were apparently within reach the Germans attempted to move the 150 officers on camp to an Offlag (Officers Prison) near Brunswick. We left in parties of thirty and our party caught a train from Fallingbostel** to Soltau** around six in the evening. Half way there the train stopped at a small village and everyone in the train dashed out into the open country for cover – Typhoons were circling and the Germans fear them more than anything else. Our guards took us out as well. This happened twice.*

The second alarm was only a few minutes later and this time the Typhoons attacked the village where the train stood. They swooped down from about five thousand feet with guns blazing and straight through the German flak. At a thousand feet the leading plane released its rockets and at the same time the other three Typhoons broke off from their dives. Just then I saw two German planes streak past at tree top level. They had been hoping to catch all four Typhoons from the back at the bottom of their dives. Since the Typhoons had noticed them the Germans lost the advantage and the next day I saw the wreckage of a FW190 a few miles away.

As we returned to our train a German Warrant Officer came up to our guard and heatedly told him that we prisoners should all be shot or left locked in the train to be shot by our own planes. Fortunately the guards had no intention of shooting us but I was thankful the train passengers had not been injured as then I am sure we would have been shot.

Eventually we reached Soltau to find it too had been attacked by Typhoons that day. People were still very excited about it and as we passed through the subway someone started shouting to the crowd to kill us. Most of the people were too anxious to get clear of the railway station to worry about us and our guards took us away to the police station where we spent the night in an icy cold deep shelter. No-one could sleep and I think that day and night Saturday 7th April were the most unpleasant of my life.

About six Sunday morning we went to the railway station again and learnt the line had been permanently destroyed. The escort decided we should return to camp and we volunteered to walk the 15 miles rather than wait for a train. Since the previous nights experience we had lost all desire to travel by rail, especially during the day. We eventually arrived in camp all very tired and pleased to get off the road. The guard told us they had decided against moving us since there were only thirty officers left in the camp. Where the other 120 went to I probably will never know. We learnt the NCO's had been moved out that Sunday morning and were marching eastward.

The following week passed very slowly each day with fresh rumours and we would hear gunfire quite plainly. Then on Sunday night the 15th April the Commandant sent word down that we officers were to be moved out by truck that night. It was a shock to all of us as we were certain they were prepared to allow the Allies to overrun us. The move was to be at nine and about eight, twenty of the officers broke through the fence separating us from the main camp and disappeared into the masses. We all changed into Army Privates' uniforms and there wasn't much chance of the Germans finding us. Ten stayed for some reason and were moved on to Lubeck that night. What we didn't know was that the Germans were evacuating, and if the others had known this I am sure they would have cleared out as well. That night I slept with some Privates. Red has a better story, he was hidden by the French in a cellar under one of the huts.

On Monday morning the seventeenth we woke to hear machine guns all round the camp and concluded the camp would be captured that day. About nine there was a stampede to the gate and the news soon spread that the British tanks were at the gates. The guards offered no resistance and the scene that followed was one I shall never forget. Old men were crying with happiness and the cheers went up as each tank rolled by. The 7th Armoured Division were almost as pleased as us.

The organization had secretly been set up in camp for weeks and they took over immediately. We moved into the German administration quarters where we have a very comfortable room in which three of us share. The pantry was well stocked and for days we have been doing nothing but eat. We feel much better now and ready to leave whenever our turn comes. Most of the men have been here for years, some over five and of course they get priority.

On Tuesday night a padre from the 7th Armoured asked four of us to dinner at their mess, it was up near the front line but far exceeded our expectations. We had roast chicken and champagne. It was wonderful for us after those three weeks of the barest necessities (mainly dandelion soup).

I hope I haven't given you the impression that we had a terrible time. It wasn't very pleasant, however we came through very lightly compared with others. We now realise what others went through and have seen prisoners starving and dying of malnutrition. Those seriously wounded had little chance of living as the Germans had no medical supplies. I am very thankful that my burns were slight and healed in a few weeks. In all it has been a great experience and one I shan't forget. We lived with some brave men and it would take too long to tell you about them. Nearly everyone had an interesting story. The army captain whom I met the first day had been surround (sic) in a house and managed to shoot seven before he ran out of ammunition. Two Dutch officers from their underground army, some young French marines, one whom (sic) had escaped to Spain at the age of seventeen and was put in prison. Another French airman whom (sic) had buried his dead comrades and burnt his plane, only to be beaten and had his jaw broken by the Germans who had caught him doing that.

In a few days I will be returning to England and will be pleased to leave this country for I dislike the people and never want to return. They are attempting to create the impression of a misunderstood race dictated by a minority of Nazis. However I have seen their cruelty and had dozens of first-hand accounts and know they are all the same. I feel sure they will never again be given a chance to wreck Europe.

So far I haven't heard anything of Ken and sincerely hope he is back at base. The NCO's are still out on the road somewhere east of here but should be safe even if hungry. What will happen to us on return, I don't know and hope I can get repatriated. I am sorry for the worry I must have caused you but there wasn't any way I could advise you before I did.

Your loving son, Harold
20th April 1945

p.s. This account is just for the family and we have been warned against giving away information to newspapers

* 'Red' refers to David Locke, Dad's navigator. Red was a Welsh national with rather firm views about the future destiny of Wales, which did not necessarily include continuing unity with England. Despite this outlook, David remained in the RAF until his retirement, becoming a Wing Commander. Ken [Bruce] the wireless operator, alas did not survive the day. He was shot from the ground while descending on parachute, as were many paratroops. After the war Dad went to visit Ken's parents who lived in Sydney to let them know what had happened.

** Fallingbostel is now known as Bad Fallingbostel. Soltau was not clear in the handwriting, but the town of Soltau is near Fallingbostl.

At some stage during the war Dad was decorated ... by the Americans! He received the American Air Medal. As I understand it he was towing a glider containing American paratroops at the time when it was hit by flak from the ground and became uncontrollable. Dad tried to maintain flight but either the towing line parted or it was released and the glider crashed. I tried to find out more information, but the records archive in the United States where the World War Two details were stored was destroyed by fire in the 1950s, before they could be microfiched or digitised.

By 27 April, Dad had been repatriated to the United Kingdom, and in May, married my mother. Mum told me that Dad had deferred any wedding plans until hostilities had ceased. Apparently he had seen a number of airmen who had been badly burned, and that worried him a lot.

My mum was in the Wrens, the Royal Women's Royal Naval Service (WRNS). I know she was based for a period of time on the Isle of Man and worked as a clerk for an eye specialist who used to assess the vision of naval recruits. How on earth she met my father, I never found out given that they would have been such a long way apart. As they say, what happened on the Isle of Man stayed on the Isle of Man.

I wonder how things would have turned out if he had been posted to the north of Australia instead.

Dad returned to Australia soon after the war and my mother followed by ship in 1946. After he was demobbed Dad rejoined Meggitt and was transferred to Adelaide to manage Meggitt's South Australian branch, located in Port Adelaide. Both my brother and I were born in Adelaide so we didn't get to know much about Dad or Mum's parents. I have a very recollection of the family flying to Sydney (before I had started kindergarten) and staying at the Abbotsford house. I think that the occasion might have been my grandfather's funeral. Dad's mother visited us in Adelaide only once, so I didn't get to know her particularly well. My mother's parents lived in the United Kingdom and never came to Australia at all.

At first we lived in fibro 'trust home' in Brighton, then Dad built a house in St Georges that we moved into in the early 1950s. There must have been a big building boom on at the time, because there were only a few houses where we lived at first, and over the next few years the street steadily filled up. I went to Linden Park from 1955–1960.

Dad busied himself with work and expanded the South Australian business significantly. School holidays were often taken up with travel to the Naracoorte and Mount Gambier region to visit farms and look at crops and see the harvesting being done. Knowing Dad, I think he liked to maintain something of a personal touch with the farmers and their families.

After hours Dad spent a fair bit of time with Legacy. He used to attend regular meetings at Legacy House in the city and possibly held some kind of administration role there because I remember that the dining table at home was often covered with piles of newsletters, envelopes and sheets of stamps and my brother and I had the job of putting all the stamps onto envelopes while Dad folded up the newsletters and put them inside.

Once a year there was a Legacy camp at Clarendon on the banks of the Onkaparinga River. Dad and a whole lot of Legacy volunteers used to go up there every year about a week before and put up tents on pre-prepared sites. From appearances the Clarendon site was possibly a former army camp because there were a number of permanent buildings already there, one of which housed commercial-size kitchen equipment. The whole idea was to provide the children of servicemen (and women) who didn't return with at least some form of Christmas holiday.

In 1965 the family left Adelaide and moved to Sydney. The introduction of decimal currency in 1966 saw me starting at a new school. Dad was already at work in a management position, still with the same company, this time setting up a new manufacturing site out near Parramatta. The Legacy days were over and now

Dad was into Rotary, doing work for local projects and exchange students. Gradually we were going our own ways. My brother was planning to go overseas and I was headed into more years of study. After a few more years, Dad retired with Mum up to the New South Wales north coast where they lived until health issues brought them back to Sydney.

Mum died in 1997 after a long illness and Dad died in 2003. Dad visited Mum every day while she was in aged care and I used to go and see them both on weekends.

In 2005, I was in Canada and met up with some of the Canadians who had been in 644 Squadron with Dad. I had been in contact with these guys for a couple of years because one of them was the unofficial historian for the squadron and had just completed a book on the squadron's history. An aircraft that had belonged to 644 Squadron and Dad had flown on one occasion had been recovered from a lake in Norway and restored was being installed in a museum just outside of Toronto. All of the people I spoke to who remembered Dad said the same thing, 'he was a real gentleman'. That's how I remember him too.

Robin McConville

Robin is the younger of two brothers who both had their early schooling at Linden Park Primary School. Thank you teachers all.

Robin completed a B.Sc. in Sydney with a major in microbiology, then spent 35 years working in different sectors of the pharmaceutical, chemical and cosmetic industries. He is retired and still lives in Sydney. Forsaking scuba diving after 20 years (he decided one day that he had been cold and wet for the last time), he has sailed from Sydney to Hobart and across the Atlantic Ocean, from Portugal to Barbados. At home, he spends his time cycling or 'mucking about in boats', rather large ones.

Robin's brother Andrew and his wife Gayle live in coastal Queensland.

George Selwyn COLLETT

(1924–2013)

by Andrew Collett

George Collett was not a captain of industry, community leader or war hero. He did, however, run his own small business for 30 years where he was highly respected, contributed substantially but with modesty to his community, and played his part in World War Two. At the age of 17 he joined the British Merchant Navy as a cadet, sailed in the treacherous mid-Atlantic convoys for three years until the end of the war in Europe and was home in time to celebrate his 21st birthday. Until Alzheimer's disease took hold of him in 2006, his life revolved around his family and friends. He made friends effortlessly and continued to nurture those relationships.

George was born in Perth in 1924 – the third of four sons born to Harold Collett of Perth and Muriel Tipping of Bunbury. Harold served in the 32nd Battalion AIF in World War One. At Fromelles in France on 19 July 1916 he led his platoon across No Man's Land, secured the first two lines of German trenches only to be captured in the counter attack staged by the 6th Bavarian Reserve Division – which included a corporal Hitler.

Harold spent the next two years in prison camps in north-west Germany before being repatriated to Holland in 1918. His POW experiences – including the stigma of capture and rheumatic fever contracted when his gaolers punished him by standing him in the snow for three days – left him with very strong views about the legacy of war and whether any of his four sons should ever enlist for service in the next war.

Harold and Muriel brought their family from Perth to Adelaide in 1930 and found a way to send them all to St Peter's College. Harold had worked with the Perth firm of wholesale haberdashers, Goode Durrant, since 1911 when he commenced as a storeman. In 1930, given the prevailing economic conditions, Goode Durrant merged with an Adelaide draper, Mr Murray. Harold was told that his only prospect of continuing employment was to come to Adelaide to manage the new business.

George enjoyed his time at Saints. He did well in maths and German. His German teacher, Werner Hebart, taught me 25 years later. The Collett family had no car, which made the boys self-reliant. George's fondest memories of his early teenage years were of their Boy Scout excursions, weekend jaunts and camping holidays in the Adelaide Hills on their 'pushbikes'.

World War Two impacted on George long before he joined up. His Scoutmaster for the First Fullarton St Chads troop, Tom Robins, enlisted at the outbreak of war – leaving the troop without a Scoutmaster. At the age of 15 George and two others took on the role, giving rise to many happy times and fostering George's talent for organisation.

George's oldest brother Doug tried to enlist in the RAF as soon as he turned 18 but Harold, by now heavily involved in Legacy, was adamant that he would not give his parental consent. So Doug waited until his 21st birthday, when parental consent was no longer required, and joined up immediately. After the second son, Clive, made it clear he would do the same, Harold relented and allowed

George to join the British Merchant Navy even before he turned 18. George had developed a love for the sea so this enabled him to serve at sea earlier than the Australian Navy would permit.

In June 1942 George signed his indentures as an apprentice officer with the Australind Steam Shipping Company Ltd – a British merchant shipping line with whom his uncle, Herbert Parkes had served 30 years previously. Before the war, the company plied much of its trade around the Australian coast and consequently named some of its ships after Western Australian coastal towns, including the *Australind*, the *Ardenvohr*, the *Ashburton* and the *Armadale* – on which George served. The *Armadale* was a small, slow cargo ship of 5066 gross tonnes, which made a maximum 12 knots.

Life for the most junior crew member of a small merchant ship was difficult and lonely. George was given the midnight to 4.00 am watch at the wheel where he staved off sleep, loneliness and boredom by pretending the ship's wheel and compass were brass band instruments on which he could belt out a tune. He spent much of his spare time in the company of the Chinese cook who taught him how to cook and to improvise with very limited ingredients. He was even more fortunate to have been taken under the wing of the third mate, the jovial John Allez, a Guernseyman. In time, this gave rise to the most tender of George's very many lifelong friendships.

The *Armadale* travelled the world carrying cargoes of wartime goods and materiel, including armaments. Liverpool was its home port but it sailed to ports all over the world including Basra, Abadan, Port Said, Haifa, Calcutta, Capetown, Freetown, Glasgow, Colombo, Vizagapatam, Port of Spain, Gibraltar, Halifax, New York, Galveston, Aden and Mombassa. The *Armadale* even made it back to South Australia on one occasion. George describes seeing a solitary man standing at dusk on the Wallaroo jetty as the ship came to – only to realise his father Harold had caught a train from Adelaide to meet him.

For a 17-year-old, the Merchant Navy in wartime provided unparalleled opportunities for travel and experience. George certainly saw it this way. His wartime service was perilous, but not by reason of conventional combat. His was a peril over which he had no control and no capacity to defend himself.

The *Armadale*, as a slow ship steaming across the North Atlantic in large convoys, tried desperately to keep up. These convoys, and particularly the slower ships, were easy prey to the many German U-boats tasked to destroy the convoys carrying cargoes vital to the allied war effort. All merchant mariners lived in dread of the U-boats. George described how one night in mid-Atlantic the ship next to his in the convoy suddenly exploded – hit by a torpedo – with all lives lost.

On another occasion the *Armadale* was in a line of 15 ships waiting outside Haifa harbour to unload its cargo. When the first ship had discharged its load of oil and started its engines, the sound detonated an acoustic mine below her. There was a violent explosion and the ship, a tanker, broke in half showering the next two tankers in burning oil and causing them to explode. The next ships, the *Armadale* and a Russian minelayer were very lucky to get away without also exploding.

George saw his career post-war as an officer in the Merchant Navy. In 2008, when I was cleaning out Mum and Dad's house as they moved into a nursing home, I came across two 1945 letters which summarised his naval career.

The first, dated 23 February 1945 was from the Australind Steam Shipping Company advising him that he had passed his final exams extremely well and was to be taken on as an officer, and considered for an Award of Merit. The second, however, dated 10 May 1945, ended his naval career. It was sent by the Ministry of War Transport, which had recently conducted his medical examination for an officer. The letter advised that he had been deemed medically unfit by reason of colour blindness. The ministry offered him the opportunity to attend a further eye examination 'on payment of a fee of five guineas provided that you bring with you a friend (who may be an ophthalmic surgeon) to witness the examination'. George had neither a lazy five guineas nor an ophthalmic surgeon friend.

Thus the young sailor who had manned the midnight to 4.00 am watch for most of the war was deemed not fit to sail. Devastated, he joined the queue at Australia House looking for a berth back to Australia. The clerk at the counter asked his name and, without looking up, said, 'Not Harold Collett's son? I was a prisoner of war with him in Germany.' George had his passage confirmed within days and was back in Adelaide in time to celebrate his 21st birthday. Back at home, George did not take up the Australian government's offer to retrain, unlike his oldest brother Doug. Instead, he obtained employment in Adelaide as a shipping clerk.

In 1949 he married Peggy Andrew. I was born in 1950, followed by my sister Diana in 1955.

George commenced building a house funded by the War Service Loans Commission in Craighill Road, St Georges in 1953. This was our family home for the whole of Diana's and my childhood. Fellow Linden Park students lived nearby, with Robin McConville next door and Rick Frolich and Michael Kryvoviaza further up the street.

In 1954 George joined his father-in-law Burns Andrew in business as a manufacturer's representative and indentor – or agent in common parlance. They represented Australian and overseas manufacturers of goods (ranging from electronic components to German pencils) who did not have an Adelaide office.

In 1962 George and his close friend and colleague Jack Cant went out on their own, commencing business in Halifax Street under the name Collett and Cant Pty. Ltd. Their long partnership was respectful, affectionate and productive. For the ten years after his retirement in 1980 Jack held the position of office gardener with charm and great humour. At the same time George coaxed his father Harold out of retirement to be his storeman as well as employing several nephews.

George was an old style businessman where his word was his bond, and integrity and friendship were far more important than profit. George retired at 70 in 1994 to spend more time in the new house, which he and Peg had commissioned on the esplanade at Port Willunga.

George's pre-war and wartime experiences forged a self-reliant man of simple pleasures and instinctive warmth and generosity. His self-reliance extended to doing much of the building and all of the maintenance of our house, along with establishing a full vegetable garden at Craighill Road. He was the only one of his friends who did this. The garden's produce, doused in George's secret recipe chicken manure fertiliser, regularly included onions, potatoes, string beans, capsicums, zucchini, grapefruit, passionfruit, peaches, apricots and nectarines. The ongoing competition for space in the backyard between George's fruit and vegetables, Peggy's roses and hydrangeas and my cricket pitch was intense.

George's simple pleasures were dominated by fishing. He loved everything about it, except actually eating fish! So Christmas holidays were generally spent fishing at Port Willunga. Eventually with John Nolan he built a boat, a Heron class wooden sailing dinghy. He never rigged it with sail but attached the smallest Mercury (3.9 hp) outboard motor. The Heron needed at least two people to launch it and manage the surf at Port Willunga. So when no one else volunteered to go, I was conscripted. I vividly recall sitting in its bow turning green from seasickness with George blissfully fishing in the stern, leaning forward conspiratorially and shouting, 'This is living, pal!'

Family and friends were of the utmost importance to George. I was supported in whatever I chose to do – even if our politics differed – which they did in spades. From when I was aged eight until about 25 he was always out watching my sport, and often coached our lacrosse team. So average was my sporting prowess that George and his father Harold were often the only spectators. When I renovated my house and later established a vineyard George was always there to help.

All the friends he made, he devoutly kept. They came from Highgate Primary School, the Merchant Navy, the Sturt Lacrosse Club and the Apex Club of Norwood. So strong was his bond with his Apex Club mates that after they all tuned 40, the compulsory Apex retiring age, he kept them together by founding the 'Early

Marchers', a group of a dozen mates who took holidays together in the first week of March for the next 30 years. In alternate years they would base themselves at our shack at Port Willunga and fish (washed down with more than the odd red and Coopers Ale). In the other years they mounted an expedition. George, christened 'Bosun' by the Early Marchers, organised every detail of these expeditions, although it helped having Mac Cooper of Coopers Brewery and Norm Walker, a great red wine maker, as part of the team. Their expeditions took them to Quorn, Venus Bay, Innamincka, Port Lincoln, Streaky Bay and the Flinders Ranges.

The pleasure of the company of men doubtless started with his Boy Scout days and was reinforced by his wartime experiences. However he was not afraid to institutionalise it in his life thereafter. George had many great friends, but he never spoke of best friends. All his friends were equally important, and to them and his family he was loyal to a fault.

His friendship with John Allez was unique because of its circumstances. There was no reason for the young jovial Guernseyman, an officer, to take George, the most junior crew member, under his wing on the *Armadale*, apart from John's natural goodness and generosity. However, a strong friendship did grow from John's almost paternal care, but after the war they went their very separate ways. George returned to a shore job in Australia, and John to the important office of Harbourmaster of Guernsey.

Communication was very different in 1945 – no Skype or email and no one could afford regular long distance phone calls. So the friendship subsisted by irregular aerograms. In the 1970s when George and Peggy had no children at home and were able to afford travel, they decided to take holidays in England and visited John and Elizabeth Allez in St Peter Port, Guernsey.

The friendship came alive, giving rise to two further trips to Guernsey by George and Peggy, three by me and three by John to Australia – the last when he was 92. I have a photo from John's last trip, which I cherish, of two very happy old boys arm-in-arm in my vineyard – doubtless contemplating the next product of the vineyard they were about to savour. When John died in 2010 there was no doubt that the Collett family would be represented at his funeral in St Peter Port.

George's wartime experiences had left their mark in another way. In 2001 he sought a War Veteran's Pension. Someone at the RSL suggested that he claim he had post-traumatic stress disorder (PTSD) from his merchant navy experiences. I thought he had no hope given that 56 years had passed. However, he was examined by Professor Sandy McFarlane, an Adelaide psychiatrist and world expert on PTSD. Professor McFarlane expressed the opinion that George was suffering from a chronic PTSD as a result of his World War Two experiences in the Merchant Navy. It was only then that I realised that a number of George's 'habits' (like sleeplessness, waking very early every day, and his growing remoteness) were, in fact, symptoms of his PTSD.

Unfortunately George began to show signs of cognitive impairment and subsequently dementia soon after, such that by 2006 Alzheimer's disease had been diagnosed. He was admitted to a nursing home along with Peggy in 2008. In 2012 he was moved to the dementia wing where he died in July 2013.

Alzheimer's disease is an awful affliction, particularly as memory, recognition, the ability to communicate and continence steadily but inexorably disappear. However, as these faculties deserted George, his dignity and warmth remained unscathed – a sure sign of a good man.

Andrew Collett

Andrew Collett studied Arts/Law at Adelaide University during the Vietnam War. Consequently he looked for something that combined the practice of law with political activism and established a practice in Aboriginal legal rights, which still keeps him off the streets.

He has lived in the Adelaide square mile since 1975 and carried on his Linden Park sporting pursuits of lacrosse and cricket to university and beyond as well as running some slow marathons far from home. However, his sporting highlight was catching up with his old Linden Park pals Don Cranwell and Phil Higgins to play cricket for Kensington and football for Sturt.

In the 1990s he established a small shiraz vineyard in McLaren Vale, which produces a palatable antidote to the rigours of the law.

In 2014 Andrew was awarded an AM for significant service to the law, as a supporter of Indigenous legal rights, and through contributions to professional organisations. He is married with two sons.

Ross Hector MACPHERSON

(1918–2007)

by Judy Macpherson Kent

I'm about to listen to a recording made by my dad in 1990. He died five years ago and I'm only just finding the courage to listen now. Why? Am I afraid I'll find out things I should have known? Or that there's nothing more to say? Might it destroy the myth I have of him or enhance it? Let's begin.

Ross Hector was the youngest of four boys born to Edward John Macpherson and Ada Pearl Muriel Shaw at the end of World War Two in 1918. The brothers, Murray, Raeburn and Wally had a sister, Airlie, but she died of a childhood illness at about the age of two. Dad occasionally expressed regret at the death of the older sister he had never known and yet sometimes I wondered if he would have made it into the world if she hadn't died. I also wondered if he had felt guilty about not being the replacement girl and whether this is why he had always maintained that he was so lucky to have had three daughters.

His parents were shopkeepers and I have vague memories of

the smallgoods shop they ran in Adelaide's inner-southern suburb, Westbourne Park. I can remember the flour and beans in sacks on the floor, the scales, and the jars on the walls, the musty smell, but not much more. It was set at the front of their house opposite the railway line on a large block which housed chooks, two sheep and a couple of tennis courts, one bitumen and the other lawn. All the boys and their wives were good tennis players and the extended family used to assemble there on Saturdays. In fact Andrew Collett's mother, Peg Andrew, reminisced recently about playing tennis with the Macpherson boys before they went off to war; she even wrote them letters while they were away.

A few years later, after they had all married, the brothers kept up the tradition of Saturday afternoon tennis. After they had limed the lines and hung the net, they and their wives would play and laugh while we cousins roamed around the property, climbing the enormous gum tree and watching in horror as big cousin Rob put penny bungers in the ant holes on the crumbling bitumen of the second court. Sweet white tea in an oversized pot would be served into tin mugs during the break along with the numerous cakes and slices brought along by the women. As I write I can smell the gum leaves, the soil and the freshly cut grass and see the women in their white tennis dresses and hats, and the men in their long white pants and vests. Even though it was a family affair, customs were observed in those days.

While the parents broke for afternoon tea, we kids picked up their racquets and learned to play. Dad invariably sacrificed his break to hit us some balls, hence developing in us a growing passion for the sport. Dad's brother Wally was President of the SA Lawn Tennis Association for many years and my sister Jan and I were overjoyed to be selected as usherettes for the Davis Cup (in those days girls couldn't be ball girls!). I went on to play tennis for Beaumont Tennis Club and at Unley High School, Barbara Grimm, another 1962 Linden Park friend and I were an invincible double act when we played on Wednesday afternoons at Memorial Drive.

If that all sounds a tad idyllic, Sundays were another story, when we were expected to go to church or Sunday School. My memories of Hawthorn Presbyterian are mixed. On the one hand there was the mad, unforgiving minister with out-of-control eyebrows preaching hellfire and damnation out of the pulpit while Dad's brothers solemnly handed round the polished wood collection plates lined with purple felt. On the other, I remember Dad laughing about how he'd hope we kids would start crying so he could take us outside into the fresh air. And the friends I made at Sunday School and the Presbyterian Fellowship Association were enduring. My sister Jan even married the boy she met there when she was 14-years-old. When I was approaching 13 Dad didn't seem perturbed when I declined to be confirmed in spite of the fact that he and Mum had 'taken the pledge' not to drink or smoke in their 20s. That was the environment they grew up in. A God-fearing Scottish Presbyterian environment of stoicism, austerity, meanness of spirit and pessimism.

But there must have been times when my parents played hooky from church because my most vivid childhood memories are of weekends and holidays at our shack at Moana which Dad built from the ground up. I was two when he built it and we were still living in our first family house at Gertrude Street, Glandore. Dad must have been pretty good with his hands – he was always up and down ladders fixing things, oiling the boards, digging trenches or holes with his post-hole digger, pouring concrete, building pergolas. I just thought it was what dads did. One of the lingering family stories is of me, aged about two, falling down one of the trenches Dad was digging because I had been fixated on a plane going overhead. Dad, at the bottom of the trench just picked me up, still curled in a ball, and placed me gently on the top of the trench. He then went on digging!

When he wasn't working on the shack we'd spend long hot days at the beach. Mum would pack the blue and white esky with sandwiches and Woody's lemonade and we'd drive onto the beach and set up the tartan rug in the shade of the latest company car. We had Holden FXs, FJs and EHs, EJs and FBs, all courtesy of the Savings

Bank of SA where Dad worked his way up from teller to chief city valuer. My recollections of my dad are that he never refused to play beach tennis with us or come for a surf. 'Please Dad!' my sisters and I would wheedle, and he'd willingly give up his sunbathing to accompany us. He was also a powerful body surfer. He'd beat us to the shore every time, even when we were allowed to hire the tightly blown up black surf shooters from the surf club for two shillings an hour.

We moved to Glen Osmond on or around my fourth birthday, in the December of 1954. Ours was the second house in an olive grove next door to Woodley Wines and from our back patio and kitchen we had a vista of the sprawling city and surrounds that was breath-taking. From the front door we looked up to the hills, which were bare of houses and sported the scars of old galena mines. We kids and the neighbours' kids would roam the hills all day long during the holidays and Mum would occasionally call out a 'cooee' and we'd 'cooee' back. We'd climb down the old mineshafts and collect gleaming galena treasures or we'd ride our bikes and billy carts hell for leather down the hill, defying cars to come round the bend. We'd also spend hours picking olives which we'd sell for a pittance to the Italian immigrant who made oil from them and who had a small factory up past Sunnyside Road. Our own olive oil came in a small bottle from John Dixon, the chemist, and was kept purely for medicinal purposes in those days. This was the life Dad had determined for us when we moved to Glen Osmond. This was the 1950s and Linden Park was the primary school of choice for all of us post-war, aspiring 'upper middle class' (his words) kids.

In the garage were all of Dad's tools and a leather greatcoat, now paint-stained, but which gave a clue of his army days. There was also a helmet with a hole in it, and a rusted army rations tin that apparently still contained bully beef. So I was aware that he had had a life before us, but he didn't talk about it much. Dad never marched nor mentioned the war. It didn't seem to be a part of his life now although he had a couple of albums with sepia coloured photos that showed he'd been to far away exotic places. There he was astride a camel in front of the pyramids; in another he is framed by the Sphinx. They didn't seem like war photos to me, even the ones of him in army uniform flanked by other smiling youths, their arms around each other's shoulders, all sporting the same bad haircuts. Any stories he did tell were about the shared camaraderie and the jokes they played on each other, as when one of them would wake the others up in the middle of the night and ask if they wanted a piss. So of course they'd all end up having to go outside into the cold.

I became more aware of his war service in Year Seven when we were asked whose fathers had served during the war and Andrew Collett and I were chosen to represent them on Remembrance Day. The grainy pictures show us in our school uniforms, laying a wreath at the War Memorial flanked by our proud fathers wearing their war medals, and other family members. It was then that I found out that our families were not only linked by war and Linden Park Primary School but also by marriage; our grandfathers were cousins.

Dad had a fascination for the world and every inch of the dining room walls were covered with the maps, which accompanied the National Geographic magazines. There were maps of Europe, the Americas, Africa and Asia, and we girls grew up with a longing to see it all and welcome others of another culture into our lives. From the time I could remember Dad and Mum were involved with learning a language – first French and then German. Their first overseas trip together was to Asia in 1964 and they brought back wonderful treasures from Hong Kong, Bangkok and Singapore. In Singapore they stayed with Dad's cousin and namesake, Sir Hector McGregor. Hector was our family hero. Born in New Zealand a few years before Dad, Hector had gone to England and joined the RAF at the outbreak of war and was knighted for his courage flying Spitfires in the Battle of Britain. A delightfully mild mannered man, he had stayed in the RAF, married an Englishwoman, and after a stellar career had been appointed Air Marshall General of Far East Forces, stationed in Singapore and Butterworth.

Dad was proud of Sir Hector and no doubt wished his war service could have been as notable. He sometimes mentioned that he regretted not going to New Guinea with his 2nd 27th Batallion but a shrapnel wound to his right hand and wrist took him out of the war, and in 1943, after six months of recuperation in Palestine, he was shipped home to Adelaide. I was hoping Dad's recorded memoirs might tell me more about his wounding but he skips over it and I will have to rely on my memory. Dad was a radio linesman, which meant that he used to have to run a communication line out from the base to where the troops were fighting. It was while he was engaged in this activity that, as he says, he 'got too close to a mortar' (a 'friendly' one courtesy of the British at that) and shrapnel hit his hand and head. Luckily his helmet was firmly attached and I still have it with the shrapnel hole right through to the webbing. Apparently he had quite a long trek over the mountain back to the base, nursing his hand, which seemed to be hanging from a thread. He was then taken by ambulance to Haifa where he was bandaged up and sent by train to the 7th Australian General Hospital at Rehovat. There they left the bones to mend and gave him physio for the next six months to help repair the nerves that had been badly damaged but not severed. Luckily he managed to get most of the movement back but for the rest of his life he wore a leather brace on his hand and apologised for his rather spidery handwriting. One other thing I remember about his wounding was that he became separated from his rifle and when he did get it back, someone had substituted their faulty one for his. It could have been problematic if he had had to use it again.

Two of Dad's brothers, Murray and Wally, were also involved in the fighting in Palestine. Dad tells the story of meeting Wally when he was preparing for his first assault and Wally was returning from battle. Wally asked him if he had any money to which Dad replied, 'Yes, how much do you need?' And Wally laughed because he hadn't been asking for money; he had been going to offer his little brother some of his own! On his tape, Dad recounts that the Australian troops were fighting the Vichy French, which included the French Foreign Legion, because Rommel was coming across the top of Egypt, preparing to take Cairo and they feared a pincer attack on Syria.

So Dad's active fighting didn't last long but he did manage to see a bit of Palestine as he was convalescing, sometimes accompanied by one or other of his brothers if they were on leave or suffering from gastric trouble which, as he said 'we all suffered from'. They were befriended by a young Sabra couple, Haim and Tikva, whose names translate to 'life' and 'hope'. They showed them around Jerusalem, the River Jordan and other historic sites, having to negotiate the blackouts at night. Dad remembers Tikva serving them black tea and lemon and he didn't understand why she kept filling up his glass until he twigged that he had to put it upside down to show that he had finished.

Dad was repatriated to Australia but was considered not fit to accompany his regiment who were destined to walk the Kokoda Track in New Guinea in 1943. Instead, he rejoined the bank, married his sweetheart and became a father to the first of his three daughters, Rosslyn, at 25, setting in train a lifetime of conservative responsibility. Janet and I followed after in three year intervals. Both he and Mum worked to give their daughters the opportunities they didn't have and there were times in later life when Dad wished he had taken more risks, retraining as a teacher or starting up his own real estate business. And yet in later life I have come across two of his banker colleagues who extolled his virtues as a mentor to them. One of them described him as 'easily the most decent leader for whom I worked'.

If Dad's life was tinged with regret for things he didn't have the opportunity to do, there were a few times when I really saw him come alive. One was in 1966 on a Saturday morning when the phone rang. I answered it and a man with an accent asked if this was where Ross Macpherson lived. Dad immediately took the phone and all his instincts told him it was Haim, even though it had been over 24 years since their last contact. And when Dad asked after Tikva, he said, yes, she was with him – they had married and were spending the next three years in Sydney on government business. Even though the Palestinian wars had prevented them from contacting each other over the intervening years, the friendship had remained and from that time on, our families became united as one. We kids spent time with them in Sydney. They and their two children spent time with us in Adelaide. Dad and Mum travelled to see them in Israel and when I visited them in 1994 they took me to the same biblical places they had shown my dad, some 50 years earlier.

The war defined Dad, physically and emotionally. It affected his hand and determined that he would suffer stomach and throat ailments for the rest of his life. Emotionally it contributed to his sleeplessness and anxiety, and even depression and mild paranoia in later years. As he aged, he was more able to come to terms with the war by marching on Anzac Day. I would make a commitment to accompany him to the early morning ceremonies, proud of him and his achievements, remembering his mates who weren't lucky enough to come back, thinking of the friendships that were forged, but wondering about the futility of all wars. Was he an unsung hero? In the War he was probably as scared as the next bloke but doing his duty as they were all expected to do, just as he continued to do when he came back. Certainly he was my hero as I was growing up, rarely missing an opportunity to watch a hockey match or cheer me on to win an athletics trophy. And all the while, encouraging scholarship and a love of learning.

Like most teenagers there was a time in my late teens when we did not always see eye to eye; he wanted to choose my boyfriends and my political persuasions and was not good at entertaining opinions other than his own. I also think that as he got older the effects of the PTSD were taking their toll and he became more anxious and had less patience, humour and tolerance. It must not have been an easy decision for him to let me go to America on a student exchange for a year when I was 16 and he also worried about my exposure to 'radical' elements at university. I remember him expressing relief after my two sisters were married and I realised that one of his main purposes in life must have been to marry us off before we got pregnant. He was a conservative man, politically and socially.

So what of the recording? It turned out to be 20 minutes of his war experience in Palestine. And yet it doesn't dwell on the war or on his wounding; it mainly highlights his camaraderie with his brothers and his meeting with Haim and Tikva and of their subsequent friendship in Australia and Israel. Maybe in that he is highlighting the humanity that can be found in war, even when there are no winners, only losers. Glen Osmond and Linden Park must have seemed like such a safe haven away from that madness where he could instil in his daughters and beloved grandchildren a passion for learning and an openness to the world beyond. Vale Ross Hector.

Judy Macpherson Kent

As the youngest of three daughters to attend Linden Park Primary School, Judy often found herself being unfavourably compared to the closest of her older siblings, Janet, who was much more academic and well-behaved. She had a close relationship with her father who spent hours watching her play hockey or athletics or tennis; he never missed a school sports day. It was he who encouraged her love for languages and, in particular, the English language. She studied Honours Arts at Flinders, became a teacher, moved to Melbourne and taught for a year before becoming involved in academic research when she lived in Darwin immediately after Cyclone Tracy. She now consults to organisations through Melbourne Business School, having attained her Masters and Doctorate in Organisation Dynamics in the past few years. She has been married for 40 years to Wayne and has two wonderful sons, Simon and Nathan, both in the advertising/media industry, who constantly remind her not to take herself too seriously.

Linden Park School, the connection between the contributors to this book. Below, the catchment area.

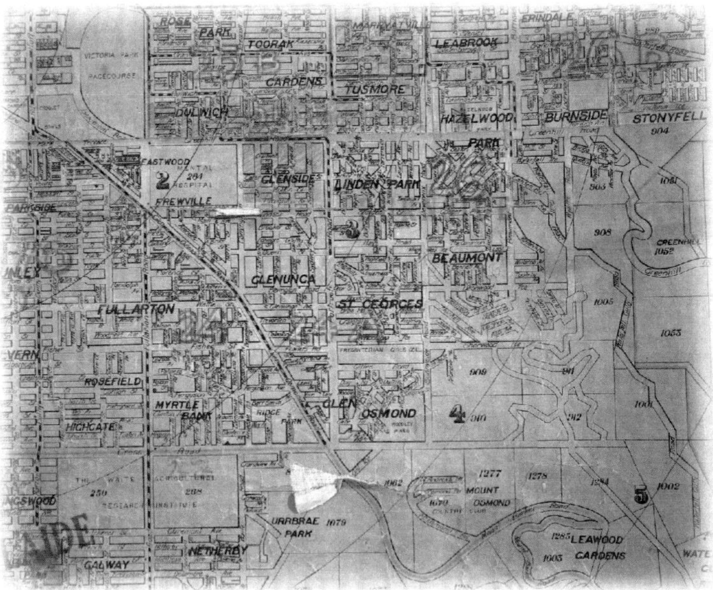

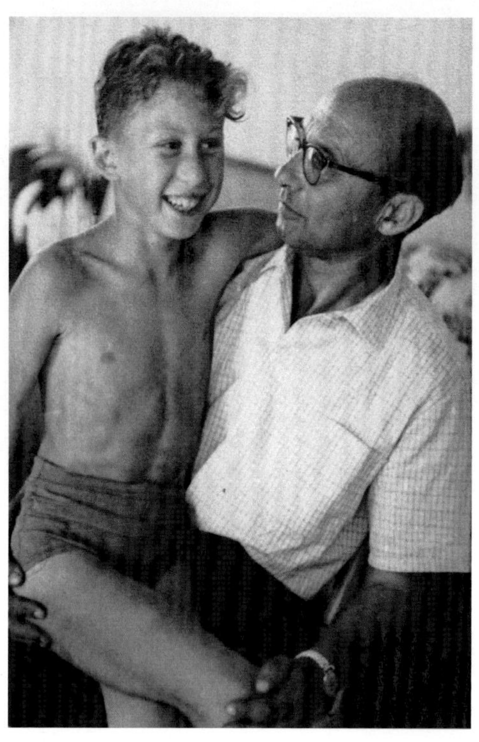

Leo Adler with his son George. Below, Leo on an AJS motorcycle equipped with a side-car, Austria, 1920s.

Right, Norm George, paterfamilias, at work in his David Jones office. Below, the George children in about 1958 sitting outside the family home in St Georges, and bottom, pictured in 2007. In both photos they are in the same positions, from left: David, Warren, Lorraine, Graeme and Bryan.

David and Warren George, aged 17.

Bill Corey at work in his Glen Osmond Road, Frewville butcher's shop, and at left with daughter Dianne.

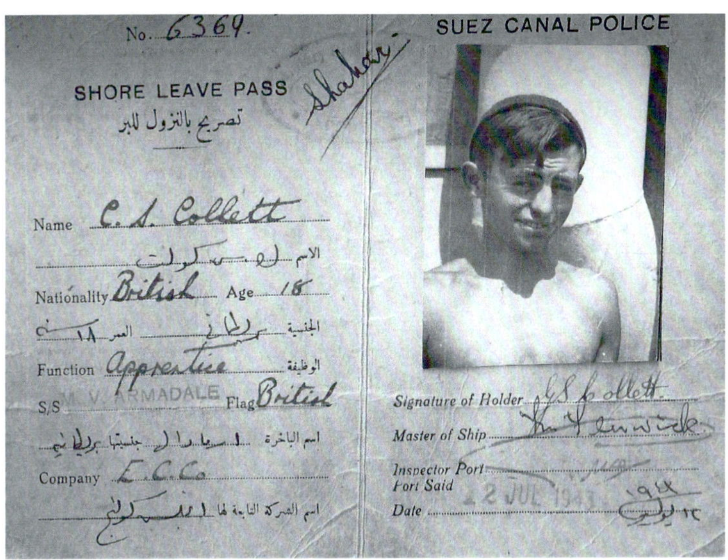

No. 6369.

SUEZ CANAL POLICE

SHORE LEAVE PASS

تصريح بالنزول للبر

Name C. S. Collett

الاسم

Nationality British Age 18

الجنسية العمر ١٨

Function Apprentice الوظيفة

S/S M. V. ARMADALE Flag British

اسم الباخرة

Company E.C.Co

اسم الشركة التابعة لها

Signature of Holder G. S. Collett

Master of Ship

Inspector Port
Port Said

Date 22 JUL 1943

George Collett's shore leave pass when he travelled through the Suez Canal on the MV *Armadale*.

George Collett with son Andrew.

Jane Hiatt aged about 18 months with her father Syd, on the stone path that Syd and his own father had just laid at their house on Highfield Avenue, St Georges.

Liz Hassold proudly showing off her school uniform.

The foundations of the Hassold's house at 20 Fifeshire Avenue, in undeveloped St Georges.

LINDEN PARK YEAR 6 CLASS – 1961

Back Row: **Anne Cramond**, Julie Shields, Andrea Barlow, Helen Tregilgas, Leonie Stenhouse, Sue Millard, Margaret Holden, Christine Curnow.
Third Row: Robert Malcolm, Laurie Cousin, Don Cranwell, **David Leonie**, Peter Conway, **David Brecht**, Stuart Main, Brian Bateup, Jane Rudyard.
Second Row: **Rick Frolich**, David George, Rodney Duke, **Andrew Collett**, John Church, Craig Dreyer, Kenton Lillicrapp, Darryl Brewer, David Turner.
Front Row: **Bryan Charlton**, **George Adler**, **Warren George**, Ula Potchies, Diana White, Lucille Wotton, Beverly Johns, **Judy Macpherson**, Esther Bennett, Tait Koldits, Arthur Lemon.
(all names left to right, contibutors' names in bold)

Physical education display at Linden Park School.

YEAR 6 GIRLS – 1961

Back Row: Ann Green, **Sandra Harrison**, Christine Ware, Roslyn Knight, Sandra Hunter, Sue Bertram, Judith Blake, Judith Lewis, **Elizabeth Hassold**.
Third Row: Christine Newcombe, Jane Greacon, Barbara Keats, Jennifer Barton, Margaret Rowland, Helene Sarap, Kay Smith, Teresa Mitchell, Susan Duance.
Second Row: Jennifer Muxlow, **Julie Gillies**, Susan Brewster, Kathryn Bagshaw, Jennifer Cheney, **Judith Hasse**, **Jane Hiatt**, **Frances Goldney**, Anna Segers, Janet Cox, Mardi Ward.
Front Row: Julie Walter, Virginia Heath, **Dianne Corey**, Barbara Grimm, Margaret Boylan, Christine Mudge, Maria Sergi, Margaret Gregg, Margaret Laws, Susan Dyson.
(all names left to right, contibutors' names in bold)

Marching into class.

Stan Joyner with son Steve on his 21st birthday

Stan Joyner (second from left) with the Blue Streak rocket that he helped design. (*circa* 1951)

Phil Higgins with his father Len.

The Macphersons off on an adventure with TAA.

Ross and Judy Macpherson, with the then ubiquitous FE Holden.

Anne Cramond and brother Stephen with parents Bertine and Bill in Aden en route to Australia, May 1961. The *Himalaya* is in the background.

Linden Park Primary footballers at Lightning Carnival, Unley Oval, 1961. Players featured include Neville Lea, John Laycock, Robert West, Craig Dreyer and Brenton Webber.

Jules Hasse wearing a promotional dress for Hoyts, for whom her father worked as a business manager, with responsibility for the refreshments. MacRobertson's products are featured.

Greg Perkin's father Harry working on plans.

Frances Goldney nursing her baby sister Celia.

Frank Goldney (at right) with Jim Moir, Wireless Air Gunner, and pilot Flying Officer John Henderson. Their Wellington Mark XIII aircraft had just landed at Rabat Sale in French Morocco, on 13 February 1944.

Gordon and Ruth Rinder on their wedding day. Ruth (*née* Iverson) composed the words and music for the Linden Park School song.

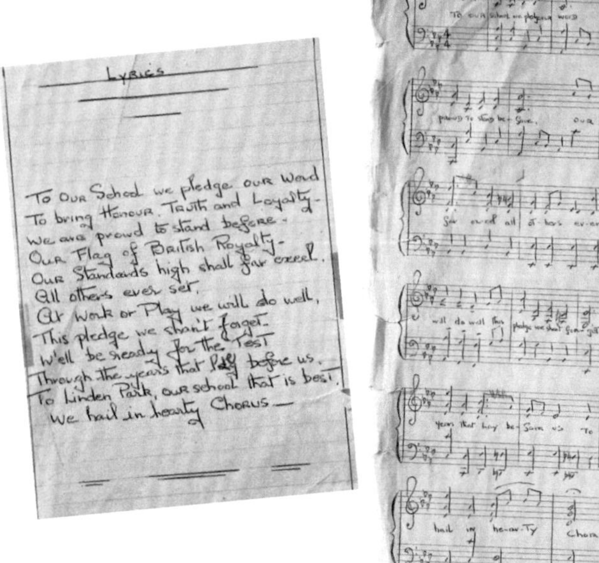

Lyrics

To Our School we pledge our Word
To bring Honour, Truth and Loyalty-
We are proud to stand before-
Our Flag of British Royalty-
Our Standards high shall far excel.
All others ever set,
At Work or Play we will do well,
This pledge we shan't forget.
We'll be ready for the Test
Through the years that lay before us.
To Linden Park, our school that is best,
We hail in hearty Chorus —

Sydney Goodwin HIATT

(1923–1995)

by Jane Hiatt

At the outset let me say that it is not vanity that insists that memories of my father also involve me. I am sure some of these memories are enhanced and sharpened by frequent repetition and inspection, and some overlooked or distorted by emotion. And sometimes the memory just fails or others don't agree.

My father was christened Sydney Goodwin Hiatt, born in 1923 in Hawthorn, Victoria. His father was John Thomas Hiatt, a World War One veteran, an artillery captain whom my grandmother said went to war with a full head of hair and returned completely bald. Syd's mother was Elsie Doris Lumb and his older brother Jack was six when Syd was born.

Syd's father had been to Prince Alfred College and that is where he sent his sons. John, or Jonner as everyone knew him, was a staunch Methodist, and his father William was a well-known lay preacher who had worked at a variety of chapels such as Warracknabeal in rural Victoria, and Moonta Mines in South Australia. He was a rather fearsome but highly respected presence and his sermons were very much praised in their day. Dad admired his grandfather and probably found him stern yet morally stimulating. I think William Hiatt was an inspiration to all his family and his faith was authentic, of the 'temperance, no gambling, no dancing and good works-on-earth' variety.

Elsie Doris, or Dor, was the third child of Thomas Lumb and Phoebe McCann, well-off settlers and storekeepers from Ceres, near Geelong in Victoria. They were also very formal and sincere Methodists and Dor often described the dinner table officiated over by Phoebe, with all the grandchildren totally silent and eating never begun without a Bible reading and Grace, read by Addison.

So the church was the strongest presence in the social and ethical lives of Dad's family and continued to be so when the Hiatts moved from Melbourne to Adelaide when Dad was seven. Jonner was manager of the Victoria Insurance Company and Adelaide was his next posting. They moved to Kensington Gardens and attended Gartrell Methodist church. Dor had won a Half Dame Nelly Melba scholarship and sung in the choir. Both Dad and his brother Jack loved to sing too and belted out hymns like 'How Great Thou Art'. They also loved the psalms and knew many of them off by heart. There was a lawn tennis court at their house and many church afternoon teas took place around social tennis.

Syd was not overly happy at Prince Alfred College. He lived rather in the academic shadow of his brilliant older brother Jack, who later trained as a criminal barrister and became a QC. Syd loved poetry and history and these joint obsessions stayed with him throughout his life, and he bequeathed an enormous love of these studies to me. Syd also drew and painted, at a time when there wasn't a role for these accomplishments in a PAC student's life.

Syd did blossom with the opportunities in sport at which he excelled. I have shelves of trophies and photographs from PAC days when he won awards in sprinting, high jumping, broad jumping, tennis, football, rowing and badminton. He was tall and lanky and won state championships in high jumping and marathon running. I wonder how he had any time left for the classroom!

We tend to forget now how unlucky Syd's generation was. In the 30s the Depression arrived, and when Dad was 17-years-old World War Two transformed Australia. It must have been shocking to have to leave school at 15 so Dad could help out the family working as an errand boy. Nobody ever said but probably the fees at PAC could no longer be afforded. Jack, who was older, described having to leave university and compete with 250 other people for a bank clerk's job. He got it and spent six years doing his law degree at night.

When Syd was 18 he enlisted in the Australian Army. He trained at Pukapunyal and the Atherton Tablelands in Queensland. This experience began a life-long worship of the lush jungles, rivers and fruit of Queensland. He taught us kids sentimental country songs like 'I was born in sunny Queensland, Up where the Barron river flows …' He fell in love with Miss Nambour and could have been entirely lost to South Australia had war not reasserted itself.

Syd trained as a commando and specialised as a signaller and forward scout. He was a member of the famous Z Corps. You had to be specially chosen for this role, over six-foot-two, an athlete and able to pass the exams. Ironic, really, how privileged you had to be to be chosen for horrific suffering and possible torture or death. No doubt he saw it differently and going to New Guinea to fight the Japanese must have seemed at first both a duty and an adventure shared with mates.

As a child it disappointed me that Syd would not talk much about the war. He did bring back mementos such as Japanese money, a flag and a set of wonderful pencil sketches of animals, feather headdresses and portraits of natives he met. He seemed to spend a lot of time sketching while recovering in Lae Hospital from malaria. He also had a mysterious lului stick in ebony that a head-hunter had given him for good luck. We've still got it.

Experiences in New Guinea did correct Dad's romantic view of jungles. The thigh-high mud of the Owen Stanley Ranges, the almost constant rain which rotted the clothes on your back, the mosquitoes and disease, as well as grasses as sharp as swords that could cut you to bits and leaves with poisonous hairs which would drive you insane with pain if you touched them, and the cannibals of the Upper Sepic, were truly appalling.

For many years while I was growing up Dad had return bouts of malaria, and pieces of shrapnel used to ooze out of parts of his body. He remembered how wonderful it was when penicillin was tested on the soldiers and how it cleared up beriberi and dysentery when he contracted them. A positive consequence of Syd's time in New Guinea was his lifelong knowledge of morse code. The negative was what was called 'war neurosis' then if it was referred to at all, but what we would call today 'post-traumatic stress disorder'. Dad had this condition and it almost crippled his life. He developed a facial twitch that embarrassed him and he had to be medicated for insomnia and neurosis. The uppers and downers created a real crisis in his mental life, and were very stressful for his family. Doctors of the day did not know what to do.

The only way I ever found out about Syd's war experiences is because he used to suffer shocking nightmares that would make him levitate off his bed, sleep walk and sleep talk. As the eldest and very close to my father, I used to get up and talk to him and take him back to bed. He told me of the time when he got inextricably lost as scout in the jungle, and heard many Japanese voices coming up a path. He climbed a tree and was silent all night and much of the next day. I can only imagine his terror, dehydration, hunger and exhaustion. Eventually the Japanese moved on, he set his compass and headed off to meet some Fuzzy Wuzzy Angels who guided him towards Australian troops. On another occasion he related a hand grenade attack at night in which his tent was torn to smithereens and every one of his mates was killed. He used to relive over and over the visual scene and condemned himself for surviving. That night he had slept the other way around from his mates.

Just one more story. Another dream involved Dad being ordered to shoot a Japanese private down by a river who was rambling in his mind and shivering and yellow with beriberi. He had him in his sights and couldn't do it. Dad used to repeat that the Japanese were just 'poor suckers like us'.

Another legacy of Syd's commando years came free with the weevilly flour, and tins of bully beef. The troops were issued with free cigarettes which they used for many purposes as well as smoking. Dad said you could trade them with the natives for garden food, and they were a sure-fire method of sizzling the leeches off the back of the mate in front of you. Maybe the Methodists were on to something when it came to dangerous addictions that the faithful pledged to avoid because Dad became a lifelong smoker and died of emphysema in 1995.

Positively, there were opportunities offered by the government for returned soldiers that benefited my father. Dad had his fees paid to train as an art teacher, and this was an ideal job for him. He worked at tough schools like Nailsworth Boys' Tech, and later at Goodwood Boys' Tech and Oakbank High School. He ran Army cadets at all those places and was a loved and imaginative art teacher. My sister and I were dragged out on Sundays quite often to forage for stone in quarries for his sculpture classes. He became a senior and was placed on a pedestal by most of his students. Of course he did apply the 'discipline of the set-square' to those who deserved it!

Dad tried out for the SANFL Norwood football team and got in, spending three wonderful years playing for Norwood as a ruckman and fullback under the coaching of Jack Oatey whom he worshipped. He used to relate how the supporters he feared the most were the little old ladies who would yell the foulest abuse and strike you as you went back to the change rooms with their brollies. One of the thrills of his life was when Norwood won the grand final in 1948 and he was in the team.

In the early 50s we had moved into our materials-rationed post-war brick house in Highfield Avenue, St Georges. The rooms were small and I shared one with my sister, but families didn't seem to need space then. I began attending Linden Park Primary School in 1955 and always loved it despite some boredom in the long summer afternoons, which saw us applying ourselves to the same old stories in the primers. I recall fondly going home for lunch and breaking off the warm crusts from the loaf the baker had just delivered in his horse and cart. Vegemite and slabs of butter were always delicious on fresh warm bread.

Life in our suburb seemed totally free. I climbed trees, made cubbies in the 40-acre paddock off Portrush Road, and if Mum threatened to wash my long plaits in the kitchen sink I would run for the back fence where I had an old tyre set up as a spring vault and be over and off in one bound. I loved our wattle tree and Dad built us kids a platform and ladder to the very top where it was blissful to sway around in the wind.

Dad spoilt us. He rediscovered his innocence in his parenting. His job was to read to us in bed, and entertain us, giving Mum a break from chores. He read us the Romantic poets that he loved especially Tennyson and Keats. We especially wanted to hear *The Lady of Shallot* over and over again. We got whole tracts of Charles Dickens because Dad liked him, especially *Great Expectations* and *David Copperfield*. I remember weeping inconsolably when Steerforth betrayed L'il Em'ly and drowned himself trying to rescue Ham in the wild seas off Yarmouth. He invented a whole group of shadow puppets with floppy ears and whiskers and projected their antics on our walls lit by the light in the passage. In the morning my sister and I knew there would be lollies hidden in our room somewhere. What an incentive to get up knowing that honey bears, black cats, milk bottles and chocolate soldiers were somewhere waiting to be gobbled before Mum knew as she would have been sure to disapprove of the effect on our pre-fluoride teeth.

Dad also taught us countless songs and played to us on his ukulele and mouth organ, songs like 'All day, all night Mary-Anne', and the 'Banana Boatmen's song'. We sang along to 'The Teddy Bears' Picnic' but he also got us to listen to the 'Nutcracker Suite' and 'Orpheus in the Underworld'. At Teachers College he had been in the 'Footlights' Review and had a natural hilarious aptitude for sending up serious situations, and pompous people, as well as telling jokes. I'm sure some of the jokes were highly inappropriate for children, but again we only knew that we were his audience and were grateful for being allowed to be present.

There was not a practical bone in my father's body despite all his love and good intentions. Dad loved nature and especially birds. He could mimic the whipbirds and bowerbirds of the bush and took me especially to the Flinders Ranges to experience the miracle of thousands of budgerigars waking and screeching in the mornings. But his attempt at construction of an aviary in the back yard was a total failure. The rusting hulk gradually decayed there for many years.

Every school holiday Dad would take the family away in the caravan. He was a real adventurer in this way. We would go to quite simple places like Second Valley, Port Augusta, Port Broughton, and Melrose. Some of my most vivid memories are of exploring goat paths and boat sheds at Second Valley, or the mangrove swamps, fishing port and old buildings of Port Augusta. A very memorable holiday was to my great aunt's dairy farm at Dixie near Terang in Victoria. We went via the Grampians and I still remember the cliffs like monster faces lit up by the setting sun. We also camped in some paddock near a cross road and my actual memory is of the only mosquito repellent my parents could manufacture – a campfire piled up with cattle dung to create stifling smoke. A child does not forget magical times like this and I adored my father who I saw as a kind of magician.

My perspective changed somewhat during adolescence. In my defence all I can say is adolescence is always a time of challenge, and I certainly challenged my father. I think I have always been a lot like him, determined on my way, adventurous, outgoing. We clashed and I was determined to win over his authority. It was the swinging 60s after all and the pop songs like that of the Kinks exhorted us to 'die before we get old' and live fully for the moment. Oddly, through all our arguments I knew he loved me absolutely and I did him, but there was too much else to distract me.

Only in his last years, after my son was born, and after I had established my own career and travelled all round the world, did I achieve the maturity to reconcile absolutely with him and acknowledge that Syd was a remarkable father who had taught me what sacrifice and love truly mean.

Again I could adore him and I feel his love with me every day.

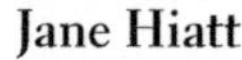

Jane Hiatt

Jane Goodwin Hiatt was born at Unley Private Hospital, now a wing of Walford Anglican School for Girls, on 10 October 1950. She was particularly thrilled to achieve the auspicious birthday of 10/10/2010 two years ago. No apocalypse occurred, but it was a disappointment that she did not win a lottery.

Jane was the elder of two daughters born to Juliet Mary nee Cobbin, and Sidney Goodwin Hiatt, and her sister Cathryn Mary Hiatt was born on 13 January 1954. Shortly before she attended kindergarten Jane moved to 20 Highfield Avenue, St Georges. She began attending Linden Park Primary School in 1955, and went home for lunch most days missing out on the gorgeous pies and pasties that more fortunate children ate in the shelter sheds.

Jane rode her reconditioned green bicycle to Unley High School in 1963 and loved the expanded world. She remembers not being allowed to go the Adelaide airport to greet the Beatles in 1964. The box pleats on her tunic occupied a lot of her time, as did hitching up the hem over a tight belt. Her favourite subjects at school were English, Latin and French. In 1967 she completed matriculation. She completed an honours degree in 1971, focusing on Spanish and English, a Diploma of Education in 1972, and began teaching in 1973. She qualified as an english senior in 1978 whilst at Glengowrie High School. In 1981 she took up a student counselling position at Thebarton, Mitcham Girls High School, and transferred to Christies Beach High School as Student

Counsellor in 1993. She retired after 19 years of service at that school in December 2012.

Jane married Syd Harrex in 1984, and they live together on 20 acres on the outskirts of Adelaide. She has travelled widely in Latin America and Asia. Jane gave birth in 1989 to her beloved only son Jaime Nathaniel, the day the Berlin wall came down. Jane loves life and is excited about all the possibilities in her future.

Eric Norman GEORGE
(1916–1989)

by Warren George

The Georges of St Georges

No matter who we are, high or low, people of great human achievement, or those whose life have been associated with the simple things.

The above epitomises the life of my father Eric Norman George, known to his family and friends as 'Norm'. What is the estimate of a good life? Varying judgements may be offered but for those of us who have known good men the answer must be that those passing from this life leave everyone richer in some way. Such was the man who preferred to be called Norm.

Norm was born on the 26 October 1916 at Parkside, Adelaide to gentle country folk from Woodside, Adelaide, near the famous Oakbank Racecourse. In those days the farm ownership passed to the eldest son, and so it was Norm's parents who moved to Adelaide in search of work. I recall a few visits to Woodside farm in my early youth, the rolling hills, the sheep, the dogs and the ferrets we used to trap rabbits.

In his youth Norm played cricket for East Torrens, Adelaide and was a state lacrosse player. World War Two interrupted his sporting hopes, his career ambitions and his family aspirations.

Norm and his wife Claire married during the war after he returned from the Middle East and prior to a further posting in the Pacific Campaign. After the war, and between 1947 and 1951, Norm and Claire had five children, one daughter and two sets of twins 14 months apart. We lived with my mother's parents in an old 1920 bungalow at 27 Bevington Road, Glenunga for the first four years of my life. I remember the house quite distinctly. It was replaced by units many years ago.

In 1953 we moved up the road to St Georges and lived in a small three-bedroom 'war commissioned' home at 13 Woodcroft Avenue. This estate was on the verge of Adelaide housing development in the eastern suburbs. The roads were dirt, and vacant paddocks were predominant to the Adelaide foothills. 'Georges of St Georges' had a certain connotation, and was often used in reference to where our family lived.

The early 1950s were a time of world uncertainty. The family unit was the prime focus. Your circle of friends lived close by. If you travelled more than six miles from the centre of Adelaide you were in the country. Times were tough then. Choices were limited. Life was not complicated though and the simple things of freedom, fresh air, great neighbours and friends were in excess. The district of Burnside and the foothills had an overabundance of stimulating and exciting places of discovery for us kids. Hiking in the foothills, quarries, mineshafts, caves, creeks, waterfalls, hard rubbish dumps, coupled with rides on the horse driven baker's cart, playing marbles, sport and other pastime activities. Youth activities and sport were often organised by the local Church groups, ours being the Beaumont Methodist Church.

Norm was employed at Charles Birks/David Jones for his entire working life, starting in May 1934. He travelled extensively with the business mainly between Adelaide, Sydney and Melbourne. I recall many airport pickups and the anticipation of a present after each return trip. He never failed to surprise us. Norm did not like flying much, especially in those earlier days when the old DC3 planes rattled their way to the east coast of Australia. The introduction of jet planes was a blessing on his travel time and comfort.

One of his senior appointments was as the prestigious role of merchandise controller for David Jones. This included the responsibility for women's fashions within David Jones, amongst other departments. Our father was responsible for the introduction of some famous fashion designs from overseas and promotion of new designs from within Australia. There were many new faces on the fashion catwalk that could have attributed their successful modelling careers to David Jones and Norm.

Norm was a private, reserved and humble person, but nevertheless he related extremely well with people from all walks of life. He never spoke ill of anyone and one of his most memorable sayings was: 'If you can't speak well of someone, don't say anything'.

My father's life journey was influenced by some early life-changing events that shaped the person he was.

The first event occurred when Norm returned from World War Two and was declared medically unfit, termed as TPI (totally and permanently incapacitated). He was granted a pension for life. He was, however, a proud man and refused to collect the TPI pension, resuming his career with Charles Birks. My father never discussed his war service, nor gave any insight into the roles he served within World War Two. Most of his past service detail was gleaned from his war service record after his passing.

The second event happened in late January 1956, just a few days before school recommenced. I vividly remember it as if it were yesterday. It was 2.00 am and I was woken from a deep sleep by all the general commotion and people within the house. Norm's wife and our dear mother, Clare, had suddenly died. I stood transfixed by my mother's side as she slipped away. I could not comprehend the event that was evolving before my eyes. Later, the police, an ambulance, the family doctor, neighbours and many relatives arrived at different times. I recall my father sitting on his chair in the kitchen dinette thoroughly distraught and inconsolable.

We were too young to attend the funeral, however I do remember with some clarity a subsequent event some days later. It involved a visit to the family home soon thereafter by State Child Welfare requiring my father to place his five children up for adoption. In those days the State's notion was that a sole male parent could not raise a family on his own, especially the size of ours. My father surprised the State Welfare representatives by ignoring their demands and thereby keeping the family unit together. So we moved on as a family. I can also remember the first days back at school after this personal tragedy. Well-meaning comments from teachers and schoolchildren were reassuring in most cases. They say children can be cruel and some were.

My father remarried some three years later, and thus began another chapter for the 'Georges of St Georges'. Our mother's name was Veronica (Vera). In hindsight, anyone who takes on a young family the size of ours had to be admired. It was tough in terms of attempting to appease everyone all the time. Vera was a strong-willed individual and quite a beautiful woman. Our extended family took care of her in the later years after Norm died. She just treasured and loved travelling interstate to visit each of the family from time to time even though there was a fear in flying. Dad lived to the age of 72. Vera died a few years ago at the ripe old age of 91. The immediate family were again by our mother's bedside as she slipped away peacefully. She was so clear of mind and strong to the end.

Our family values endured during the days when Norm and Vera took in his aged parents for approximately ten years rather than institutionalise them. In those days the extended family usually took responsibility for aged and respite care. Australian aged care culture has changed somewhat now. The expectation for the government to support the aged in institutions seems to be the reality now. That was not even a consideration in years gone by. Both Norm's parents lived to a ripe old age in their 90s. Imagine nine adults living in our small house. We all made sacrifices. I can truly appreciate the meaning of being a part time carer.

Put all that into the framework of one life, an unassuming life, a family man and you have a story of a good man in Norm George. Life was not easy but we all survived and prospered. Whilst the extended family is now spread throughout Australia – in Perth, Brisbane, Sydney, Melbourne and Adelaide – we continue to be quite close. It certainly saves on accommodation costs when travelling interstate.

In those days of changing values it was the strong character of my father, a man with purpose, that held his family together. Such people are the true builders of a worthwhile society and the future of Australia.

Norm died on Easter Sunday 1989 from a heart attack. He fell off his favourite kitchen chair positioned next to the breakfast bar. One desire he had shared with me from time to time: 'I don't want a stroke or any lingering health problems. I've seen enough suffering to last a life time … let it be quick'. When he died his faithful dog was sitting by his side, licking his face and gently whimpering.

Is it not unusual to find out a bit more about a person after their death and so it was for our father. About ten years ago I read Dawn Fraser's autobiography, *Dawn: One Hell of a Life*. To my great surprise I noted some references to my father going back to the late 1950s and early 1960s when Dawn Fraser worked at Adelaide's David Jones. As it turns out, my father employed Dawn during her formative years as a swimmer. He would have been chuffed to read the following book extract as noted by Dawn:

> They were good to me and the Managing Director, Mr George, tolerated my training and need for extra leave for competitions … I was paid full wages instead off part time, even if I was not there much of the time. In the lead up to any serious competition I'd be training in the middle of the day, too. They were good to me and whenever I came back to Sydney during the winter they'd get me a job at David Jones in the city. I always felt comfortable with Mr George and we had a strong rapport even though others were frightened of him.

Obviously, Dawn Fraser recalled the favourable treatment she had received by my father some 50 years earlier. She had a need to swim and train at the Olympic-size pool in Adelaide. Norm played a small part in the development of one of the world's greatest Australian Olympic swimming champion ever. The David Jones' culture was a 'family friendly' work ethic. In those days institutions respected staff, people valued their job, and it was not unusual for a male wage earner to remain loyal to one company throughout their lifetime. It's quite a different culture these days where the value to a company is the experiences within the field of excellence rather than years of employment. Norm retired from David Jones in October 1981, aged 65, a few months short of 48 years of service.

As mentioned previously our father served commissions in World War Two, initially in the army before transferring to the RAAF No. 3 Squadron, North West Area shortly thereafter. He served in both the Middle East and Pacific campaigns. Any information regarding unit activities, battles, areas of operation, campaigns, histories (where appropriate), prisoners of war, are rarely confirmed and in my father's case he never ever talked about or released any personal details of his service.

He never attended an ANZAC march to my knowledge, but watched every march on TV, sitting on his favourite chair with a Southwark beer in his hand. My occasional glances towards him during these times saw tears streaming from his eyes. Norm received honours for his RAAF service. A partial transcript of the 'Mentioned in Dispatches' was obtained in his personal papers following his death.

Sergeant George enlisted in the RAAF on the 3rd January 1940, in the mustering of medical orderly.

After consistently good service on training units, Sergeant George was appointed medical orderly on an island (Burma conflict) within the perimeter of enemy lines. In the execution of his task of maintaining the health of his Force, he showed devotion to duty and ingenuity far beyond his rank and mustering. His efficiency and untiring energy resulted in the continual fitness and wellbeing of the party even though they were working under most difficult circumstances.

In addition, finding the native health at very low ebb, Sergeant George trained native nurses and carried out treatment of the natives, bringing about a marked improvement in the general state of health over the entire island and, in the process, undoubtedly saved many lives. His work during this period will be reflected in the life of this island for many years to come. It vastly added to the prestige of the Australian party, contributed greatly to the success of the mission, and brought much credit to the Service.

Apart from Decorations consisting of the Campaign stars and medals, 1939–45 star, Africa Star and the Pacific Star, together with the War Medal 1939–45, Norm also received in July 1946, a citation from His Royal Highness (King George) and the Governor General in recognition of his services. This was promulgated in the Australian Gazette on 27 June 1946. These awards were discovered amongst Norm's small treasure of personal belongings after his passing and have been restored for family posterity. They are prominently and proudly displayed in my home in Sydney, together with the war records of my wife's parents.

Shortly before Norm's retirement he purchased a 24-foot caravan, quite huge by the standards in those days, and a Holden V8 to tow it. Later he purchased a boat, a Deep Hull Offshore 16. They loved staying at Stansbury, York Peninsula. The van was always on the same site, 5 metres from the water. He went fishing much to the angst of Vera. She disliked boats mainly due to motion sickness I presume, and never put a foot on that boat. She never cleaned the fish, usually King George whiting and garfish, but cooked it to perfection. She enjoyed the people and the 'happy hours' with their group of friends and family. In the winter they would move the van and boat to Mannum Caravan Park and go there every second weekend.

Finally, Norm was president of the Beaumont Indoor Bowling Club (probably referred to as a 'Men's Shed' these days). The club was incidentally the meeting place for the 1962 Year Seven, 50-year Linden Demonstration School Reunion, held on 7 September 2012.

In fond memory of Eric Norman George, father of Lorraine, Warren, David, Graeme and Bryan.

Warren George

Warren is one of five children, and one of two sets of twin boys born 14 months apart. There is also a sister. Lorraine is the eldest sibling and is the matriarch of the unique George family. Warren was the second born of the elder set of twins, Graeme and Bryan being the second set of twins. Warren credits himself with letting David be the first born as this facilitated his easier passage into this world.

The George household was quite competitive with plenty of testosterone flowing. It was a challenging time for their parents and particularly their father. Nevertheless, both the immediate and extended families continue to be very close despite geographical challenges of reunion from time to time.

Most of the extended family live in different Australian states except for Lorraine and Graeme. Both have returned to Adelaide after working internationally, or in other states or cities over time. All siblings were very successful in their chosen careers. Warren is a Fellow of the Institute of Public Accountants (FIPA) and has worked in Adelaide, Wellington and Sydney. His career had a leaning towards senior management in accounting system implementations, industry superannuation solutions and risk management, together with due diligence, company amalgamations and subsequent business process consolidations. He retired some six years ago. Sport, mainly tennis and travelling continues to be an important part of his life, but his family is the prime consideration.

Warren has been married to Wendy, who is still as beautiful as the day he met her, for 40 years. They have a son, Mark, who lives in Brisbane and a daughter, Tracey, who resides in Sydney with her husband Daniel and son Riley, who was born on Mother's Day, 12 May 2013.

Life is good.

Hugh Cecil GILLIES

(1917–1961)

by Julie Gillies Kernick

My father lived a short life. I don't remember a time when he was in good health due to the meningitis he contracted while serving in the war. He did, however, manage to achieve many things, and I have some fond memories of our short time together.

Hugh Cecil Gillies was an only child who grew up in a duplex house in Opey Avenue, Hyde Park. He attended Unley High School, which he left during the Depression to assist a boot-maker with errands. It was here, incidentally, that he learnt a lot about feet and found inspiration for his future career as a chiropodist. As a lad he enjoyed his time with the Scouts and went on to be a leader. I remember his stories of camping adventures that involved runaway trailers holding their equipment and supplies; there were also some rather interesting photos of nude bathing in rock pools.

Dad had a few hobbies that he enjoyed. He was a keen photographer and developed his own prints at home in the days when this was quite a process. He was also a keen trout fly-fisherman and had a stint as president, among other roles, of the South

Australian Trout Fly-Fishing Association. He was passionate about every aspect of fly-fishing and participated in regular fishing trips while working to establish fly-fishing in South Australia. He also collected a vast array of boxes and packets of bits and pieces, which he used to make his own flies for fishing. I can remember discussion about acquiring a peacock feather, among others, via contact with the Adelaide Zoo. All were sorted, labelled and immaculately stored. His acquisitions were well researched and he displayed great pride in them. My mother was called upon to design and make him a vest with zip-top fitted pockets which held divided containers holding his flies, sinkers, spinners and other fishing equipment. At the time no one else had anything like it. He also invented the 'Gillies' fly. One of the weekend activities was when the fly fishing association was getting the sport established here and located its first hatchery – a tin shed – on Cross Road by the train line on the south eastern corner. Dad was on the roster to check on the hatchlings and fingerlings. I was quite fascinated with the whole process and remember using an eyedropper to pick out the eggs that had died from the racks in the troughs. We also visited farm properties through the Adelaide Hills and Dad put hessian across the streams to facilitate deeper water so trout would establish in the streams. There were a number of men in the association involved in getting things established at this time.

Being a fourth generation Australian of Scottish descent, he inherited the characteristic fair skin and red hair. I can remember tying little ribbons in his hair as a young child while he lay on the divan in the study after work before heading out to one of his various club or association activities. However, I still did not realise underneath was red hair because his short back and sides of the time was well 'Brylcreemed'. I can remember him returning from fishing on a cloudy day in a hat and long-sleeved business shirt – pre sunscreen – and having been in full sun some of the day. His skin had burnt through his clothes' fabric, and when he took it off the construction of the shirt made a sharp outline on his pale arms. After that he always wore a thick army shirt.

He had also been part of the Adelaide Rowing Club and later would reconnect with fellow member Roland Kaibel and his wife Jill (now deceased) when in practice in North Terrace. Dad met my mother through a mutual friendship with Neville Soward who married Coralie and they became my godparents. Both are now deceased but daughters Robyn and Christine also attended Linden Park Demonstration School and Robyn and I have become friends again in recent years. I now regard Robin as my 'god sister', as we shared opposite parents as godparents, and my mum has taken her on as a daughter following the loss of her mother, who we all held in high esteem.

My earliest memories of my father are of when we lived in his family home with his dad, following the death of his mother. This was while our family home was being built at 14 Glenroy Avenue, Beaumont. Because of post war restrictions and availability of certain products, it took over four years to build. We moved to Beaumont when I was four-and-a-half, but before we moved there was an earthquake in Adelaide. This resulted in the house being underpinned with beams down the main wall through the middle of the house. My dad liked everything to be well done and the house was very solid in structure. There was also a timber-floored shed that held a car and a trailer, plus had shelving and cupboards at each end to hold traditional carpentry tools and equipment. There was a wooden staircase up to a half loft that had shelving and boxes full of ropes and old wooden shoe lasts in every size – length and width. It was a wonderful place to play with all sorts of bits and pieces and provided a great backdrop for my reading of Enid Blyton's *The Secret Seven* and *Famous Five* books, and for club meetings with groups of friends in the loft. The house was eventually demolished with a pair of two-storey town houses filling the block instead. Some sections of the stonewalling remain, but the rest of it must have been quite an undertaking to demolish!

We had a big holiday one year at Bright in Victoria with family friends the Winspears. We got out to the snow one day and did a bit of fishing as well. Fishing days at Clayton were the least enjoyed – in the heat, red mud and sand flies. Some trips out around Hindmarsh Island were very successful and I remember walking back across jetties with planks missing hurrying to get back to the car and make the last punt back to Port Elliot. One Christmas Dad made each of us a fishing rod from bamboo and fitted it out himself. His workmanship was immaculate. Due to his health problems, he took a weeks' holiday every term break to help him to relax. I have memories of spending a week away every school holidays at Middleton Beach or Victor Harbor. Family friends and neighbours were also there and a number had their own beach shacks or houses.

My sister Heather and I shared the front bedroom and I had a cot before moving into a bed. I remember sitting on Grandpa's lap in the big armchair in the corner of the sitting room. I also enjoyed Noddy stories and was entranced with the idea of having my own red car that went 'parp parp' and being able to go out on adventures. We had a black Vanguard car. Mum used to take me on the back of her bike in a cane basket seat to pre-school. I remember accompanying her to a felt hat-making class on at least one occasion too. We walked to King William Street and caught the tram at the end of the street – the line is gone there now. A second cousin of Dad's lived next door with three children. I remember playing with the youngest, Philip, and being in their bathtub – much deeper water than we were allowed at home! Our laundry was beside the back veranda and I remember wool bathers and 'bubble' ones, a knitted brown wool hat and a bucket and spade for the beach.

Mum was ill for several weeks when I was three, so I went to stay with my Nanna in Mum's family home in Alexandra Avenue, Rose Park. I had silk worms to help keep me entertained as Nanna had a huge mulberry tree in the backyard. There was also a huge fig tree over the chook house. We climbed both trees in summer and picked the fruit. The chooks enjoyed the dropped mulberries and had pink-tinged eggs in mulberry season. Nanna was in her 70s and looking after me must have been quite an undertaking as I was a very busy child. Everything I asked to do she said 'directly'.

I thought it meant 'later' but discovered it meant 'later but actually never' and it took me years to work out what 'directly' actually meant.

By this time Dad was practicing as a chiropodist with a practice he established in North Terrace. We had home help to wash the surgery towels and also wash, starch and press his surgery coats with the clip buttons. He sharpened his own scalpel blades with stones, leather straps and oil, and was absolutely meticulous. This was in the pre-disposable days. I remember 'Page', as we called her, being at the house often to undertake this work. Being elderly she asked to work at her own pace and was very much a part of the household. His dad, my grandpa, was a carpenter and builder, and had a full set of trade tools including knives and sharpening implements. Dad worked with extremely sharp instruments and I remember once when he dropped his fixed handle scalpel one day while working on a patient; it dropped straight through his woollen suit pants and into his leg. There was a lot of blood and he was driven home with his leg wrapped in a number of surgery towels.

Dad joined the army in World War Two and was based for a time at the camp on Victoria Park Race Course, almost across the road from my mother's family home. He was working on establishing his chiropody practice. At the time there were no courses or qualifications he could complete that provided adequate training, so he did a three-month correspondence course available in Victoria. He acquired books and other materials from England and studied and taught himself wherever he could. At the time chiropody had a low status and he spent many years up until his death working on getting the profession established. When he died he was the second South Australian President of the Chiropody Association following Major Mitchell, and part-time lecturer at the South Australian Institute of Mines (now the University of South Australia), where a course was by then established.

Dad combined what he had learnt running errands for the bootmaker with his passion for chiropody, and started making foot supports. As with everything else he did, he researched and ordered materials from all over the world to meet specialised needs to feet.

When he was in the army it soon became known that he knew something about feet, and he became a sergeant with his own tent set up as a chiropody centre where he checked the soldiers' feet and sorted other problems while insisting on correctly fitting boots. The army surgeon who had facilitated this arrangement continued to refer patients to Dad post-war when they were both back in Adelaide in their respective practices. Unfortunately Dad contracted meningitis while in service. It had previously been a deadly disease, but sulphur injections into the spine had just started several weeks before and once the seriousness of his 'sore throat' was realised he was fortunately diagnosed and given the new treatment before it was too late. He lived, but it had a dramatic effect on his life, leaving him with chronic headaches and very high blood pressure. My sister I were born after this so never had an opportunity to know him prior to his being so ill.

I was always very keen to be involved in various activities and one of my desires was to play the piano accordion. This was not a popular choice with other family members but I did manage to have an instrument and take lessons. I remember my dad hearing me practise Christmas carols very early on and encouraging me by asking me to play several verses to the relatives at Christmas lunch at our house. Manfred Bauer, at Ron Pearce Music School taught me for about eight years.

While visiting a favourite cousin, Richard Cooper, on his family farm, we chose a puppy from a litter of their farm dog. The father was not known but somehow the kelpie cross dog looked amazingly like a dingo and had a great personality to match. Neighbourhood children asked to have a pet dog like Ritchie and when we were on holidays he was frequently sneaked inside by hosts and hidden under the table where he enjoyed a few scraps. My special photo of my dad is of him showing Ritchie a fish he had caught. He also liked the family car, but once in, getting him out could be a challenge. Ritchie learned to jump out the opened back door as we paused roadside driving up Devereux Road on our way to turn up

Glenroy Avenue. There would be a terrific racquet followed by a scuffle as he leapt out and raced us home.

Dad's dad, Pop, came to live with us at Beaumont. He continued working as a carpenter and liked to go dancing on Saturday night. He had two medals from World War One but never spoke of his service. He had a Morris Minor and my parents were always very worried about his driving as there were a series of minor prangs. He liked to go dancing on Saturday and used to get his very short hair cut every Saturday. People joked that he went for the chat with the others, but I think he liked to keep his grooming and his bushy eyebrows under control with a weekly tidy up. He used to shave with a cut-throat razor before going out and as a child I used to inspect his very smooth skin. My dad, I remember, wore tailor-made suits for work as well as causal clothes on the weekend and had waist-high fishing waders for casting a line off Waitpinga Beach.

Pop met a new partner and married, a relationship that turned out well. Dad commented, as best man at the wedding, that Pop had put his age back ten years on the marriage certificate! He continued working into his 70s but his son, my dad, was to die well before him.

Dad's desk was immaculate. He had a copperplate hand, was ambidextrous, and used to write my name on my school writing books on the cover with a thick nibbed pen dipped in black ink. I was sure that they were the neatest named books in the class. His workmanship and attention to detail contributed to his skills as a podiatrist where careful blade work and accurate foot supports were essential. It is possible that his drive to do things so meticulously contributed to his stress which, combined with his illness, ensured ridiculously high blood pressure and caused his eventual demise.

One task he undertook relentlessly was to ensure that his war service was recognised, including his part-disability (about five per cent) from his illness while on war service. My mum eventually realised why he did this when he died the day before his 44th birthday and she was eligible for a war widow's pension and other benefits. He had tried to take out a life insurance policy and found the premiums offered were 50 per cent per annum of the value of the policy.

My parents decided that my sister and I would not know just how ill my father was. We knew we had frequent family holidays and that fishing was a relaxing hobby for him. One occasion, while with his fishing friends, was not so relaxing. He had reached his daily bag limit, but nevertheless threw his line back in, catching the biggest trout ever. He had to put the fish back, but spent time after that unsuccessfully trying to catch it again.

He was in the Repatriation Hospital at Daw Park for six weeks one Christmas with blood pressure so high (both readings in the two hundreds) that he was not even allowed out of bed. He was out in the shed with a neighbour working at the bench a year later when he had a stroke. The ambulance was called and he was taken to hospital, dying that evening.

Dad had a leading reputation for his chiropody practice. When he died suddenly, his chiropodist, Heather, was about to leave the practice to be married. She ended up deferring her wedding for six months, giving Mum time to sell the practice and organise a way ahead for us. His amazing developments with foot supports helped many people and his work on the committee, which defined 'podiatry' in state legislation, set the path for the future of the profession, establishing it in the American surgical tradition rather than a more European pedicure style. South Australia was the first state to achieve this by some years. Unfortunately his complete collection of podiatry books went with the practice and that part of his history is lost. He is buried in Centennial Park in the soldiers' memorial section. Friends and family helped to sell his business and support Mum in practical ways, including selling his fishing gear and all those boot lasts. Family friends remained, and we continued to be included, something that was not always 'done' when one became a widow in the 1960s.

Dad's drive to learn and be the best remained to the end. He even had the lawnmower serviced 'just in case'. His attention to detail was unmatched. All our fruit trees in the backyard were professionally pruned, trenched, sprayed and watered well – the million dollar peaches we had growing up are still a fond memory. Just a few months ago I had occasion to speak to a fellow parishioner at St David's Burnside, Russell Greentree (who is 95 and looks about 70), about my father dying in 1961 (now over 50 years ago). In that process I had occasion to acknowledge the life he had lived up until that time and the life he missed out on. That conversation about his war service and life in general has enabled me to reach a point of forwarding my story and finally acknowledging my dad's life.

Dad's life was all too short but he succeeded in leaving a legacy of many fine achievements.

Julie Gillies Kernick

Julie is the younger of two daughters who attended Linden Park Primary School from year one to seven. She then attended Presbyterian Girls College (now Seymour College) at Glen Osmond and completed qualifications at four universities here and overseas. While her children were young she worked in education for several Commonwealth bodies in Canberra before returning to Adelaide in 1993 as Assistant Secretary of the Independent Education Union. Julie currently works as a manager at the Construction Industry Training Board, has three adult children and is very happily married to Phil. While her dad died when she was in primary school, her mum has enjoyed good health and is still living in her own home in Adelaide.

Ferdinand Frederick BRECHT

(1913–2003)

by David Brecht

My father was born Ferdinand Frederick Brecht on 25 May 1913 in one of the family homes on what was then Burnside Road, Knightsbridge, on the east side of Adelaide. A midwife came to the house, as was common practice in those days. The new baby came to be known simply as 'Fred' and that was the name by which most people knew him throughout his life. He used to say that he was born in eventful times 'between the Titanic disaster and the World War One'. In later years, to Fred's regret, Burnside Road became Glynburn Road and Knightsbridge became Leabrook. Fred's birthplace was important to him and he always reckoned that it had been compromised by having the original names replaced.

Around 1910, Fred's father Herbert accepted a government land grant and started a farm on the River Murray. The closest town was Morgan. During the years in which Herbert was establishing the farm, his first two children, sons Sheldon and Fred, were separated and sent to live with family in Adelaide. Fred spent his early years mostly in Burnside in the home of his paternal grandfather who had migrated to Australia from the city of Brunswick in Lower Saxony, Germany, many years before. The Brecht children would eventually number seven, with six boys and a girl.

In 1921, when Fred was eight, he and Sheldon were brought home to rejoin the family on the farm. The kids loved life on the river. There was swimming, boating, and all sorts of adventures. One of Fred's favourite pastimes was watching the paddle steamers go by. He had a keen interest in all things mechanical and could identify many of the steamers by the sound of their engine, even before they came into view. Dad told me of one steamer that had been put together by mounting a steam locomotive on a barge and fitting paddle wheels to it. He said it had a unique sound, like a train coming up the river. Dad sometimes spoke of how the Murray River flooded in 1931, peaking at 9.8 metres at Morgan and breaching some of the levees. The Brecht family home, built on a low ridge above the river, filled with water to a depth of over a metre. The family had to make a hasty departure to their other house further back on higher ground. Later, Herbert, Fred and several others came back in a rowboat, manoeuvring it into the flooded house through the wide front windows to try to salvage items of value that had been left behind in the rush.

When Fred was ten years old, his father decided that he was skilful and responsible enough to drive himself and the other kids to school in Morgan in a horse-drawn dray. This became a regular occurrence for a while. Fred had a natural ability for working with mechanical things and, by the time he was 12, he was driving and helping to maintain the family cars and motorcycles. His mother, an Irish woman named Adeline, didn't drive, so Fred would often drive her into Morgan to do the shopping. The local policeman was a country boy himself and understood the need for farm kids to often take on adult duties, so, as long as they behaved themselves, he turned a blind eye to underage drivers. There was always something that needed fixing on the farm and Fred became a skilful handyman, repairing everything from plumbing and electrical systems to furniture and farmyard equipment. In his spare time, he amused himself and delighted the younger children by making wooden toys for them.

As a young adult, Fred decided to head off on his own for a while and worked at various jobs on farms on the Eyre Peninsula, particularly in the region around Elliston, a small town on the edge of the Great Australian Bight. Fred used to like standing on top of the cliffs there, watching the huge waves roll in. He travelled almost exclusively by motorbike in those days and honed his riding skills on rough unpaved roads, dirt tracks and cross-country jaunts through the scrub. He became an expert at roadside repairs, sometimes completing a trip with clips and brackets cobbled from pieces of old wire and scrap metal that he found lying around. It seemed that everywhere he went, there were farm girls in their late teens or early 20s looking for husbands, often with the help of their mothers, but Fred was determined to keep moving in those days and remained single. Work commenced on the Goolwa Barrages in 1935 and Fred worked on the project on and off in several different capacities. Eventually he decided to settle down and married his cousin Roma.

By 1940 World War Two was in full swing and able-bodied men were joining the armed forces en masse. Fred was a patriot and more than ready to fight for his country so he joined the Army Signals Corps, a division of the Second Australian Imperial Force (2nd AIF), with the intention of becoming a motorcycle dispatch rider. At the army base where he signed up, some rather nasty recruiting officers asked Fred if he was joining the right side because of his German surname, but Fred told them that he was second-generation Australian and that Australia was his country. He was sent overseas to take part in the North African campaign.

As planned, Fred became a dispatch rider known unofficially as a 'Don R', an English expression also adopted by the Australians. His mount was the army version of the 490cc single-cylinder Norton known as the WD16H (WD for War Department). One of his regular delivery runs was from southern Israel, known as Palestine in those days, north to Syria. He had to maintain a constant lookout for roaming German fighter planes whose pilots liked to use Allied dispatch riders for target practice. Also, there were Arab ambushers who believed that they were helping to free themselves from the tyranny of 'British fascism' by aiding the Nazis. A band of Syrians pushed a cow across the road one night in front of Fred and it was too late for him to stop. He ploughed into the animal, killing it instantly, and finished up lying on the ground next to his bike. As the Arabs closed in, he got to his feet, whipped out his army revolver and the would-be assassins fled into the darkness. Much to Fred's relief, he found that the Norton was still in good working order so he resumed his journey, very thankful to have survived the encounter.

On another occasion, he heard the sound of an aero engine rapidly increasing in volume over the sound of his own engine, and looked back over his shoulder to see a fighter plane making a low level run up the road behind him. He stood on the rear brake, slid the bike down and rolled into the ditch, waiting for the hail of bullets that never came. The aircraft roared over him and pulled up in a big climbing turn and Fred saw the distinctive shape of Spitfire wings. An RAF pilot had decided to break the monotony of his patrol by having some 'fun'.

In 1942, the 2nd AIF left the Middle East and returned to Australia to meet the threat of Japan's entry into the war. During the interim period in Australia Fred was assigned to be an off-road driving instructor, because of his skills and experience. During a training session, a jeep rolled on him and broke his back, so Fred spent some time in hospital in a plaster body cast. He recovered, was deemed to be ready for more active service and was sent north to the Philippines where he was put in charge of maintaining a group of mobile generating sets that provided power for the camp. Fred was neither a drinker nor a smoker, and saved his beer and cigarette rations to use as trade. This was particularly useful on one occasion when one of the generator engines died and there were no available replacements. There was a temporary US Air Force aerodrome next door to the camp, and Fred bargained with the Americans for various bits and pieces to construct a generating set. He collected a good motor from a damaged jeep, the chassis of an old ammunition wagon and electrical wiring and gauges from decommissioned aircraft. Upon completion, the generating set worked perfectly and became one of the main units of the camp's electricity supply.

The army camp was right alongside the American runways and Fred used to watch hundreds of fighters and bombers taking off each day, heading north to attack the Japanese invasion force. Some of the planes would come back damaged from the conflict, the fighters with engines misfiring and trailing smoke, and the bombers with holes shot in the wings and sometimes with a motor missing altogether. Fred watched one day as a badly damaged bomber ditched into the ocean and he admired the pilot's skill as the plane slid across the water and came to a stop on the edge of the sand. The crew were able to step out on to dry land, doubtlessly marvelling at their good fortune.

The war ended and the Army asked for volunteers to go north through the Pacific Islands to help gather up Australian prisoners-of-war from the various Japanese camps, so Fred became part of the recovery squad. He would tell stories of the walking skeletons they found and those who begged to be given a gun to settle the score with their former captors, many of whom were still there, having been abandoned by their rapidly retreating forces. Non-stop food kitchens were set up and the starved men were fattened up before being taken back to Australia. This was done in an attempt to limit the outrage that people already felt as a result of the many widespread reports of Japanese cruelty. It had already been arranged that we would trade with Japan in the post-war years and nothing was permitted to spoil those plans.

While Fred was away on military service, his wife had become involved with another man so Fred found himself single again. He left the Army and went to work in Adelaide for a motorcycle sales and repair firm known as Lenroc's. The company sold Triumph motorcycles and entered a team in the annual *Advertiser* 24-hour road trials. The team consisted of two solo bikes and a sidecar outfit. Special skills were required to handle the outfit over rough terrain so Fred was recruited as the rider and won the *Advertiser* Trial four years in a row from 1947. Lenroc's made much of his victories in their advertising, referring to Fred as 'The Unbeatable Man and Machine'. Three of his victories were with his young nephew Gordon in the sidecar as navigator.

During those early postwar years, Fred met an attractive brunette named Marjorie Illingworth who had come to Australia as a two-year-old in 1919 with her family, from Coventry, England. Marjorie was also a returned service officer, having spent her time as an army nurse in Port Moresby, New Guinea, and then in Katherine, in the Northern Territory, after her group was moved back to Australia to escape the Japanese invasion. Marjorie and Fred were married in 1947. A daughter, Helen, arrived in 1948 and was followed by a son, myself, in 1950.

In 1952, the Brecht family moved from their rental flat in Tusmore to their brand-new house at 4 Seaton Avenue, Hazelwood Park. My mother had spent the early part of 1950 looking for an affordable block of land in a nice neighbourhood. As a child, she had lived in Queenstown and found certain aspects of it to be rather squalid. She had attended the Queenstown Primary School and remembered walking home past the Alberton Hotel on Port Road and seeing drunks staggering around and, on occasion, lying in the gutter. Mother was determined that her future children would grow up in a much nicer environment. One of her older sisters, Gladys, had married in 1926 and was living on Heathpool Road, just a few doors from Tusmore Park. Mother visited Gladys often. The lovely homes in tree-lined streets appealed to Mother, as did the nearby park. It was the sort of place to raise children and she intended to have the same. Prior to purchasing our block, she had done a thorough inspection of Hazelwood Park, noting the close proximity to the park itself. Here, children could climb trees, play in the creek and generally run free. She had noted the brand-new Linden Park

Primary School and decided that it would be suitable for educating her little daughter and baby son, when the time came.

Construction of the Brecht house had taken two long years. The builder was an obstinate old Englishman, Horace Waterman, who wouldn't be hurried or told what to do, so the more Mum and Dad tried to encourage him to get on with the job, the slower he went. My parents would visit the house each weekend, hoping to see some signs of progress and steeling themselves against disappointment if nothing had been done. Horace had a Lightning cement mixer and had painted his name above and below the brand name so that it read 'Horace Lightning Waterman', which became a grim joke to my parents as the building time dragged on.

Eventually the house was finished and we moved in. Mother and Dad revelled in the spaciousness compared to the Tusmore flat, and enjoyed the freedom of owning their own place and getting away from their grumpy former landlord. The house was standing on a bare, muddy, sloping block, but for years Dad toiled ceaselessly after work at night and on weekends, landscaping and building retaining walls, laying concrete paths, building a large garage and workshop and establishing lawns and the garden. He also made built-in wardrobes, cupboards and shelving for the house. He loved his garden and planted fruit trees, grape vines and many different types of vegetables, so we always had a supply of fresh, perfectly ripened food to supplement the bought goods. Mother was an excellent cook and Dad planted a special little garden for her with parsley, mint, chives and various other herbs.

When Lenroc's closed their doors in the early 1950s, Fred rejoined the Army as a member of the Royal Australian Electrical and Mechanical Engineers division known as 'Raymee'. He was stationed at Keswick Barracks and commuted each weekday, up and down Greenhill Road, on his trusty Austrian Puch motor scooter, which we named 'Pooky'. During this period with the Army, Fred studied at night, sat for written and practical exams, and gained a number of trade certificates, formalising different aspects of his mechanical skills. In 1962, he left the Army and worked for a short time at the Magill Reformatory as a group supervisor, but his old back injury started to give him chronic discomfort and he couldn't take the hours of standing when the boys were working outside.

Fred went to work as a mechanic for George Bolton, then mayor of Burnside. George owned a Kawasaki motorcycle dealership and general service and repairs workshop on the corner of Fullarton and Greenhill roads. Fred worked on everything from lawn mowers and motorbikes to quarry trucks. He wore a back brace in those days and would come home for lunch every day and spend at least 20 minutes lying flat on his back on the kitchen floor. This used to ease the pain so that he could go back to work. The Puch scooter had been replaced by a little Goggomobil sedan, which provided much more support for Dad's back and protection from the weather on cold wet days. In the tradition of his own childhood, Dad taught me to drive this car when I was 12.

Fred had a love for cars, motorbikes, airplanes, speedboats and just about anything mechanical. 'Anything with an engine in it,' my mother used to say. I inherited this passion, and Dad and I would talk happily for hours about cars, motorbikes, and motor racing. He took me to many race meetings to watch motorbikes, go-karts, and speedboats, and we regularly made the trek out to the Mallala road-racing circuit and the Collingrove hill-climb. Friday night was 'Speedway Night' and we were regulars at Rowley Park, thrilling to the sight of the racing machines, the crackle and snarl of their engines and the smell of their special fuel.

We were not wealthy by any means and any 'new' family cars were second-hand and always required a lot of fixing up. From the age of eight, I would help Dad to work on the cars, watching and learning so that I could repair and maintain my own vehicles in later years. When my sister and I bought our first cars, Dad and I worked on each one, doing whatever was necessary to make the car safe and reliable, and minor repairs and maintenance were an ongoing job. Dad was our 'RAA' for years if anything went wrong with our cars while we were out. He was just a phone call away and would always arrive with tools, and a jerrycan of petrol, if needed.

He also had a towrope if all else failed and we needed to get the car home for serious repairs. Dad was always the backstop in everything and there was rarely a problem that he couldn't fix.

Dad loved his grandchildren and they loved him. He would play with them for hours, and he and my mother would take my sister's daughter and my son to Victor Harbor for summer caravan holidays, which the children loved and remember vividly. I'll never forget the sight of my 88-year-old father down on the floor with his two-year-old great-grandson, both of them pushing little Hot Wheels cars around on the carpet and making engine noises.

By 1995, my mother was chronically ill and spent the last two years of her life in bed. She had told my father that she wanted to stay in her own home so he looked after her with my daily help and regular visits by nurses and the doctor. Mum was sometimes a difficult patient but my father's love for her never wavered and his patience was infinite. After she passed on, I looked after Dad so that he could stay in his own home with his beloved garden where he spent so many happy hours.

One afternoon in May 2003, a week short of his 90th birthday, Dad slipped peacefully away after a lifetime of devotion to those people whom he loved. I'll always remember the countless gifts he gave us down the years, the many hours that we spent together, and his steadfast willingness to help in whatever way was necessary. I know that he suffered from his back injury but I never heard him complain. He had a keen sense of humour and, rather than grumble when things weren't going right, instead he would say or do something to amuse us. How do you thank someone who selflessly gave so much for so long? I don't know, but I hope Dad is watching me write this and knows just how much he was loved and appreciated.

David Brecht

David Gordon Brecht was born in Toorak Gardens, Adelaide, on 24 January 1950 to Marjorie and Fred Brecht. He was their second child, having a sister, Helen, who was 17 months older. David received his primary education at the Linden Park Demonstration School and then moved on to Norwood High. In January 1969, he joined the then-Department Of Civil Aviation as a clerical officer and spent the next 23 years working in a number of positions and locations, helping to ensure the safety of civil and commercial aircraft operations in the South Australia/Northern Territory region. During this time, he was married twice and the second union produced a son, Adrian, born in 1971. David was a keen surfer and motorcyclist and had a passion for writing and producing his own pop songs on multi-track recorders. He was mostly a 'one-man band' and played guitar, piano, keyboards and drums and sang lead and backing vocals. He became adept at building electronic audio devices and built much of the equipment that he used in his recordings. In 1991, the aviation department was subjected to a 56 per cent staff cut and David's entire section was made redundant, along with many others. David left the department in 1992 and spent the next two years taking care of his girlfriend who suffered a long illness. Then he helped his father to take of care of Marjorie who was bed-ridden for the last two and a half years of her life. Following her death in 1997, David looked after his father for the next six years until Fred's death in 2003. These days, David spends his time with friends, hobbies and a large collection of favourite books, movies and music.

Philip Mercer HISCO

(1923–2009)

by Garrie Hisco

Philip was born on 6 August 1923 to Charles Thomas Hisco and Elizabeth Jones Hisco. They resided in Keyes Street, Linden Park. Charles was an antique restorer and wood-turner of some note. He held the contract for Government House to maintain the furniture at that time. He was a Freeman of Bristol and held the key to that city. Elizabeth was a Scot born in Edinburgh. The big, beautiful Tudor-style home they built was a family centrepiece and the three boys played in the grounds and the workshop where Charles would French polish and build and repair all manner of exquisite pieces.

Philip was bought up in that tradition. His schooldays were spent at Rose Park School. Weekends were always fun as he would practice roller skating on wooden wheels that he would turn himself on his father's wood lathe. At that time the OBE (Our Boys Institute in the city) had a skating rink.

He attended Adelaide High School and later began work in Newton McLaren Pty Ltd, Leigh Street, in the city. He began in that company as an office boy and later became a representative.

He joined the Army as World War Two began along with his two brothers who joined the Navy and the Air Force respectively. He was soon transferred to accompany the ninth division as a signaller.

This period of his life took him first to Queensland for training; then to Tarakan to help defend the island against the Japanese. During that time, as a member of the Signals he spent much time in appalling conditions constructing, repairing and ensuring the communications were in place. He experienced a bomb attack when his jeep hit a landmine. Along with his mates, all were thrown from the vehicle. He sustained a hearing injury at that time. He spoke very little about the Tarakan experience as was the way most returned soldiers coped.

I do remember him mentioning the mud, the humidity and the swamps, where he would spend days at a time waist deep in mud and leaches. He contracted Malaria amongst other things. He did comment that the Japanese prisoners were of the same thinking at the time and that nobody really wanted to be there. It was a terrible experience for all concerned. He took an interest in the locals, the Fuzzy Wuzzy Angels, as they were called. On his leaving they presented him with a beautifully carved and bladed machete for his kindness to them. I still treasure his memento.

He returned to Australia eventually with Red Cross handkerchiefs with Japanese illustrations and written messages passed through the wires to him from prisoners who were grateful for the humane treatment they were shown by our soldiers.

At that time he would write as often as possible to his sweetheart back in Adelaide. Ronda Venus was also in the Army by then. She enlisted in the AWAS and was stationed at Woodside Camp and later in Seymour in Victoria. Philip was 19 years of age at that time. He returned to Australia and recommenced his relationship with Ronda Venus. They were married in 1947 in Scots Church on Adelaide's North Terrace.

He had an interest in motorbikes and they would travel everywhere that way with Ronda riding sidecar! His career blossomed and his many friendships made during the war experience made for excellent business connections and mateship. Two children followed. The family home in Hazelwood Park built by them in 1948 still stands. My mother still lives there.

Family life was well provided for with many people always visiting. My father made many friends amongst the Linden Park School community. Many longstanding business connections were made. He was a member of the Tusmore Freemasons Lodge. Local names like Collett, Blanchard, Marchant, Toombes, Roe, Stacy, Nottage, and Cribb were amongst his contacts. All of these families had children attending Linden Park School at the time.

My father had a special interest in micro switchgear and provided much equipment for the original installations at places like Holden, Kelvinator and the West End and Southwark breweries. He was a generous man very well liked amongst the business community. Many of his orders were taken in hotels after work with his colleagues. At that time hotels closed at six o'clock in the evening. The bars were always packed.

He very much enjoyed his working life. After 38 years in the electrical wholesale business the company closed. His many long-term friends moved elsewhere and he finally retired after a few years working at Seymour College in the maintenance department.

Throughout his life he was a devoted husband and father ensuring his family had everything we needed. Annually, we would go snow skiing. He delighted in the fun and antics in the snow. Many more business relationships developed whilst we teenagers were enjoying the slopes and he would often return home with more orders for equipment. My memories of him, immaculately dressed in tailored suits and always with a new motor car, are indelible.

At one time he helped me restore a vintage car. I was only 12 but the two of us pulled the tiny 1925 Austin Seven apart and reassembled it to as-new condition inside the garage. I was very anxious to drive it. It took some time for me to realise that he had seen that coming and had ensured that the end of the garage had to be removed before it could be taken outside!

On my 16th birthday he finally relented and both car and I

were free! It started me on a long and enduring life passion for the manufactured object and only a few years later I studied industrial design at art school.

My father was a totally amusing man, full of jokes and fun. He would often have us all laughing at the dinner table; always entertaining. His easy nature enabled many local family friendships to be made. At that time it was the early 60s and our home always seemed to be having parties and family gatherings. This was an era when the Australian larrikin still existed. It would be fair to say that many of his friends could have been described that way. When a fence was to be built or a concrete path to be laid, or if there was a fishing trip to Black Point or Victor Harbour or Port Vincent, groups of friends and relatives would appear to share the fun.

It was a time when sense of community still existed. He would take us on picnics, tennis days and all kind of events. Our lives were full and happy. Each Friday night the family was treated to the Speedway where we would watch the likes of Moss Marchant, Ray Skipper and Clem Smith race each other in their stock cars. Many of us boys became addicted to motor sport at that time (not to mention Chiko Rolls!). A number of lads at Linden Park followed the lead and some to this day are still engaged in that sport inspired during their schooldays. Whitrow, Marchant and Cribb come to mind!

As a role model my father always made a big impression on me, along with my grandfather. Both instilled a love of craftsmanship, order, and an interest in perfection. As a child I picked up on these things and without doubt it led me into my own careers and interests. In his retirement years he and my mother travelled the world many times visiting Asia, Europe, England and the United States of America. He developed a keen interest in motoring holidays. A motorhome was purchased, and the two of them would often travel to various parts of Australia in it.

At 86 he enjoyed his four grandchildren. He would amuse them with his musical talents learnt way back in the trenches. Just about any tune would come from his mouth organ on demand. He would love to take requests!

He passed away three-and-a-half years ago of a sudden illness. Sadly missed and never forgotten.

He was a gentleman.

Garrie Hisco

Garrie's background since schooldays has been in a range of areas, but always to do with art and design. He studied at the South Australian School of Art on leaving The Adelaide Technical High School. He also qualified as a high school teacher in the specialist field of design. He spent seven years teaching design in schools before being appointed Design Education Lecturer to Torrens CAE (later known as the University of South Australia).

He worked in the School of Design and School of Education for over 20 years teaching various areas of study from product design, philosophy of design, art and design history, graphic design and clinical in-school teacher training, and studio subjects like drawing and CAD.

It was a long and enjoyable career from which he resigned in 1998 to begin his own business. He chose to develop a Japanese ryokan in Adelaide. For eleven years it held a five star rating and was known as 'Allessandro Maandini's Ryokan'. It was a lot of fun and many interesting people, celebrities and business groups were entertained there.

Garrie has written two books: one published and the other still in process, with a third book underway. His big passions in life have been exotic sports, vintage and racing cars.

Since 1986 he has been a world traveller/adventurer. Many tours of Europe, Asia, the Middle East and the United States have taken him to the world's most fascinating places. Garrie lives in the Adelaide Hills with his collection of motor vehicles and his cat!

He still owns the ryokan, which is now leased to corporate groups.

From Country to City

Gordon Samuel RINDER

(1919–1985)

by Greg Rinder

On 12 June 12 1919, Gordon Samuel Rinder was born to parents Edward George and Ida Blonde at Maitland on the Yorke Peninsula, South Australia, the second of two children. His father ran the town picture theatre and was Maitland's first Ford dealer, opening and operating the town's first garage where the new motorcars could be serviced. Gordon often made trips across to Adelaide with his parents and sister Nance in the T-model Fords, a journey over rough dirt wagon tracks that took two days to complete if all went well. According to Gordon it was not uncommon for the wheels to detach themselves from the early Model Ts and the family usually stopped overnight with a relative living at Wild Horse Plains, often to undertake repairs. Little remains of that once substantial dwelling whilst the small township by the old Adelaide Road has now almost vanished.

Gordon spent his early years in the country before the family shifted to Adelaide so that Gordon could attend Prince Alfred

College. Though he did not excel at college, he enjoyed literature and mathematics, winning a number of awards. After leaving school Gordon went into business with his father. After settling in Adelaide George had purchased Humphrey's Canning Company, a manufacturer of, amongst other products, an excellent tomato sauce.

At the age of 21, Gordon enlisted in the Royal Australian Air Force and was shipped across the Pacific Ocean to Canada for training. Once qualified as a pilot with the rank of flight sergeant, he was transferred to England for active service with the RAAF. Like most returned servicemen, Gordon rarely discussed his World War Two service but on occasion recalled some events. One dealt with the voyage across the U-boat-infested Atlantic Ocean on an old freighter that developed engine trouble halfway and was forced to drop out of the relative protection of the convoy. Gordon, together with other RAAF personnel, manned the deck guns during the terrifying hours that the ship sat motionless in the water, each minute expecting to see a periscope or torpedo speeding towards the stricken vessel. Fortunately they survived and finally reached the United Kingdom where Gordon was posted to a billet in the historic Lygon Arms Hotel at Broadway in the Cotswolds. Charles I and Oliver Cromwell had both stayed at the hotel during the English Civil War so Gordon was certainly in good company. He joined a nearby RAAF squadron and flew reconnaissance missions over Europe in a Douglas Boston Bomber. Failing eyesight grounded him in 1943 and he became a flight instructor before returning to Australia in 1945 to undertake operational duties against the Japanese in Southeast Asia. He was based in the Northern Territory not far from Darwin until the end of hostilities.

Gordon received his 'exemplary' discharge from the RAAF in May 1946 and returned to Adelaide where he recommenced employment with his father. After five years with the RAAF Gordon decided to take an ocean cruise along the eastern coast of Australia from Sydney to Cairns in 1947. It must have been an extremely relaxing contrast to his wartime adventures on both the Pacific and

Atlantic oceans. It was on this voyage that he met Ruth Iverson and a shipboard romance developed. Ruth and Gordon were married at St Andrew's Church in Brighton, Victoria on 11 December 1948, and returned to Adelaide where they lived with Gordon's parents in a large Tudor house on Greenhill Road, Toorak Gardens. I, Gregory Edward, was born in 1950 and grew up with both parents and grandparents.

After working with his father for a number of years, Gordon decided to purchase John Farmer Pty Ltd, a manufacturing business that produced saws for companies such as Black & Decker. He had virtually no experience in this field but wanted to improve his position in life as well as securing a better future for his family. After years of hard work, long hours at both the office and factory, interstate travel and many sacrifices, his efforts paid off. With ongoing contracts and now a comfortable income, Gordon and Ruth purchased their first home in 1956, a little stone cottage at Linden Park.

I was attending the nearby Linden Park Primary School when Gordon applied for membership of the Royal Adelaide Golf Club. Every Saturday he would travel down to Seaton to play on what he considered to be one of the finest courses in Australia. He was a proud member and often recalled sharing drinks at the 19th hole, the bar, with a number of famous South Australians including Sir Donald Bradman. Gordon was an excellent golfer playing off a handicap of six in his younger days. He cultivated an intimate group of wonderful golfing associates and friends who attested to the fact that he was an excellent competitor: the more pressure he was under, the better he played. He was a great sportsman in every sense of the word, playing always to win whilst accepting defeat like a gentleman, without excuse or grumble. Golf was his passion and together with Ruth they played at affiliate courses in Victoria and New South Wales. He also enjoyed tennis, watching local Australian rules football matches together with the sport of professional boxing, attending many bouts whenever the opportunity arose. I joined him in later years.

In the 1960s Gordon purchased a larger home at Glenunga where his elderly parents came to live after selling the old family home on Greenhill Road. A comfortable granny flat was built onto the original house and the extended Rinder family were reunited under the same roof again until George and Ida passed away. By now I was attending Prince Alfred College, a school that both my father and grandfather had attended before me.

Gordon had always wanted to return to England after the war but unfortunately could not convince Ruth to leave Australia. In 2007 my wife Rosalie and I made the pilgrimage. Our first port of call after landing at Heathrow Airport was Gordon's old billet at the Lygon Arms Hotel in Broadway. It was a moving experience to enjoy an English beer at the same bar that had served the RAAF airmen back in the early years of World War Two. Gordon finally convinced Ruth that they needed to see a little more of the world and in 1969, we all boarded a passenger/cargo ship in Fremantle to sail up the Western Australian coast to Singapore. Though a wonderful experience for all, it was to be Gordon's last voyage.

By the mid 1970s Gordon decided to sell his business and planned to retire, however, a long-time friend Dr John Bundey, encouraged him to accept an accounting position with a group of Adelaide based doctors. This part-time role proved to be literally 'just what the doctor ordered' as Gordon had always enjoyed a new challenge. He continued to look after the practice's financial affairs until finally retiring altogether in 1983 when he and Ruth moved from their third family home in Glen Osmond to a beachside property south of Adelaide at Silver Sands on the Fleurieu Peninsula. He now played golf at the Willunga Golf Club and explored the local area together with wife Ruth. Their granddaughter Emily and I joined them regularly at their lovely home near the beach.

Gordon kept in touch with a number of old Air Force mates he had met in the United Kingdom during the war, together with a close circle of golfing friends and neighbours that he and Ruth regularly socialised with. The move down south introduced a whole new lifestyle for Gordon, something that he adapted to very quickly, forming strong new friendships with many local residents. Their Silver Sands sea change was brief but extremely happy and fulfilling. Within two years of moving down south, Gordon developed cancer and passed away on 29 December 1984, after a short time in hospital. He was 65 years of age. His wife Ruth survived him into her 94th year, passing away nearly 30 years later in November 2012.

Throughout his life Gordon had always enjoyed the company of wonderful friends. Dr John Bundey survived most of them and wrote the following words for his funeral service. They are the recollections of a dear friend who knew him well:

Gordon's kindness and generosity, especially to those less fortunate than himself, is well attested to by those who knew him best. As a friend he was always there when most needed. He was excellent company, possessing an excellent sense of humour characterised best by his ability to relate humorous stories against himself. Above all a sense of dignity pervaded his whole personality making him one that would stand out in a crowd. It was a privilege to have known Gordon Rinder and those of you who counted him among your close friends were lucky indeed. To those who were closest to Gordon and knew his love as husband, father or grandfather we can only acknowledge the greatness of your loss. May you be strengthened in your loss and may you treasure the memories of a wonderful human being.

From a son's point of view, my father will always be remembered warmly as a man with high standards and convictions. He was immensely proud of his military service and of Australia's defence forces. He had a great sense of humour and was a staunch and loyal friend to the special people in his life. He was a hard-working man who made the most of every opportunity in order that he care for his family and provide them with a comfortable and happy lifestyle. Banjo Patterson once said: 'A man who's done his best has done enough.'

Gordon Samuel Rinder could easily have been that man.

Greg Rinder

Gregory Edward Rinder was born on 19 April 1950, the only child of Ruth and Gordon Rinder. He attended Linden Park Primary School and later Prince Alfred College. Greg studied surveying and geological mapping whilst employed by a Canadian mineral exploration company in the late 60s. His work took him to the outback and he has continued to explore the remote vastness of Australia for both work and pleasure ever since. He joined the CSIRO in 1972 and throughout his 40-year career with that organisation, has worked as a cartographer, photographer and graphic artist in the field of communications. During this time Greg was also involved in the hospitality industry as a part-time working partner in two Adelaide based businesses. Greg's only child Emily, from his first marriage, died tragically in 1999. Fortunately he met a special lady, following his marriage breakdown, who helped him through an extremely difficult decade. Greg and Rosalie were married in 2000. After accepting early retirement at the age of 55, Greg was given an honorary fellowship with CSIRO and continues to work with that organisation on a contractual basis. He and Rosalie spend much of their free time on their River Murray houseboat with friends and family, touring outback Australia and exploring exotic locations around the world. In their 17 years together they have managed sheep stations in the Flinders Ranges, a country hotel at Mt Mary and a houseboat company on the river. They are making the most of every moment.

Gréham Richard LAYCOCK

(1926–2010)

by John Laycock

Dad was born in Port Augusta, South Australia in 1926. He was the elder of two children born to Frank and Hirell Laycock.

The history of our Laycock family in Australia dates back to the mid 1800s when three brothers arrived from London, United Kingdom. One brother, Richard Laycock, settled in Gawler in the 1870s and married Elizabeth Ann Riggs. Dad's father, Francis Kingsley Laycock, was one of 12 children, the ninth child of Lizzie and Dick and known to me as 'Pop Laycock'. He was born in Gawler South on 29 May 1897 and, prior to enlisting in the Army on 2 October 1917, was a grocer. He served overseas from March 1918 and returned to Australia on the *City of Exeter* on 21 August 1919. He probably didn't experience much active duty as this war ended in November 1918.

On Anzac Day 1922, Frank and one of his older brothers, Roy, left Gawler and arrived in Port Augusta to set up a business together. This was the Apex Motor Company. They had the Ford dealership and franchise for the north of South Australia and did very well selling the old Model T Ford. This was a very popular vehicle with farmers from cattle stations in the outback and was renowned for its reliability on the rough roads. Frank used to go to Adelaide and drive the new models back to Port Augusta at 25 mph to run-in the engines. Frank and Roy also ran the local Port Augusta Taxi Service in the 1920s.

Frank (Pop) met his wife Hirell Florence Oswald when she was transferred to the Commonwealth Bank in Port Augusta from the Port Adelaide branch. She was the first woman in the bank ever transferred so the story goes. They were married in Adelaide on 28 February 1925 and drove back to Port Augusta in a new Model T Ford to run it in. They had two children, my dad Gréham born 27 September 1926 and then my Aunty Margaret born 22 October 1927. Dad was born in Port Augusta and lived there at 23 Langsford Street until he was 15 years old. He attended the local primary and high schools. Port Augusta, then a small railway town of about 2000 people was known as the 'gateway to the outback'. Dad's parents were quite well off as a result of their thriving Ford dealership and were the first household in Port Augusta to acquire a kerosene-powered refrigerator. All the kids used to come around after school for his mum's home made ice-cream (aided by their new fridge). The family participated actively in community life – Dad and his sister Margaret both gained bronze life-saving certificates and Dad was a member of both the Port Augusta swimming team and the school A-grade football team in 1942. The team played against the other school footy teams from Whyalla, Quorn and Wilmington. The family had a fishing boat, and often spent the weekends out on the gulf or driving up to Pichi Richi Pass on the Quorn Road for family 'chop picnics'.

Dad was a good student at high school, always at the top of his class. His best subject was mathematics and one of his teachers suggested he should become an accountant, due to his uncanny skill with figures. I remember, as a child, watching him add up a column of figures in a ledger book as he ran his finger down the page. He didn't add up the units, tens and hundreds as separate columns. Somehow he could do what we do today with calculators and when I checked the total by my school-taught method, I would always find he had calculated the correct answer in just a few seconds.

Even though these extraordinary skills probably weren't a prerequisite for accountancy, he took his favourite teacher's advice and, having completed year 11 (probably then called 'leaving'), my grandparents arranged for him to go to Adelaide where he became articled to a firm of chartered accountants while he studied. He completed his diploma of accountancy and within a few years started his own business. I remember it as G.R. Laycock & Co.

When Dad first moved to Adelaide in early 1942 aged fifteen-and-a-half he initially found private board and lodgings in Sydenham Road, Norwood before moving into Carrington Street in the city to board with a lady by the name of Mrs Asherton. It was while he was living here that he met my mother. Dad had a strong interest in singing and as a result of living initially in Norwood, he attended the Norwood Wesley Church on the corner of The Parade and Portrush roads, where he joined the church choir. The accompanying December 1943 photograph of this quite renowned choir singing Handel's Messiah at Christmas features both my parents. This was how they met. Mum was nearly three years his senior but didn't know how young the tall, handsome chap in the back row was. And he wasn't about to tell her – well not at that stage anyway. Apparently at 16-years-old he had one of the best tenor voices in the entire choir. The family still has a copy of an old 78 LP recording of Dad singing a solo of 'The Serenade' from *The Student Prince* after this 1920s operetta was made popular by the 1954 MGM movie starring Mario Lanza.

Mum and Dad courted for about five years, spending their time between Adelaide and Port Augusta. In about 1946 Dad acquired his first car, a 1937 Morris 8/40 soft-top two-door convertible, purchased for him by his father Frank. He was still 19. He often used to talk about it and it features in many of his early photos (it's probably no mere coincidence that my first car was a 1950 four door Morris Minor that Dad purchased me for $100 when I started university).

During their engagement Mum and Dad took their new car over to Kangaroo Island for a short holiday. Their little Morris was lifted onto the deck of the local passenger and cargo vessel the SS *Karatta*. This vessel did the Port Adelaide to Kangaroo Island run from 1913 to 1961. The photo shows the car coming off the deck from in amongst the sheep onto the wharf at Port Adelaide.

During the first two years of their relationship World War Two was in full swing. The first bombing of Darwin occurred in mid-February 1942, when Dad was only 15. Dad's sister remembers that the Port Augusta High School had regular air raid drills in the schoolyard and in Langsford Street, Pop had dug an air raid shelter on the vacant block they owned, which was next to the family house. The bombing of northern Australia of course continued well into 1943 with 62 more raids recorded up until November 1943. By this time he had just turned 17. When he turned 18, Dad decided to enlist in the Royal Australian Air Force. He went off to the Air Training Academy in Melbourne to learn to fly but had not completed his training by the time the war ended in May 1945. I think I was fortunate to have a young father who didn't serve in active duty, unlike many of my friends at school. Dad had just turned 24 when I was born. I certainly remember some of my friends at school talking about their fathers having served in the war but I don't recall too much of the detail.

Straight after they were married, Dad and Mum resided for some time with an aunt and uncle of Mum's at 137 Beulah Road, Norwood. They had a big house and plenty of spare rooms. Dad's parents had sold up in Port Augusta to settle in Adelaide. They purchased two blocks of land at 53 and 55 Kyle Street, Glenside and built a sandstone fronted art deco home at number 55 on the corner of Broughton Street. The house was completed in 1950. Pop Laycock had just sold his business in Port Augusta to move to Adelaide. He had just retired aged 54. By coincidence Phil Higgins' father Leonard grew up at 57 Kyle Street, Glenside which was called Knoxville in the 1920s and 1930s. And his father was also an accountant, and his ancestors came from the south of England as did mine.

In 1950 Dad had just started his own accountancy business and money was tight. His father was helping him look for a house close to theirs in Kyle Street and happened to find a property with a council demolition order on it at 40 Cator Street, Glenside. It was a 1920s bungalow – very cheap and needing extensive work due to cracks that were so typical of early houses built in that area. Mum and Dad bought it and moved in just two weeks before I was born in December 1950. It was three blocks to the babysitting grandparents in Kyle Street, walking distance to the local Knoxville Kindergarten in Allinga Avenue (at the Knoxville Jubilee Bible Church, which was recently converted into a family residence), and not too far from the highly regarded Linden Park Demonstration School. Interestingly, the once condemned house still stands opposite Burnside Village Shopping Centre, despite all these years of development in the neighbourhood.

One of my earliest recollections of this house is of Dad arriving home from work in 1952 in a brand new cream coloured FX Holden sedan. He proudly parked it on the front lawn and Mum took a photo of me in his arms beside the car. He wasn't a 'car nut' but following this he bought a new car every two or three years when a new shape came out. It was always a Holden. After the first sedan the new cars became station wagons so the growing family could pile into the back. Two younger sisters followed me – Janette was born on 22 April 1954 and Alison on the same day, three years later, on 22 April 1957.

My memories of Dad in the early days at 40 Cator Street are a little hazy. I know he was out working a lot at night-time. In those days accountants used to visit their clients at home after hours probably going through the shoeboxes of purchase receipts. Once a year around tax time he would head off to country South Australia and Northern Territory to visit clients in these far-flung locations.

I never actually thought about it too much until now but his contact with these outback families would have been as a result of my grandfather selling his Fords throughout northern South Australia and into the Territory. In those days, as well as his many clients in and around Port Augusta, he also used to call every year on others in Maree, Angas Downs, Alice Springs, Curtin Springs (near Ayers Rock/now Uluru), Tennant Creek and Katherine. Looking back I think those journeys and the opportunity to experience temporarily the way of life of his outback clients were particularly important to him. They connected him to his early days in northern South Australia and he always enjoyed and marvelled at the desert landscape.

Once when I was 14 I went on one of these excursions in the September school holidays right up to Katherine and back. The unsealed roads in outback South Australia were pretty rough back then and Dad let me 'take the wheel' to my absolute amazement. 'Do you think you can drive?' he said totally out of the blue. Wide eyed I said, 'Of course I can.' Dad had just sold his last Holden, an EH station wagon and purchased a brand new Chrysler Valiant AP6 station wagon in mid-1965. We always had automatics so with no clutch or gears to worry about my introduction to driving on these outback tracks was pretty uneventful. You would only see three or four cars a day coming in the other direction around Maree and Oodnadatta, even though it was actually the main road between Adelaide and Alice Springs.

During the late 1950s Dad joined forces with another accountant, Brian Blunt. They initially had offices at Melbourne Street, North Adelaide and then at Greenhill Road, Wayville. They set up a branch office at Kingscote, Kangaroo Island and Brian purchased a quite luxurious home by Kingscote standards with four bedrooms and a tennis court. I remember when I was about 12-years-old, the two families swapped homes during the Christmas vacation. By this time we had moved from 40 Cator Street, Glenside and purchased a brand new home at 23 Russell Avenue, Hazelwood Park. We had moved into this house in 1956 just before the birth of my youngest sister, Alison. In the next street, Seaforth Avenue, lived my best mate Geoffrey Webber who also attended Linden Park up until 1960. Geoff and I had somehow managed to talk our parents into allowing him to come to Kangaroo Island for this house swap vacation.

Back in the early 1970s Dad had sold his business premises on Greenhill Road, Wayville and moved to an old bluestone villa with bigger rooms and more space at 167 Goodwood Road, Millswood. There is now an Indian Restaurant on this site on the corner of Clifton Street. The house was huge and he used to lease out separate rooms to various businesses. My sister Jan used to work there in the late 1970s and provided secretarial services to his many tenants.

Returning to my memories of my early home life, by the time Alison was born we had moved into a brand new house built by The Keen Building Company in a newly subdivided area of Hazelwood Park. Dad and Mum managed to raise a deposit by selling a vacant block they had purchased in Tennyson Drive, Beaumont in 1954. I have clear memories of the open culvert and bridge that linked 23 Russell Avenue with the street. All the local kids used to catch tadpoles there, as well as in the swampy corner of the opposite vacant block where there was a natural year round spring. When not at school – and we all went to Linden Park School – we seemed to spend a lot of time exploring the area on our bikes with other kids in the neighbourhood. There was plenty to explore with the Burnside Brick Kiln (then on Waterfall Terrace, Burnside), Waterfall Gully, Beaumont Common and the vast expanses of Hazelwood Park. There were various neglected old 'mansions' including one on the common and a rusted out plane in an olive grove somewhere. We could do what we wanted as long as we were home by 6 o'clock for dinner.

Through those early family years, Dad and Mum were active members of the Tusmore Methodist Church on Portrush Road. We three kids attended Sunday school there and I have recollections of the annual Sunday school picnics in Belair National Park, and the church Christmas carols at the Burnside Town Hall every year.

Church sport also featured regularly as part of our weekends in those days.

Another of Dad's interests in the early 1960s was Rowley Park. I think he may have been mates with someone on the organising committee and I have enduring memories of being there with him on a Friday night. The demolition derby at the end of the night was definitely the highlight. At about the same time Dad was also involved with the South Australia Cricket Association at Adelaide Oval and had a supervisory role at the Main Southern Gate. I recall being allowed inside the old historic scoreboard during a West Indies test match. Mum's father used to work on the turnstile at the same gate and had befriended Gary Sobers. Pop asked the great man if he had a souvenir for his grandson and he pulled out a brand new bat from his sports bag, autographed it and gave it to him. I cherished this bat and begged Dad to let me take it to school to show everybody. I was finally allowed to take it one day but I didn't keep a close enough eye on it. Unfortunately it vanished from my life that same day. Dad was right and I was devastated.

Another feature of these early days was the annual family holiday, when Dad and Mum would pack us all into the car and set off for a couple of weeks. Usually it was a holiday in a seaside environment somewhere – I recall Port Victoria, Port Fairy, Wallaroo, Port Lincoln and Kangaroo Island (three times). We also had driving holidays further afield, to Sydney, and the Victorian highlands and also to Geelong. In later years after I had left home, there were family holidays to Perth and New Zealand. I think the golden rule was to visit a different place each holiday until 1972 when my parents bought a shack on the south coast at Goolwa. The shack became the focus of family holidays after that. Lake Alexandrina was the perfect place to indulge Dad's interest in boating and fishing and the nearby surf kept younger members of the family happy.

In the early 1970s, Dad became an involved 'riding-club dad' and the Burnlea Riding Club events became the focus of his Sundays, rather than the church choir. My youngest sister, Alison, was a keen equestrienne and had three horses through her high school years. Dad was a supporter of this interest and, while he didn't ride himself, would often spend most of the weekend towing the horse float to various gymkhanas and sometimes to agricultural shows in country South Australia. He seemed to enjoy the opportunity to nurture his genuine interest in horses.

Throughout the years of my parent's married life, Dad maintained his interest in singing. He joined the Adelaide Philharmonic Choir in the 1950s and in these early days Mum sang in this choir as well. In fact, Mum joined in 1941 aged 17, long before Dad. She was the youngest person at that stage to be accepted into the choir and still remembers the gruelling audition. My memories of this period include the annual Carols by Candelight on the lawns adjacent to the River Torrens in Elder Park with the choir and the Adelaide Symphony Orchestra belting out all the old traditional Christmas carols from the sound shell. Dad and Mum were both up on stage and my sisters and I sat with Nanna and Pop (grandparents on Mum's side). Dad was president of the Philharmonic Choir for many years and actually held this position until 1975 when it ceased to exist under that name. This occurred when the ABC withdrew its annual funding. The current Adelaide Philharmonia Chorus was formed in 1981 but by this time Dad had lost his passion for singing and didn't re-join.

Much of what was happening in the Laycock household in the late-1960s to the mid-1970s is a bit hazy. Dad and Mum's relationship had been a bit strained in my teenage years and Dad seemed to find it difficult to communicate. I was a fairly typical teenager, rejecting authority and wanting to make my own decisions on simple things. Such as who I went out with, how long I could grow my hair, what time I could come home at night and what clothes I could wear. As is often the case, I decided the best way to avoid all this angst was to find my own place to rent. I was 17 and just about to sit for my first year university exams. Most of my contact with Dad over the next ten years or so was outside of the family unit. We were both very stubborn and didn't go out of our way to stay in touch. He was a long-term member of the Sportsmen's Association on Greenhill Road, Unley and we would sometimes have lunch together there to catch up.

In 1977 my parents split up, with Dad moving out. Nobody saw it coming and it was a shock to all of us. Back in those days most couples seemed to just stick it out when the relationship soured. Dad was 50 and it was time to move on. Mum stayed on in the family home and Dad seemed intent on starting a new life.

Over the next ten years or so Dad became very reclusive and for a while nobody even knew where he lived. I don't think he wanted to explain his actions to my sisters and me and it was a difficult time for all of us, particularly Mum. My recollection is that it was several years after the split before Dad and I had a meaningful conversation regarding what really went wrong with the marriage. Most of the details about his new life came back to me via my sisters who had a bit more contact.

Over the next phase of Dad's very interesting life he rented a home unit in Glenside, purchased a holiday shack in Port Julia, on York Peninsula in 1982, and purchased 40 acres of land at Gumeracha in the Adelaide Hills. He moved his 4.8 metre cabin cruiser that he had built in his mid 30s in the back shed at Hazelwood Park over to the peninsula and spent most of his weekends over there. He had formed a relationship with a new partner in life and together they built a new house on the land at Gumeracha on Checker Hill Road. He worked from home and became a primary producer as well as continuing to look after his loyal accountancy clients.

Dad and his new partner, Marie Jordan, set up a horticultural business called the Australian Bulb Company. They spent their weekends selling bulbs and plants at the various markets and field days around South Australia. They attended flower shows in Victoria and New South Wales winning many prizes for their exhibits. I would often call in to see them at The Royal Adelaide Show horticultural pavilion. They both loved the lifestyle and thrived on the hard work. Marie also had her own bridal fabric business in Adelaide Arcade in the City.

In 2008 the Gumeracha property was sold and Dad and Marie moved their business to Monbulk Road, Silvan in the Dandenong Ranges near Melbourne, where they had purchased a couple of acres with a house and ready-made nursery. He was now 82 and still working, but his good health was finally deteriorating. He was suffering from osteoporosis and suffered a broken leg following a fall from which he never fully recovered. He passed away on the 23 November 2010 in Melbourne. Dad had cut a lot of ties from his earlier years. He was obviously happy with his new life and had a good circle of friends, but I know he had deep regrets that he hadn't maintained closer contact with his kids, his sister, and wider family members, and I think even Mum.

I had the pleasure of spending some quality time with him on a short holiday to New Zealand in May 2009, when my wife Helen and I attended a real estate conference in Christchurch and Queenstown. Dad and Marie (who is a New Zealander) decided to join us there for their first real holiday in 20 years. Dad and I talked at length one night after dinner, just the two of us, like we had never talked before. He got many things off his chest regarding the break up and we reminisced about the old and good times. I think we both needed that moment and it was very emotional. I told him that I loved him and he responded accordingly. I couldn't remember ever saying that before, certainly not in my adult life.

Dad didn't want a funeral. On the anniversary of his cremation, Marie came over to Adelaide with his ashes. Four of us drove to Port Julia where Marie, my son Tim, my sister Alison, and I cast his ashes to the wind in St Vincent's Gulf. We went to the end of the little jetty next to the launching ramp where he used to launch his beloved fishing boat. It was his dying wish. A fitting farewell to a wonderful man.

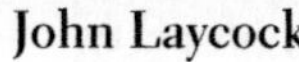

John Laycock

John was born in December 1950, the oldest of three children. He attended Knoxville Kindergarten, Linden Park Demonstration School and then Unley High, matriculating in 1967. He also studied at Adelaide University and graduated in 1971 with an Applied Science Degree in Secondary Metallurgy.

John first entered the work force, while still at university, as a part-time technical trainee at British Tube Mills, Kilburn. From there he moved on to Chrysler Australia as a Quality Control Metallurgist at the Lonsdale Engine Plant. Retrenchments at Mitsubishi in 1977 resulted in his dramatic career change.

In 1978 John entered the real estate industry with a small firm in Plympton. Today Gary J. Smith Pty Ltd employs 40 people and John is still passionately involved with this company, and has won numerous industry awards over the past 35 years.

After two unsuccessful marriages, John finally met his soul mate in life about 20 years ago. They married in Queensland's Palm Cove in 2007. John has a son Timothy now aged 27, and Helen has two daughters: Chanelle (same age as Tim) is also in real estate as John's personal assistant; and Megan, 30, is married to Darren with three sons. Grandparents at last!

Donald William WAKE
(1924–1956)

Colin DYSTER
(1932–2011)

A tale of two fathers

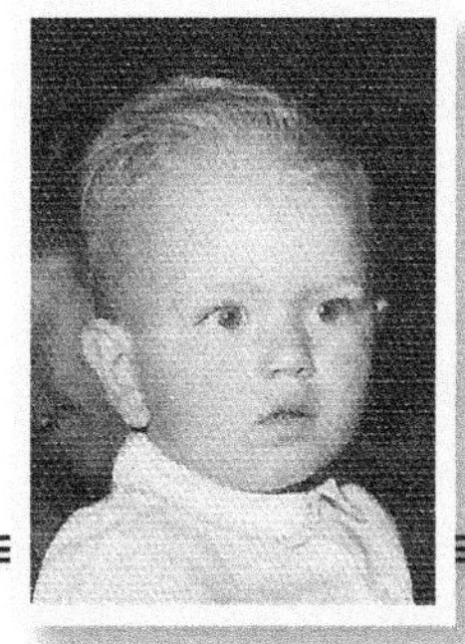

by Colin Wake-Dyster

A young eight-year-old lad came up to me recently and said, 'Mr Wake-Dyster, you had two fathers?'

'Why, yes,' I replied a little astonished. 'Who told you that?'

'No one! I worked it out myself. It's quite simple really. You have two names joined together. Therefore you must have had two fathers.'

Oh! To have the clarity and perception of an eight-year-old!

He had in fact hit the nail on the head. In my lifetime I have had two fathers, my parental father and my stepfather, who later become my father through adoption. But that is for later.

Donald William Wake was my paternal and obviously my first father. He was born in 1924, the fifth child of four boys and two girls, to Tommy and Emmie Wake. The family moved in 1928 to Buckleboo on the Eyre Peninsula and began farming there. Gradually Tommy increased the farm acreage to provide sufficient living for him and his family. My father, Don, grew up on this farm and at the death of his father in 1949, began share farming the property with his younger brother and mother.

It was also at about this time that Don met my mother, Verna Kitto. Verna was also from a farming background at Pekina near Orroroo in the mid-north of South Australia, but pursued a career as a governess and teacher. Her first teaching appointment was to the Buckleboo School. Don and Verna courted and married in September 1949. Interestingly I still have the watch Mum gave Dad as a wedding present. Also interestingly is the superstition that double weddings will come unstuck or have bad luck befall them. Verna and her sister Elma celebrated their marriages at a double ceremony at the Anglican church in Orroroo.

If 1949 was a tumultuous year, 1950 was a great year. I, Colin Raymond Wake, was born in the July of 1950. It was a Saturday night and Don was at the picture theatre. Apparently at intermission the words 'It's a boy!' were flashed up on the screen. Nothing stays sacred in a close farming community very long. Also, I'm not sure if my brothers Kevin, born in 1953 and Trevor, born in 1955 had such an introduction to this world.

Saturday night was all joy but Sunday brought a different story. By nightfall on Sunday, my father had provided his blood as a blood transfusion for me and I had been baptised by the local Anglican priest. I wasn't expected to pull through. However, being of resilient fortitude and with the help of many prayers I made it through the day and beyond.

I have some recollection of time from 1950 to 1956, the year Don was killed in a tractor accident. I was nearly six years old having just started school at the reception to Year Seven Pinkawillinie School. Don had bought a new set of Yakka overalls, which he was wearing while trying to change the moving drive belts on a welder powered from the power take off on the tractor. The overalls caught in the drive shaft and Don sustained severe injuries. They became fatal when he died a week later. I still shudder when I think of all the exposed moving machinery that was used in those days. It was just an accepted part of the job, but very costly! I have very little memory of this, other than Dad was there one day and gone the next. Even though I knew of the events I think the adults shielded me from the gory details to such an extent that I didn't go to Don's funeral service or burial. Looking back I think this was the done thing by adults believing that kids in those days could not handle such emotional trauma. For me, not grieving my father's death, in itself, was a part of this tragedy.

My other recollections are of playing and hiding in the headlands of a mature wheat crop – wheat doesn't grow that tall these days; our first home, a four-roomed house made from pug and pine with the kitchen being the social hub of the home – this house is still standing today and is a heritage listed construction; nearly stepping on a snake on the footpath as I went out to help Mum hang clothes on the line; Don combing my hair in front of the bathroom mirror; Dad killing a sheep, then hanging its carcass in a linen bag under the veranda to allow the meat to set; standing on the front driver's seat in the new FJ Holden and steering while Dad worked the pedals; Don holding my new 24" bike with my feet just reaching blocked pedals as I learnt to ride a bicycle – there were no trainer wheels, I just kept falling off until I could steer and stay upright – tough stuff!; Dad going to the pub on Friday nights in Kimba – Friday was the day everyone went to town!; sleeping on the back seat of the FJ parked in the street while Mum and Dad went to the pictures; spotlighting in the new FJ and rubbing the paint off the front passenger window frame with the rifle stock; riding on the mud guard of the tractor; helping Don lay a new hardwood floor in the Buckleboo Hall; the flood when the dam bank broke and the house was surrounded by water – I had never seen so much water in such an arid area; the leather strap that hung behind the kitchen door and which was never used but often offered as a threat; Dad putting sauce on almost everything including ice cream if he was allowed; the single cylinder diesel engine which supplied electricity to the home; the steel moulds used to make bricks to build the new home. Today I still see myself as a jack of all trades and master of none, and I think this is part of the heritage of being a farmer's son.

As a consequence of Don's death, my mother was widowed with three boys aged nine months to six years. Because my father had predeceased my still-alive paternal grandmother who was still receiving an interest from the farm, my mother was left paying death duties on a property that she could not sell. Somewhat destitute both financially and mentally, Verna and her three boys moved back to Orroroo to live with her mother and father, Ina and Reg. As there was no such thing in those days as widow's pension or social security, our family was reliant on the gracious generosity of my grandparents. To a large extent this sadly ended my relationship with Don's family until only just recently, in the last five to ten years. It also ended any further influence of Don on my life. Don's gift to me was life, in more ways than one.

Transitioning from a life with a father to one without took some doing. Even at the age of six years, being the oldest child and with my maternal grandmother having said to me something like: 'You're the man of the house now', I unknowingly began to assume responsibility for my mum and brothers. Therefore for two years till 1958 I unwittingly assumed this role, developing the characteristic of self-reliance along with the need to protect those around me, particularly my mum. On the flip side, a boy growing up without a father tends to become unruly and 'a bit naughty'. Grandpa Reg did well to accommodate this, but it was not the same as having a dad. It was also during this period that Mum restarted part-time teaching at the local school. This gave her both a physical and emotional outlet, while also supplementing the family income.

At that time Colin Dyster was also a teacher at the school and took a shine to my mum. For a man to marry a woman with three sons, in any era, is some feat. But Colin persisted against all opposition from outsiders, and with the support of my grandparents he and Verna were married in 1958. I can truly boast that I saw my mother and father sing to each other at their wedding. I can also boast of having my three grandmothers at my wedding. To the very end of his life at 79-years-old, Colin loved Verna passionately. They say that 'the best thing a man can do for his kids is to love their mother'. Colin was the epitome of that man.

Initially, having Colin on the scene posed a threat. He was stealing my mum and straightening out my behaviour, and I wasn't too flashed on the idea! In discussion with him some years later, he said it took about two years before I had fully accepted him into our family and saw him as my father. My life had taken another turn and I was gifted back my boyhood.

Unlike most of my family, including my grandparents, who were farmers, Colin Dyster was from teaching stock. Born and bred in itinerant places like Koolunga, Winkie, Berri and Port Noarlunga in South Australia as his teaching father moved around, Colin was at heart a country boy who had a passion for the literary things in life. Reading, writing, literature, language, history, and music were big on his agenda. Therefore, he graduated from Adelaide High School and teacher training with a view to teach English and the like and build young people's lives as a primary school teacher. He enumerates in a story 'My loneliest day' of how he obtained his driving licence (no practical test back then), bought a new Vauxhall car and proceeded to roll it on a dirt road as he drove up to Orroroo to his first teaching appointment. His introduction to the community was them rescuing him and his car! Facing an unknown journey with unforeseen disaster, for a relatively quiet, retiring sort of guy, brings out the best in survival skills.

These skills were to stand my new dad, my stepdad, in good stead early in his married and our family's life. If 1956 was a sad year, then 1960 was almost as tragic. There was good and bad as there always is in most situations. The birth of my sister, Julie, in

Orroroo in January 1960, with the temperature over a hundred degrees Fahrenheit and red plum juice dripping from Colin's elbows as he helped to make plum and raspberry jam was the good. I might add that the temperature remained over the century mark further than a week. I don't think the fresh plum jam lasted much longer with newly baked bread, scalded cream and hungry boys around. Having a girl amongst three boys definitely changed how we boys did life!

Later that January, while we were visiting Dad's parents at Port Noarlunga, he suffered a ruptured appendix and his life hung in the balance for some time. You may well imagine the effect this had on my mother. It was devastating! Having lost her first husband only four years back, with the possibility of losing her second husband and suffering post-natal blues after giving birth to her daughter, Mum suffered severe depression lasting many years. Again her parents pitched in to help look after us kids while both my parents began recovering from their respective illnesses. After his recovery, Dad's survival skills again came to the fore as he worked full-time and raised four kids virtually on his own. We had also moved into a new house and it was at this time that I learnt to make beds, light the chip heater in the bathroom to have a hot shower, hand pump water from the underground tank to the overhead gravity feed tank to provide pressurised water, make semolina porridge on a wood stove without soot falling down the chimney into it, do dishes, cut wood, prune the vegetation along the pathway to the outside toilet to minimise being attacked by spiders at night, be chased by jumping jacks at Guy Fawkes, listen on the radio to West Adelaide beat Norwood in an SANFL grand final and many other things to contribute to the running of the household. My brothers and I learnt many life skills during this period. It is said that every man at some stage in life has an Everest to climb! My father 'hung in there' as the going got tough, never once giving thought to abandon his wife and family. So much for the bad!

To obtain the best health care for Mum, Dad transferred to Adelaide to teach at the Mitcham Demonstration School. He bought a house in Glenside and so began my journey into city life. So, too, did my schooling move to Linden Park Primary School when I was in year six. It was also at this time that, as Mum's health improved, Colin continued his studies for an arts degree majoring in English and Latin. He had started this by correspondence in Orroroo but it was much easier being near facilities in Adelaide. Dad duly graduated with his Bachelor of Arts. It was also the time that we children continued to learn more about home chores. It was also the time when a TV landed in the home, I drank my first cup of tea, was given a four speed chain geared bike from which I still managed to fall occasionally, and was allowed to wear my watch as I progressed to Year Seven.

As Mum's health continued to improve, Dad received a posting to Allendale East Area School as year five teacher. Therefore in 1963, having completed my first year at Unley High School, we moved to the south east to Port MacDonnell. One doesn't realise the extent to which the 'floating population' i.e. teachers, bankers etc contribute to a community until you are a recipient of their efforts. In the two years that we lived there, Dad started a Scout group, with Mum's help set up a Saturday night dance, and contributed to the local church life. It was also the first time that I had had my father as a teacher other than at home. In the first year there, he tutored me in Latin, which I did by correspondence, and the second year, my intermediate year ten, he was my class and English teacher. The Latin exam in year ten was the only exam from which I have exited early in all my life. Dad gave me heaps for he thought I could have done better. It was okay though. I got a 'C'. I also never forget the day he taught us through the outside open window as the room was filled with smoke, the result of trying to light damp pine wood in the classroom fireplace.

These years were perhaps two of my finest. I was transitioning from boyhood to manhood and my father was crucial and influential in this process. I was learning that people placed me in positions of leadership and all the responsibilities and blessings that meant. I broadened my skills through scouting and through playing colts football for the town and cricket for the school. I also began to notice the female of the species. I know that my dad's relationship with my mother taught me well in how to relate to and treat young ladies. Also being in a co-ed class of nine boys and five girls, of which my dad was class teacher, enhanced my social and relational skills.

This was also the time I became Colin Raymond Wake-Dyster. In 1964, Mum and Dad decided that the three boys should be adopted. My paternal grandmother, who died in 1974, was obviously still alive. If my mother died then it was my paternal grandmother who would have legal custody of me and my two brothers. To circumvent this, my mother relinquished her birthright to her three sons and Colin Dyster and his wife (my mother) adopted us. It was also at the point of adoption our names could be changed. Having the surname Wake while my father's was Dyster always caused some confusion. This did not change when my surname changed to Wake-Dyster.

From the south east Dad moved to various schools including Cambrai on the Murray Plains, Tailem Bend on the overland rail line and Modbury North, before his final appointment at Klemzig. During this time I was hived off to board as I completed my secondary education at Unley High School and entered Adelaide University to complete a pharmacy degree. Also during this time my dad was completely supportive of my choices, particularly in choice of profession. His contribution during my uni days was both emotional and financial, as his motto was: 'You provide for your children educationally as much as you are able.' He was there when I crashed my car in the wee hours of a Sunday morning and was also there when things got tough at uni.

Of all the things that Colin contributed to my upbringing, his introduction and fostering of my Christian faith has been a tremendous blessing. Tommy and Emmie, my paternal grandparents, were devout Anglicans and this faith was encouraged and handed down through the generations. Colin built on this during my life such that I could return the gift later in his life as we shared enquiringly different aspects of walking in this faith. This resulted in Dad giving a statement of his faith at his 70th birthday party.

In the latter part of his life, he and Mum resided in a retirement village where Dad formed and conducted a choir, wrote the village newspaper, was involved in the residents' management body, lay preached at the local church and made many, many amazing friends. That, along with caravanning and family, filled a very busy retirement schedule.

To conclude, I reiterate Colin's unswerving love for my mum and for her three sons whom he took on as his own. This was not just a wishy washy love but a love that was translated into practical processes that built and maintained the family in which I grew up. It exhibited sacrifice, a willingness to enter areas in which Dad was not always comfortable, a fairness and impartiality, persistence and perseverance. I am eternally grateful that he was the man he was.

As Don had given me life, Colin taught and raised me to make that life fruitful and generous.

Colin Wake-Dyster

Colin was born in Kimba, South Australia to Don and Verna Wake in July 1950. The first six years of his life were spent as a country boy on a farm. Verna moved to Orroroo in 1956 after Don's accidental death. Colin's life consequently took a dramatic change of direction, moving in with his grandparents for a couple of years. Despite his father's death life was good for Colin, consisting of homemade go karts, fossicking in Grandpa's shed, and generally getting up to mischief as young growing boys do. As luck would have it, soon he would have a new father. Verna remarried a school teacher in 1958 and thus began for Colin a sojourn around the state of South Australia as a child of a school teacher family. Amidst these travels the family landed

in Adelaide and Colin survived years six and seven at Linden Park Primary School graduating to secondary school at Unley High School (years eight, 11 and 12) where he matriculated and met Elizabeth, his wife to be. After graduating as a pharmacist from Adelaide University in 1970 and marrying Elizabeth in 1972, Colin spent six months as a guest of Her Majesty's armed forces as a conscriptee. After learning to shoot someone, Colin then spent the next 40 years helping people in his capacity as a community pharmacist in the southern suburbs of Adelaide finally retiring from paid employment in 2011. The 40 years were also punctuated with three children – two boys and a girl, all of whom have married and collectively produced two grandsons and a granddaughter. Retirement sees Colin enjoying grandchildren, mentoring, archery, sailing, building a house, a good red wine and holidaying at home and abroad with his wife Elizabeth.

War Stories

William Thomas COREY

(1917–)

by Di Corey Skull

My dad was a country boy, living his first ten years at Tarlee, about 85 km north of Adelaide in the Gilbert Valley (born 7 August 1917). He was the fifth child in a family of six (four boys and two girls) born to Muriel and Arthur Corey. His father was a butcher and they lived in what is now called the Grasshopper Restaurant (a building which began as a butter factory). Dad loved the country life – the freedom, the simplicity of everyday family life, and the events such as the local show, sheep sales and sports.

Dad's mother was brought up by her grandmother, Marion Baird, who arrived in Adelaide in as a 13-year-old with her family in 1837. She married her first husband in 1842 and together they had eight children and founded the town of Nuriootpa. Her unfortunate husband died of thirst in the north of the state and Marion married again and had three more children. They lived at Hamley Bridge and later at Booleroo when that area was developed. She took Muriel, aged 17-months, to help her daughter cope with her second child. Upon her 36-year-old daughter's death, she also raised her fourth child, while the other two were looked after by one of her son's family. Dad is a descendant of two pioneer families in South Australia, the Bairds, and also the Watts family in 1840 on his paternal grandmother's side. In fact all Dad's ancestors were here before 1853.

The family moved to Gilberton, Adelaide in 1927 for the benefit of their children's future (better education and work opportunities). Dad attended Walkerville Primary School for year six and seven and then Adelaide High School in the city. One of his high school teachers, Mr Williams, later became a good customer in his butcher shop and his wife taught me typing at PGC (Presbyterian Girls College) many years later.

Dad began his working life by working for a local butcher – no apprenticeships in those days; you just worked alongside an experienced butcher. A local boat builder, Mr Medwell, lived in the same street and introduced Dad to the world of sailing through the Port Adelaide Sailing Club. Dad was later to own his own 20-footer yacht, *Nomad*, for 25 years and was a member of the Royal South Australian Yacht Squadron. All Saturdays in summer were spent there with his crew – Ralph Cranwell (his children went to Linden Park Primary School, Don Cranwell in the class of 1962 with me), and Len Norman (married to my mum's cousin) of Norman's Wines. Our families spent many Sundays there. I remember many occasions when I went sailing with Dad. It was where I swam – it was very rare to go to the local beaches, as there was only one car in a family and mothers didn't drive in our childhood days.

Dad also loved motorbikes, and for a period of time was the proud owner of a Harley Davidson – much to his mother's horror.

The Great Depression of the 1930s meant that his father went back to Riverton during the week to work for his cousin in his butcher shop, returning to his family at weekends.

1939 was a horror year for the Corey family. On 13 August Dad's older brother Aleck died suddenly, aged 29, with a blood clot, following a fall from a motorbike. On 3 September Britain declared war with Germany. On 13 November (three months to the day after Aleck died), his younger sister Muriel died suddenly, aged 20, of meningitis.

On 17 June 1940, Dad voluntarily enlisted in the Army and was a foundation member of the 2/43rd Battalion which was formed firstly at Wayville Showgrounds, then after a few weeks, at Woodside. Around the same time Bill's older brother Jack joined the Australian Military Force (part-time), later resigning and enlisting in the Australian Imperial Force (AIF) in 1941 for overseas service.

After six months of training in cold wintry conditions at Woodside Army Camp he travelled by train to Melbourne to board a ship for overseas service via Fremantle and Ceylon (now Sri Lanka). Sleeping was in hammocks. At Ceylon they changed to a smaller boat to travel to Egypt, where conditions were of a lesser standard and a shortage of food and water resulted in local food being procured and, found not fit for consumption, being thrown overboard. Dad experienced his first air raid when an enemy aircraft dropped mines in the Suez.

After the long trip on a primitive train he reached a desert camp near Gaza in Palestine and spent a couple of months training there with one day's leave in Tel Aviv, before going to Libya on trucks to replace the Sixth Division in March 1941. The first job was to guard the Italian prisoners of war, then put up barbed wire defences. Holes were dug in the ground and these became Dad's home for the next eight months. As well as protection they provided some relief from the intense heat of the desert climate. Water was scarce (a quart of water every other day at one stage) and flies were deadly as they bred on dead bodies, so dysentery was a real problem for the men.

The siege of Tobruk began at Easter when the Allied troops were surrounded. There were about 1100 air raids during this time. To start with the Germans patrolled, bombed, machine gunned at will as there was no opposition from Allied planes as they had been shot down in the first few days. Time was spent at the front (red line) and alternated with periods behind (at the blue line). With changes in position more holes needed to be dug. Dive-bombers would come in with the sun behind them and drop bombs. Men patrolled at night as well as the day, and sleep at night was interrupted by enemy planes repeatedly circling around for about an hour before dropping bombs. Dust or sand storms presented more difficulties, visibility was poor and there was no movement from either side. Land mines were everywhere. Reinforcements were brought in by the Navy as well as people or supplies in or out.

Spiders, scorpions, fleas and rats used to get into the blankets so they needed to be shaken before being used. There was no water for washing, the men cut each other's hair with blunt scissors, and they sharpened razor blades to shave. Dad had two washes in those eight months when trucks took small parties down to the sea to have a swim, when not in the front line.

2/43rd Battalion statistics: 51 men were killed or died of wounds, 156 wounded, four prisoners of war, 236 injured in accidents and 367 in sickness (with many more who just carried on).

After being evacuated from Tobruk in October 1941, Dad spent Christmas in Palestine and the battalion then moved to Syria. From there Dad had leave and he took the opportunity to visit all the biblical places. Having been brought up in a strict Methodist home he knew all the bible stories. He visited the place where Christ was born, the Mount of Olives, Sea of Galilee, the holy spot where Christ was interned and rose from the dead, walked down the old cobble stone street where Christ carried the cross etc., and in Egypt saw the pyramids and all their historical places.

Dad took part in route marches to keep the men fit and some of these were over the old battlefields of World War One. The battalion then moved to Lebanon and they constructed defence positions. Then news of the fall of Tobruk shocked them all and the Germans were on their way to Egypt. Then the Ninth Division (of which 2/43rd was a part) was recalled to the North African desert once more to help stop the Germans from taking the whole of the Middle East with its oil supplies.

In July 1942 Dad found El Alamein different from Tobruk in

that they were not cut off, they had better supplies and were better armed, including an air force. But he still lived in holes in the ground. Dad spent his time on supplies, with mine fields, shells and aircraft the biggest worries.

On 23 October at 2140 hours exactly, 1000 guns opened up and continued for 15 minutes, then stopped for five minutes before starting up again. The sky was lit up like daylight. Before this hundreds of aircraft had pounded the enemy with bombs all day long for several days. The enemy resisted until they finally retreated.

2/43rd Battalion statistics: 104 killed or died of wounds, 225 wounded, 31 prisoners of war and five died of other causes.

Dad moved back to Palestine and it was Christmas and he spent seven enjoyable days in Cairo seeing the pyramids and other places of interest before returning to Australia on the RMS *Queen Mary*. There were 11,000 men on board with two meal sessions a day. Dad volunteered to work in the butcher shop to help pass the time and he was well fed. After being away for two-and-a-quarter years, seeing the Sydney Heads was an unbelievable sight. So too was coming through the Adelaide Hills on the train and seeing the city of Adelaide. After some leave the battalion marched from the parade grounds up King William Street, Unley Road, then to Daws Road with an estimated 200,000 people welcoming them home.

After a period of leave he travelled to north Queensland by packed train for jungle training on the Atherton Tablelands out from Cairns. Dad sometimes slept on the luggage racks, it was so crowded. Here they made camp in the scrub and also did landing exercises from barges on Trinity Beach.

Then Dad's war against the Japanese started at Milne Bay, New Guinea. The romantic vision of the beach with coconut trees soon disappeared as the rain poured and poured and Dad found himself walking around in water about six inches deep. Then the mosquitoes attacked. Next he was moved by boats up to Buna to prepare for a landing behind Japanese lines at Lae, the first landing by Australians by ship into enemy territory since Gallipoli.

Dad landed very early in the morning, waded ashore and pushed on to Lae about 15 miles away. After leaving the beach the Japanese bombing caused about sixty American casualties. And still it continued to pour with rain (ten to eleven inches in one night). Lae was a complete mess, flattened by the air force. Fighting in New Guinea was very different to the desert patrols and air raids. It was a one-on-one meeting with the enemy at any time in the jungle.

After Lae there was a landing again at Finschhafen. Just after landing, three Japanese bombers welcomed them. Still the rain fell. Dad said if you weren't wet through with rain you were wet through with sweat. The heat of the wet humid conditions drained the life from you. Also the stress of not knowing when you would come face-to-face with the Japanese was a constant worry.

After five months Dad became weak with dengue fever, losing three stone in weight, and was flown back to Port Moresby in a DC3 cargo plane to spend time in hospital with a couple of weeks in a convalescent camp up in the mountains. After flying back to Port Moresby Dad's plane had a near miss from crashing into the jungle – the pilot, a 19-year-old American lad, told them when they landed how close they came. Coming home in the Coral Sea they met a cyclone with winds of 90 miles per hour, and sea sickness was common, although Dad never suffered from it; perhaps his body was used to sailing.

Dad then had leave in Adelaide, and after travelling back to Queensland went down with malaria and was hospitalised in Brisbane. This happened again after another period of leave. He spent 18 months on the Atherton Tablelands doing a variety of exercises out in the bush and more amphibious training at Cairns, before embarking on his last campaign in Borneo.

In April 1945 Dad left on a ship for Moratai, an island south of the Philippines. There were 5000 on board, with two meals a day, and severe blackout restrictions – shut down at 5.30 pm and not allowed up top until after daylight next day. Lighting in the holds was confined to a couple of blue lights, bunks were four high, with minimal space between, and the heat was overbearing. There was a submarine scare, but fortunately nothing happened as there would have been no hope of getting out.

The invasion of Brunei Bay was the operation that also involved taking Labuan Island and securing the northern part of the mainland. It was an impressive sight to see 85 ships moving through the Celebes Sea into the South China Sea, finally landing on the beach at Labuan Island.

Naval gunfire, aerial bombing and rocket barges all let loose, sending the Japanese away. Dad and the others all climbed down the rope ladders to the barges and the barges were able to land. Some men then moved over to the mainland and arrived at the village of Beaufort, while Dad's barge continued up the huge river to land at Beaufort. Here they met with the local people who were very pleased to see them and assisted by giving information about the Japanese and their movements.

Dad missed five-and-a-half years of his life giving service for his country. His 22nd birthday was spent at Woodside (South Australia), 23rd at Tobruk (Libya), 24th at El Alamein (Egypt), 25th at Finschhafen (New Guinea), 26th and 27th on the Tablelands (Ravenshoe), north Queensland, and 28th at Beaufort (Borneo).

It was another three months after the ceasefire before Dad returned to Australia in November 1945. His brother Jack, who served with the Eighth Division Ammunition Sub Park in Singapore, returned after being a prisoner of war on the Burma Railway and Changi Prison, following the fall of Singapore. He became an active member of the Ex-POW Association of South Australia.

Upon returning home Dad took time to adjust – he had lived with men for five-and-a-half years and didn't mix with local people during that time except in Beaufort, Borneo when the war finished. He had had little experience with the opposite sex. He did, however, meet Iris Sullivan, marrying her on 19 October 1946. He always maintains this was the best thing to happen to him as he had much to organise and didn't ever dwell on his wartime experiences.

Everything was in short supply after the war and so the newly married couple lived with Dad's parents for four years. Within 12 months they had their first child, a son, Donald, who was spoilt by all the attention placed on him by doting parents and grandparents.

Dad set up business in the trade that he knew – his own butcher shop on Glen Osmond Road in which he worked for the next 25 years, making a good and honest living. Every customer was a friend to Dad and he went to great lengths to please them. He says today you have to see every customer as a dollar to survive. With the assistance of a war service loan they built a new house in Frewville, opposite the Glenunga ovals, and a short walk from his business. In 1951 I was born, a couple of months after moving into their own home.

Upon returning Dad joined the 2/43rd Battalion Club and maintained contact with his mates over the years to the present day. He was the last veteran president of the club for a number of years in his 80s, handing over to a younger man to keep it going for the remaining veterans. He is currently vice president. In December 2008 Dad returned to Borneo with Veteran Affairs to honour those who did not return. In October 2012 Dad returned to El Alamein to celebrate the 70th anniversary of the Battle of El Alamein, the turning point in World War Two, compliments again of the Veteran Affairs Department. It was a very emotional return for 21 veterans, including Dad.

It has only been in Dad's latter years that he has talked much about his wartime experiences, as no one really was interested in the early years of his return, especially us children, who had not really appreciated what he did for us and our country. But with so few left, a new interest in that part of our history has enabled him to share his experiences with a number of school children and other groups. He travelled on the Ghan for its first Anzac tribute train in 2011 with his son Don who also spent 20 years of service in the Armed Forces as a result of being conscripted as a 20-year-old when his birth date marble was drawn out. However Don was an officer, reaching the rank of major, whereas Dad was a private.

Dad prospered sufficiently in his business life until the advent of the supermarket when butcher shops began to decline. He ensured that both his children had a good education and he always encouraged us to do well. He was a justice of the peace for about 20 years.

Dad continued to sail regularly, eventually selling his boat and buying a caravan in which he and Mum spent a number of years visiting various parts of the state. They moved from their home of 43 years to a retirement village where Dad still lives independently following the death of Mum in March 2007. He is now 96 years and enjoys sharing his experiences with those who want to listen. His first grandson, Will, has just arrived.

Di Corey Skull

Dianne Corey Skull was born on 9 February 1951 to parents Iris and Bill Corey of Frewville. After attending Linden Park Primary School, Presbyterian Girls College, and Metropolitan Business College, Dianne graduated from Adelaide Teachers College as a commercial teacher. She was posted to Quorn Area School (six years) and ended up spending the next 33 years living in the town of Quorn. She married Mark and subsequently had three children, Julia, Michael and Matthew. Although Mark was a train driver with the Commonwealth Railways, and drove trains in the outback of South Australia, he and Di bought a pastoral property north of Quorn for sheep and cattle grazing, and later a mixed farm closer to the town. As well as bringing up children, helping with the farm, and being involved in community work, Di worked at Caritas College in Port Augusta for three years, then in administration and finance at the Quorn Hospital and Flinders Ranges Council for 11 years. After Mark's death Di sold the property and moved to Adelaide in 2004. She now works in patient services at Calvary Central Districts Hospital and is semi-retired.

James Harold LEA

(1915–1998)

by Neville Lea

It is some 18 years since the passing of my father whilst my mother, Jean, is 93 years of age. She naturally struggles to recall details about Dad (known as Jim), but fortunately he kept a war diary from which I have drawn extensively to bring his war service to life.

The Lea family tree can be traced back to one of the first ships that came out from England in 1836 named the *Africaine*. On board that ship was a Deacon, and a Deacon married a Lea three years later. Jim's place of birth is listed as Semaphore. He had two sisters Grace and Rita (both deceased). The Lea family moved to Toorak Gardens when he was eight and then to an almond property in Hackham. There is a Harold Lea Way as a street named in honour of his father.

Jim attended Rose Park Primary School and Thebarton Technical School up to intermediate level. He would recount stories of the animals he kept at Hackham (Pennys Hill) including a pet magpie, which he fed with meat and a kookaburra. On Friday nights he would ride his bike to Rowley Park Speedway. Wow, now that's fitness!

The outbreak of war saw many families send off their loved ones. Dad was one who enlisted on 27 November 1939. As he had been still living on an almond orchard of some 40 acres, and was very close to his sisters and parents, this next chapter of his life was to test all his skills; strength and luck would also play a big part. If it started off as an adventure then this was about to rapidly change as the army discipline kicked in. For the record Jim was posted to 7th Section Royal Australian Engineers and at time of discharge the records show that he was a sapper in the 2/3rd Field or 9th Division.

On 13 May 1940 Jim travelled to Sydney for training at Ingleburn and from there he boarded a boat at Long Cove for the journey to Fremantle. The next leg of the journey was to Cape Town, South Africa. The ship was in full blackout with some 200 in hospital with flu and mumps due to the poor travelling conditions. He finally arrived in Scotland after six weeks at sea. The unit moved around, setting up camp with tents as their sleeping quarters. When leave was granted the boys headed to London for sightseeing. In November 1940 he set sail from Glasgow to Sierra Leone and Durban for more leave. He spent good times with Claude Bright, a friendship which was not to last, and writes that he went to a picture show instead of playing up as his stomach was feeling a bit queasy after a recent stint in hospital.

Durban was described as a seaside resort of the big island town, very modern with concrete hotels and wide streets and a population in 1940 of about 80,000 (white and black). Christmas day was spent on guard duties. And by the end of month the troop ships were heading to the Suez Canal. Their ships travelled through the Straits of Aden whose bare rocky hills provided a stark backdrop. The boys apparently made the most of the slow travel playing 'two up'. They disembarked at El Katara, the desert sands enclosing them from both sides, and all they could taste was the grit of sand. The train then took them to Ikings, about twenty miles from Alexandria.

The whole convoy of troops was now camped in the outskirts of Alexandria in tents that extended for miles. There was no vegetation in sight. Always there was the marching drill – down to the Mediterranean for a swim and a march back to camp – 15 miles for the round trip.

It turned out there was an Australia Club in Alexandria. The place was full of nightclubs with young boys pestering them to see 'can can' and other dance routines. Hawkers were on every corner selling cheap leather wear. In mid-January 1941 Jim and his mates hired a Ford V8 and headed for Cairo. They only managed to go two miles before a dust storm prevented further travel, the sand being so thick that visibility was less than five feet. Back at camp Dad received some letters from his sister Grace dating back to May the previous year (22 in all).

The convoy was finally off to Tobruk along the coast road. The rough roads had been partly repaired by Italians and there were thousands of Italian prisoners lined up on the side of the road with plenty of booty in sight. The boys enjoyed firing off the hand grenades. Tobruk had been destroyed by naval bombardment and the town looted. Cognac and dry wines were plentiful.

The boys were set to work on the roads with Italian tractors, the heavy rains having forced them out of their dugouts. They travelled to Benghazi and camped seven miles to the west. In February 1941 the men dug pits in the sand so that they would not be seen from the air – dugouts that threw no shadow made it difficult for air reconnaissance to detect. Dad's diary was poor on detail for reasons that if it fell into enemy hands their positions and history of movement would be hard to track.

The sections were scattered in the desert with no roads or tracks to guide them and they drove by compass and maps (what, no Tom Tom?). During the day Stukas dive-bombed and dropped their load of bombs. There was little resistance for the Allies had few fighter planes at Tobruk. Dad's unit had been asked to clean out wells, so that the armoured unit wouldn't have to travel miles for water. There were 300 mines on his truck, which were used for destroying anything of use as they made their retreat. According to his diary, one day in March they were working on the roads and they had to walk home as their truck was machine-gunned from the air.

The relieving convoy travelled at night with no lights, knowing the Germans were only a mile behind. They arrived back in Benghazi to find the fuel drums ablaze. The army had decided to make a stand, so the mines were set. On the night of 9 April the men were working all night helping to mine the road at the approach to Tobruk. The bridge and road were blown up on 10 April 1941 at 11.40 am. As German tanks approached, the 25 pounders opened up. Duties now included helping to erect barbed wire defences on the second line of defence. The Stukas were coming in waves and the men saw some good dog fights – more than four shot down. Although they were exhausted from laying hundreds of mines they were now feeling really fit and began putting up hundreds of yards of apron wire fence – day and night. Bill Coyoth lost his hand and four others received shrapnel wounds from setting mines. The sky again became active with bombs being dropped on hospital ships in Tobruk harbour. Dad's mate, Claude Bright (nicknamed the Colonel) was killed and buried in Tobruk Cemetery.

Desert sores became a problem for the men as there were no vegetables to eat. They were also wearied by 14 days of consecutive sandstorms. One night they were on another patrol detonating booby traps and laying small mines with the 2/48th Battalion covering party. The Germans who were nicknamed 'Jerries' because their helmets were the shape of English jerries, or chamber pots, were only 250 yards away, so they had to work very quietly. A destroyer picked the men up in pitch dark and took them to El Katara. There they were able to take some leave and see the sights of Damascus having spent the past nine months in the desert.

They continued with road works; the weather was very cold, but they had plenty of time for touring. They were taken by truck to Beirut from Tripoli for the day. But back at camp there was continuous guard duty, rifle drills, lectures and more road works leading to much boredom. Reveille was at 6 o'clock every morning, followed by parade, and a three-mile march. An evening was spent in Haifa. Again they were kept busy constructing pontoon bridges and landing gear.

According to the diary they were then sent back to the desert again at El Alamein digging dugouts and watching Hurricane planes getting shot down. They kept shifting camps, keeping busy with fencing and laying minefields. In one night, 2667 mines were laid. The artillery was very active and quite deafening at times.

The 2/15th and 2/17th battalions pushed hard and took 200 prisoners. Casualties were also heavy on the Allies' side. Jerry also made a push up to the 2/43rd Battalion and suffered heavy casualties as a consequence. Eighty prisoners were taken, and two planes were shot down near their position. The pilot of a Jerry fighter landed 30 yards from their position and Dad took him back to headquarters in the truck. Early September 1942 the men were laying minefields for consecutive nights, 1000 yards in front of the Allies' front line – all work under cover of darkness. The infantry was intending to move up when the minefield was completed. They were doing a few patrols at night but otherwise, during the day, there was little to do.

Dad described the camp as being 'like the sandhills at Christies Beach'. They had been busy every night widening the gaps in the minefields. Then their responsibility was to guide the 20th Battalion through the minefields. The infantry made it through with only a few casualties. Another night of action and this time they had been attached to the 8th platoon and to the 2/32nd Battalion opening up the minefield and making track for the armoured vehicles.

Following the artillery barrage the infantry went in, with Dad and the men following 30 yards behind. The machine gun fire and mortar were intense. They advanced 1500 yards and soon hundreds of prisoners were taken. A corporal and two sappers were lost. There were some lucky escapes from machine gun fire and mortars.

The second stint in the desert was over – four months and everyone was sick of the weather, fleas and dugout life. They packed up and headed to Palestine for a break, moving camp regularly.

Christmas Eve was spent in Bethlehem. Every night they went to the pictures as there was nothing else to do in Palestine.

After spending so much time in the desert they were repatriated and found it a welcome relief to be back on Australian soil. Leave was granted and family and friends were eagerly sought out. However, their leave was not long lasting.

In May 1943 the call to jungle training began. Dad started on courses for bridge building and learning how to do lashings. There was always another marching day – 25 miles in humidity – to help with acclimatisation. Again no real detail was recorded, just that they were north of Cairns. Next came training in the use of Amphibians – landing craft that would take them to the jungles of New Guinea. The Americans or 'Yanks' as they were affectionately called were assisting with their training, which lasted day and night. They were lectured on malaria (for what good it did – they all seemed to get it!).

They left in the cargo ship, *Vanderden*, for New Guinea. The seas were very rough and Dad writes that keeping food down was a real problem. The troops arrived at Milne Bay at 7.00 pm at night. They disembarked the next day and headed for camp near the aerodrome fashioning beds out of bush timber. It was pouring with rain. Milne Bay gets 272 inches of rain a year. It was August 1943 and the men continued road and bridge works.

Dad was attached to 2/17th Battalion, which got their movement orders to land 17 miles north of Lae. There were 'Jap' bombers above and they were strafed on the beach. By now they were working with the Yanks with dead Japanese soldiers lying everywhere. Dad reported that 'a Yank soldier took out a Jap sniper in a tree'. They shifted camp again, repairing roads or tracks and building more bridges.

Once when the truck was packed up, Dad and others were offered a lift back to camp. Most of the boys took up the offer but Dad and three others rode on the bulldozer that had to follow. He saw the Japanese bombers approaching and thought they were going for the artillery, but when they reached their camp they found

16 killed and 23 injured. Of those who rode in the truck, very few escaped – that is luck in war, Dad observed.

By October they were digging graves for 2/13th Battalion to whom they were attached. The bulldozers were busy burying Japanese. Food was poor and boring – usual bully beef and jungle crackers, but Dad had been successfully fishing in the local creek with hand grenades, thus providing a welcome change of diet. The opposition diminished daily and duties lightened – the men were now working on memorial foundations while waiting for a ship to take them home. In February 1944, the American cargo ship, *Sea Snipe*, finally arrived. Dad was back in Australia on 3 March 1944 and headed for Adelaide the next day by train.

As if the last four years of service weren't enough, Dad was soon off to Borneo. He kept no record of his duties there but survived which is all that matters. After the war had finished Dad was discharged from the army and he set about making a new life in peacetime. Jobs were scarce. He met Mum through a church contact and they partnered each other for an occasional dance, and from there a romance blossomed. Jim took up a work opportunity at Symons and Symons (glass merchants) previously located adjacent to Webb Oval in Glenunga. He worked there through to retirement, riding a bike to and from work every day.

After their wedding, Mum and Dad set about building the family home at 16 Torrens Street, Linden Park. I can remember Dad bringing wood home (from the glass crates at work) and spending many evenings planing the wood to make furniture for the new home; cupboards, shelving, built-in beds and the like. It was Dad's time in the army that gave him many skills and confidence to have a go at making things. Jim also dug a pit in the shed and lined it with bricks, which was hard work in the clay soil of Linden Park.

From an early age I remember Dad was always busy and he loved his bees; he had four hives and we always had honey on the table. I liked to cook the honey and make toffee with all the almonds we had. Yes, he grew almonds in our backyard too. Friday night was Rowley Park Speedway night and now that we had a car we could all go. For some reason Mum lost interest. Jack Young and Kym Bonython and the New Zealand rider Ivan Mauger were the names to recall. Jim also loved his Monday RSL nights where he would share a beer with his old mates.

In his shed he had souvenirs from the war – mines that they used to set, hand grenades etc. Over the years his mate from the RSL had taken all of them away. One other passion he had was fishing and much to Mum's disgust he decided to (as Dad would try anything) breed his own bait. Yes, you guessed – the best bait for tommy ruff fishing is maggots. After a few days in the ground Dad had plentiful supplies. We would set off for Port Giles where he taught us the finer art of 'burleying' the water adjacent to each other so one of us would get a bite.

Dad had two sisters, Rita and Grace, both now deceased. There were many cherished memories of family get-togethers with cousins. Rita and Jack Highett ran the successful Kyton's Bakery in the Central Market. We always collected a block of sultana cake from a visit, so that a slice would always go into our school recess pack.

Jean and Jim both loved gardening, Dad with a view to providing for his family. In retirement Dad enjoyed holidays with Mum until failing health. I saw Dad the Monday morning he died – by the afternoon he was gone. There was a large gathering at his funeral and needless to say his mates from the RSL turned up, and guess what they played.

Neville Lea

Neville Lea was born on 24 June 1950 and is the eldest of three boys born to Jim and Jean Lea. Brothers Jeff and Chris also attended Linden Park. His first job saw him working with Rob West, also of Linden Park School, with an importer and exporter company. Opportunities in Western Australia took Neville to the bush, working with a geophysical team searching for nickel deposits. When working for Gilbarco as a costing analyst he luckily missed a flight to Moomba when all on board died. Later, bored with a lack of promotional opportunities, Neville joined the Hindmarsh Building Society. Here he was encouraged to study and completed his landbroking ticket before being duly promoted to a middle management position. With Hindmarsh heading for a merger with Co-op he decided to leave and do conveyancing. At age 40 he decided to leave the bank and trade as a conveyancer and is still practising now.

Neville married Evelyn aged 25 and the marriage produced a daughter Vanessa. The marriage was to eventually end in divorce. Then he met Lorraine Brewer from Port Lincoln and they enjoyed each other's company for many years until cancer took her life in February 2012.

Neville follows the Crows, is building a new home, assists his 93-year-old Mum, and travels to the Gold Coast to see his daughter.

Ross Haldane RAGLESS

(1920–2011)

by Jeff Ragless

On 21 November 2011 we farewelled my father, Ross Ragless, at a funeral service at Alfred James on Marion Road in South Plympton. Over 90 people of all ages attended – friends and relatives came from near and far to say goodbye. I know Dad would have appreciated it, but at the same time would probably have wondered what all the fuss was about. He was a bit like that – an unassuming man, somewhat reserved, but always ready to help family and friends in need.

Ross Haldane Ragless was born 2 February 1920 at Rose Park Private Hospital – the third son and fourth child to George and Berta Ragless. His siblings were Don, Peter and Betsy. His early years were spent on the farm near Port Germein, to the north of Port Pirie. Parental health problems forced the family to move off the land and into the city, when Dad was about four or five. His father George suffered from chronic rheumatoid arthritis that would render him an invalid for the remainder of his days. Berta was to develop breast cancer and she passed away when Dad was 16 years old.

The family took up residence at 39 Chatsworth Grove in Toorak Gardens, which was on the very fringe of Adelaide suburbia, and probably quite different from the beautiful leafy suburb it is today. The bungalow-style house remained in the family until the mid 1980s, and is still there today. Dad commenced school at Rose Park Primary, along with his brothers and sister. They say that friends come and go, but in Dad's case they seemed to come and stay. At about the age of six, he found a good friend in the girl next door, Lina Kurger, and when a little older, he discovered great mates in Keith Burr, Keith Claridge, Milt Pascoe, Ray Roberts and Lindsay Croser. These were friendships that lasted their whole lives. Croser children were also students at Linden Park School. There were many and varied social occasions over the years that were enjoyed by the group and their families, as they grew together.

Dad also had an older friend that had a billy cart, and this enterprising mate used to take it around, collecting horse manure from around the streets, selling it for threepence a load (handy pocket money in those days). Dad used to help out with the 'business' and his commission was a ride in the billy cart on the way home. I think he came to realise eventually that it wasn't such a great cut of the profits. I just hope he had a bath before tea on those working days.

Rose Park Primary gave way to Adelaide Technical High School, and much adolescent mischief. Dad's mate Keith Burr related the story that one day he went to visit Dad and as he walked up the drive, he heard the intermittent sound of gunshots coming from the garage. He found Dad engrossed, using a length of copper tube secured in the vice as a makeshift rifle – the tube was just wide enough for a 22 bullet and a hammer and nail did the rest. Both Dad and Keith were most amused at the holes in the shed roof. They never did say if Grandpa George ever found out.

As you can imagine, kids made their own fun in those days and a two-wheeler bike was blissful freedom. Kids from all over used to gather around the River Torrens, behind the Adelaide Zoo and ride their bikes up, down and around the many dirt tracks and through the creek (as it was in those days). Dad loved to impersonate the vicar on his pushbike and would wear his shirt backwards to imitate a clergy collar, and ride bolt upright through the tracks and river. The crowds of kids loved it and demanded many a repeat performance, according to his mates. A successful but simple one-act play.

Dad and another friend, Ray Hunt, decided late in their teens to join the local militia (today known as the Army Reserve). It seemed a rather adventurous thing to do at the time, although they didn't realise until too late that they would be required to do much of their training on horseback – a prospect that was rather horrifying to both of them apparently. But they went ahead and became reserve soldiers, learning horsemanship and many other military skills. This for Dad, led into World War Two – his biggest adventure was about to come.

He enlisted in February 1941 and was posted to South Australia's 2/43rd Battalion. The 2/43rd had been formed the previous July, and was already on active service, as part of the Australian Ninth Division. Training was at Wayville and then Woodside in the Adelaide Hills, before they embarked for the Middle East in April 1941, arriving in late May for further training before joining the main battalion in Libya in July. What followed was the famed defence of Tobruk.

German propaganda (during radio broadcasts) derisively referred to the Allies as the 'poor desert rats' of Tobruk, as they lived in extensive tunnel networks and shelters, attached to their trenches. The propaganda backfired and, typical of the Australian dry sense of humour, they took the insult as a badge of honour, and The Rats of Tobruk were born. The title became part of Australian folklore.

Even in the height of warfare, some lighter moments arose. German equipment was much sought after by the Allies, as it was often superior quality. Dad relayed one instance. The Australians had captured a German position and were in the process of scrounging souvenirs and useful equipment, when one wag came out of a foxhole and shouted, 'I've got the boots – anyone want the socks?'

After months of fighting, the division was relieved and withdrew by sea to camps in Syria. Then followed rest and further training, before the El Alamein conflict, that legendary Allied offensive that halted Rommel's charge across North Africa and eventuated in victory over the Afrikakorps.

Dad didn't escape completely unscathed from the fight, being slightly wounded twice. The first was a small piece of shrapnel in the shoulder that was treated quickly at the aid post, before he was sent back to the line. He made light of the second wound, saying that at least he was headed in the right direction – another small piece of shrapnel got him in the butt cheek. Once again he was patched up and sent back into action.

By the end of 1942, Dad had been overseas for more than 18 months and many of the Australians more than two years. The Ninth Division was relieved in early 1943 and headed home, as threat of Japanese invasion of Australia was ever growing. They disembarked in stages at Fremantle, Melbourne and Sydney.

South Australia's 2/43rd Battalion arrived in Adelaide by troop train on 1 March 1943. It must have been quite an experience – the battalion arrived at Mitcham Station, and marched down to Springbank Camp on Daws Road (opposite the hospital). Apparently thousands lined the route. It must have been a wonderful homecoming.

After several months of respite and then retraining in jungle warfare, the 2/43rd headed for New Guinea and fought against the Japanese, returning to Australia in January 1944. It was about this time that Dad applied to transfer to the RAAF with an intention of learning to fly, but late in his course the Empire Air Training Scheme was disbanded. Apparently there was a surplus of trained pilots at that stage of the war. Dad was promoted to sergeant, and saw out the war as an airfield defence instructor.

It is ironic that his transfer application from Army to RAAF was processed in 1944 by Heatherlie Payne, sister-in-law of his great mate Keith Burr. Heatherlie would many years later become Dad's second wife. But more on that later.

During his time in the RAAF Dad met Gloria Thomas. They were both stationed at Port Melbourne in Victoria, and romance blossomed. Mum described this dashing airforce sergeant, with ribbons on his chest and looks akin to Tyrone Power, 'the movie star'. They were married at Glenelg's St Peter's Church in June 1945.

After the war ended, they both returned to civilian life. Dad returned to the Motor Vehicles Department, and they built a home at 5 Blairgowrie Road, St Georges, and looked to start a family. Mum unfortunately was unable to have children, so they elected to adopt and I was the successful candidate. Someone told me once that they then proceeded to spoil their new baby boy rotten, but I don't think that was quite right. Didn't everyone have train-sets?

Dad was always a doer. There were always things to build or repair and he seemed to be a master of all. He built a brush fence and stone wall around the house and extensive retaining walls and garden beds within. Inside the house he built bedroom and kitchen cupboards throughout, along with wooden Venetian blinds for all nine windows. The asbestos-clad single garage also went up quickly with help from brothers, Don and Peter – nothing was too tough to create.

Sadly the house at 5 Blairgowrie Road has now gone, as has the brush fence. However the stone wall does remain in its original form and seemingly as strong as the day it was built. The number five that was attached to that wall was reclaimed during the demolition stage by persons unknown and became a fridge magnet for the original owner, RHR. It now forms part of my treasure collection.

Dad also readily helped with the establishment of the Beaumont Tennis Club – a community effort that actually built courts, fencing, retaining walls and clubhouse from scratch. He then held the position of club secretary for the first three years. His significant contribution earned him life membership, along with other local names, Jack O'Shaughnessy, Rolly Buttery, Noel Shakes, Clem Gunner and

Neville and Coralie Soward (later Mayor of Burnside). Dad and Mum played tennis there for a number of years, and enjoyed many resulting social occasions.

Dad continued in the public service with the Motor Vehicles Department, and then moved to the Police Department in the late 50s, in charge of the records section – still as a public servant. I remember getting carried away at school and telling a couple of mates that 'my dad's a policeman'. I nearly came unstuck not long after when one of those mates, Stephen Jones, came over home and seeing Dad in the garage, asked him: 'Mr Ragless, are you a policeman?'

Dad never batted an eyelid and said, 'Yep, sure am.'

I never did tell Dad how much I appreciated his flippant reply that day, but it was a good lesson learnt – I was wary of stupid boasts after that. I guess Stephen Jones still thinks Dad was a cop.

Dad's love of woodwork continued. He built various pieces, including furniture and wooden toys. I asked him once what a tommy gun looked like and he proceeded to build one for me out of about five pieces of wood. The result was an incredibly accurate replica of a Thompson submachine gun (barrel magazine and all).

He built two wooden desks, one for himself and one for me. His idea was that the desk would inspire me to be more scholarly. That didn't quite work out, but the four-drawer desk, with the two-tier bookshelf at one end, built from meranti and pine still sits in our den, over 50 years on.

Binky, a small black and tan terrier cross arrived on Guy Fawkes night 1961, and became a much loved part of the family and the neighbourhood. Dad built a run alongside the garage to keep the dog in during the day, but it wasn't long before Binky crashed out on a daily basis and made the neighbourhood his own. Phil and Andrew Mugge, our neighbours, even called the dog 'St Georges Binky' in the same vane as 'Greyfriars Bobby', a Disney movie of the era, that told the true story of a small dog that was granted the key to the city of Edinburgh. Binky seemed to own St Georges, and always managed to evade the dog catcher. Dad had great affection for that little dog and admitted only recently that it was one of the saddest days of his life when Binky was eventually put to sleep.

As I grew older and played school footy Dad was ever willing to load the Renault Dauphine up with rowdy kids, and take us to Saturday morning matches. He would then suffer the grizzles on the way home, if we got beaten – it was always the umpire's fault. Saturday afternoons in winter, it was off to Unley Colosseum to watch the might of the Double Blues. Again if the Blues got beaten it was the umpire's fault – still is.

Dad struck health problems in 1962, having a serious heart attack. He spent six weeks in hospital and had to recuperate for many months. Further heart scares followed in 1968 and 1971; however bypass surgery in 1975 gave him a new lease of life.

He owned a couple of boats in the 70s and loved to go fishing off the bay. There was always the odd fillet of fish up in the freezer. The boat was also generously available for scuba diving and water skiing.

Sadly, Mum passed away very suddenly on 4 July 1975, which was a great shock to all, and life for both Dad and me took on quite different dimensions. Dad retired from the E&WS Department and recovered from heart surgery at the end of 1975.

During this period he reacquainted with Heatherlie Payne and happily one thing lead to another. Dad and Heatherlie married in 1976 and a whole new stage of his life began. St Georges was sold and they moved to a unit in Wood Street, Millswood.

Together they took up art classes, bowls and Dad, par 3 golf. Fishing continued and pottering about in a newly established work shed reached new highs. During this time they also welcomed Jan into my life and we were married in 1977.

Grand children came in the 1980s and Dad was incredibly proud of both granddaughters, Laura born in 1981 and Hayley in 1986. In the late 90s Dad bought and restored a 1937 Austin, which my wife Jan named Anabel. Dad responded by ordering personalised number plates that read 'Anabel' and the car's entity was finalised.

The Austin gave Dad a whole new project for a couple of years and many hours of enjoyment and achievement. He eventually drove it in the Bay to Birdwood and two years later he asked me to drive it in the same event, with him as 'navigator'. He was unable to operate the clutch due to a leg problem. It was a great day and wonderful personal experience.

When the house in Seafield Avenue began to get a bit too much work for them, Dad and Heatherlie moved to a unit in The Parks Lifestyle Village in January 2004. They both continued to enjoy bowls and other activities, but Dad's life began to slow down. He became more reclusive, with a number of health issues contributing.

A 90th birthday for Dad at the Parks Village was a wonderful tribute and attended by many family and friends. Dad thoroughly enjoyed himself. Anzac Day came and Dad laid the wreath at a ceremony, also at the Parks Village.

With Dad's consent, I had his service medals restored in 2010. They received new ribbons and were mounted correctly in their order of protocol. Dad wore them proudly (as ever) on his last Anzac Day in 2011.

His last months were mixed with frustration, at not being able to return to the activities he loved. Dad still maintained a sense of humour, but not always. He became bedridden for the last couple of months and passed very peacefully.

Dad was always a great advocate of family and we, his family, were blessed to have been such a major part of his life. I am grateful for the qualities that he impressed on me, throughout, and I sincerely thank him for his generosity and love. I will carry his memory with me, always with great respect, love and appreciation.

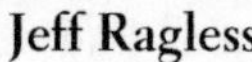

Jeff Ragless

Jeffrey Ian Ragless, only child of Ross and Gloria, attended Linden Park School from 1956 to 1962, and then completed five years of secondary schooling at Unley High.

He joined the Savings Bank of South Australia in 1968 and progressed to Departmental Manager and Branch Liaison Officer, before being retrenched in 1974, during the State Bank crisis. He joined Galaxy TV in 1974 and then Westpac in 1977, where he still works today.

Jeff lives at Flagstaff Hill with wife, Jan, who was always greatly admired by his dad. He has two married daughters, Laura and Hayley, and two grandchildren, William and Kaitlyn. Both son-in-laws, Paul and Ewan, are in the Australian Army. Jeff also served for two years with Army Reserve after leaving school.

Jeff has enjoyed numerous interests over the years, including football, scuba diving, snow and water skiing and golf, which he continues to play quite badly. Jeff and his family have also enjoyed a number of family holidays, both in Australia and overseas.

Religion

Frank Hammond GOLDNEY (1914–2000)

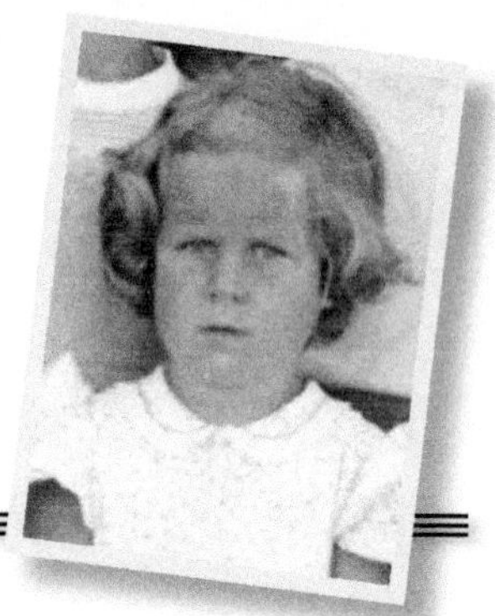

by Frances Goldney Nilson

World War Two: the reasons why men and women enlisted in the Australian Armed Forces and headed off to war were many and varied but mainly because they believed that the war was morally right, because it offered them the sense of adventure and excitement, to 'do one's bit' for their country out of a sense of duty and national pride, and to play a part in Australia's military heritage (Johnston 1996). Other people like my father joined up for possibly some of the above reasons but largely because the alternative was too horrific to contemplate. He was a Quaker, a pacifist, and this was to be his dilemma.

When my father was four years old his father, Frederick Goldney, died of influenza in the worldwide epidemic of 1918 and their nursing sister mother, Minnie Goldney, raised him and his older brother, Fred. She worked full-time as a hospital matron to support and educate her sons at St Peters Boys College, Adelaide, and they boarded at the school with the partial financial support of a choral scholarship. He then went on to become a chartered accountant in 1938, like his father who had died. It was in the same year that he became associated with the Society of Friends (Quakers) and was interested in their cause for world peace at a time when war threatened. He always had a love of history and published his *War Diaries & Memoirs of Flight Lieutenant Frank Hammond Goldney* a meticulous account of his experiences during World War Two. In his own words (1993, p. 7) he explains his anguished decision as a Quaker to enlist:

> *Deep down in all of us is a sense of responsibility to resist oppression, callous aggression, and crass cruelty. In a strange way it emanates from a pure desire to protect the ones we love and that, of course, embraces not just our own family, but all humankind. For whom the bells toll!*
>
> *I awakened from my dreams of peace to the reality that Hitler was a menace, not only to peace, but to the survival of all the men, women, and children of the British Commonwealth of Nations, and the rest of the world.*
>
> *So I came to the decision – it was between me and the Great God I worship – Hitler had to be defeated in war.*

He therefore enlisted to serve with the RAAF in 1940, which was a popular choice and attracted a disproportionate number of men at the time (Johnston, 1996).

My memories of him are of a loving father who treasured his wife and five children. I was always aware as his eldest child that he was a little different to other children's fathers in that he didn't conform to the stereotypical image of a businessman. He was artistic, detested bureaucracy and possessed a bohemian air about him. He was often seen striding around Burnside, taking his Labrador dog on his ten kilometres walks, wearing tennis shorts, long brown socks and shoes, and a cravat. He had no intentions of playing tennis and dressed to his sense of style. He worked from home as a chartered accountant for as long as I can remember and still had a couple of long-standing clients at the age of 86 years when he died.

His want of a peaceful life often escaped him. The war, as with so many men, women and children, had long-lasting detrimental effects upon him that stayed with him most of his life. He rarely slept before three or four o'clock in the morning and wrote in a letter to the Department of Veterans Affairs when applying for a Gold Card, saying: 'I have lost the art of sublime sleep.' As a child his insomnia was always a bit of a puzzle to me and it was only as I grew older that I understood. The war memories never left him and he was often intolerant of our loud noises and boisterous games. He would become quite distressed, stating that we should never fight but love and hug each other, something that was furthest from our thoughts at the time.

He became easily frustrated, and, as an example, my siblings and I learnt never to ask him for help with our mathematics homework despite his expertise in the subject. He would impatiently want to ignore the mathematics examples provided in the school textbook, despite my protestations, and would teach me a 'simpler' way to solve the problems. Unfortunately my teachers didn't approve of his methods despite having the correct answer and I would have to do the homework again, much to my disgust.

The writing of his memoirs based on his diaries in 1993, seven years before he died, is not only a wonderful legacy for our family but I think helped him deal with and resolve some of these inner torments. As he said, 'my mind was flooded with multitudes of memories which built up to a time when I became pregnant with the past' (1993, p. 1), and so he set about the daunting task of writing it all down. He was a more peaceful and very accepting man in his final years.

My father was a very spiritual person, an idealist, and not a traditionalist. As a child I would attend the Society of Friends with him on Sunday mornings to the sound of bells of the St Peters Cathedral next door. I was aware that other people thought that my father being a Quaker was quite unusual. The fact that most people equated Quakers with the man on the box of Quakers Oats breakfast cereal, and some teachers were still describing Quakers as they existed in the settling of Pennsylvania, America, in 1682, didn't help. Consequently children in my class half expected me to wear a mob-cap and talk using 'thee' and 'thou', something I found very funny. Our life at home was very conventional, certainly not puritanical, and we enjoyed all the things most families did. Although I am not a Quaker I regard the values of peace and tolerance that I learnt as a child still fundamentally important to me now.

To put the meaning of being a Quaker into context in terms of what it meant to my father when World War Two began I will explain further. The Religious Society of Friends (Quakers) was formed in the mid 1600s and was a breakaway branch of the Church of England. It is a simplified philosophy of a Christian religion where they believe that every person has direct access to God. In their view there are no priests, churches, ceremonies, gowns, creed or dogma needed (Quakers Australia, 2012). It involves each person's direct experience of God, prayer through silence, and they have had a tradition of opposing war. The first and second world wars created a crisis for the movement, which, up until this time, would have ejected any soldier from its society. It was an impossible situation for many Quakers in World War One where servicemen, who were ordered to take up arms but resisted based on religious grounds, faced lengthy gaol terms. This changed at the beginning of World War Two when many Quakers entered the armed forces in a non-combatant capacity and joined air ambulances corps and transport squadrons and were able to provide valuable support to the war effort without fighting.

He enlisted for service with Air Crew at the Old Legislative Council Chambers on North Terrace and then followed many months of lectures on all the basics for navigation in flying aircraft, mathematics, meteorology and astronomical navigation. He was called up by the RAAF in July 1941 and was posted to No. 1 Elementary Flying Training School at Victor Harbor, South Australia.

By all accounts my father was a bit of a daredevil when it came to flying a plane and he delighted in telling us, his children, of his escapades while training to be a pilot. On one very amusing occasion he was the last Tiger Moth to take off from Parafield Airport to do aerobatics solo over the Gawler River. However, while flying, a line squall (a sudden and violent change of wind) developed, and when he came to land the plane there was a 50 mph head-on wind. The Tiger Moth's stalling speed was only about 40 mph, with the result he landed the plane in reverse. Apparently this caused much laughter from all those who were watching, something he enjoyed (1993, p. 11).

Unsurprisingly, his pilot training was short and sensational. He did one too many 360 degree loops, skimmed a fence by a few feet on take-off, and generally scared the living daylights out of the flying instructors. When my father asked why he was being taken off flying in pilot training he enjoyed describing his friend, the chief flying instructor and squadron leader's response: 'Frank, the aircraft are too expensive.' (1993, p. 14)

Hence with further training he was reclassified as an observer navigator with No. 117 Squadron. Their role was as a transport squadron that would ferry supplies to the war zones and bring back casualties from North Africa, India and Burma. These flights were often conducted unarmed despite flying in enemy territory, and there were often no airstrips and little suitable terrain for landing near the front line troops, which prompted General Wingate's term for a challenging landing 'to come down the chimney' (J. Winter, 2012).

When I read my father's account of his experiences of the war he states that 'humour is one of the antidotes to fear' and I am always struck by three things in his book. Firstly the humour, with some of his accounts being very funny despite being potentially life threatening. Secondly, the comradeship amongst his fellow servicemen – he talks so fondly of these men, many of whom he kept in contact with until the end of his life. Thirdly, a sense of weariness and sickness prevails toward the end of his account. When he was repatriated back to Australia in 1944, where before the war he had weighed 11 stone, he now weighed six-and-a half-stone (45 kilograms) following repeated bouts of malaria, dysentery and other tropical diseases.

The first years after the war ended he and so many people struggled to get back to some semblance of normality, but as very different people. My own belief is that he experienced post-traumatic stress disorder, a medical diagnosis that was still to be recognised and therefore not treated. After the war he found it hard to settle down in Adelaide and travelled back to France to rehabilitate and study art at the Sorbonne University in Paris (hence the bohemian influence) and then worked in England, where he met my mother on a train to Cornwall.

They married and lived in Cornwall for a year before returning to Adelaide with me as a baby. Eventually they settled in Hazelwood Park, Burnside, where many of World War One and World War Two servicemen returned to live and bring up their families. There were many children in our street and suburb and my parents were keen for us to attend the local and reputable Linden Park Demonstration School, a training school for student teachers. We had a strong sense of community in Burnside, whether it was at the Beaumont Girl Guides, the Glenside Anglican Church Netball teams, the Beaumont Tennis Club, or the Norwood Swimming Club. We knew so many children in the area as our lives crossed paths day in and out. Our days out of school hours were full of carefree adventure, and as long as we reported back at teatime, my mother, the disciplinarian in our family, was happy. We'd often hike up to Waterfall Gully to pick blackberries, walk to Hazelwood Park when it was still a large paddock with horses, catch tadpoles in the creek beds around Tusmore Park, and on one occasion, walked to the Mount Lofty kiosk. We were too tired to walk back and rang my not-very-happy mother to pick us up at six o'clock in the evening, the time we were due back. There are many memorials to those who died in the wars at strategic points around Burnside and as children we would often come across them when exploring and wonder at them.

My memories of Linden Park Demonstration School are of a strict and structured school that provided a good grounding in reading, writing and arithmetic for the post-war baby boom population of the area. The classes often comprised of more than 40 children, and classes continued regardless, despite summer temperatures reaching more than 100 degrees Fahrenheit in the hastily erected prefabricated buildings. I was conscious of the newly-emigrated children from postwar Europe in my classes, their strange but tasty lunches, and sometimes their struggle to fit between two cultures. Life at home for other children was extremely difficult and I suspect fraught with abuse. The war had only ended 11 years earlier when I started school in 1956 (aged six years) and the consequences of war were often hidden behind closed doors but the distress still could be heard in neighbouring houses.

My father's influence went beyond the home and into the classroom on one particular occasion each year. I would dread the morning after the teacher interview evenings and not for the more obvious reasons. I would come to school with trepidation only to have my fears confirmed. There and behold, taking up the whole blackboard would be an enormous drawing of, for example, a lion's head, or an American Indian in full headdress, only just missing the times tables and important messages, and children gazing and wondering who had drawn it. Knowing my father's love of drawing it was my secret and, sadly, I couldn't wait for it to be rubbed off.

As you may have gathered my father enjoyed entertaining people and loved nothing better than to tell his stories. In his later years I would find him down at a Dulwich coffee shop having a conversation with anyone who had time to listen. On one occasion I found him with the cast of Jesus Christ Superstar who were gathered around him entranced, eager to hear his stories. They rewarded him by giving him tickets to their show, much to his delight.

The legacy of war is profound and its detrimental effects go beyond the present generation to those generations that follow. I sometimes wonder what my father would have been like had the war not left its mark, something I will never know. I do know that I miss him every day and the older I get the more I feel indebted to him for his love, guidance and the opportunities he provided me. I know at times he struggled, but his love of life and positivity always shone through. He left the Society of Friends after about 35 years as a member. I'm not sure why he left; possibly because he just decided that he didn't need any formal organisation to practice his faith in God.

He was in England in 1943 when he heard of the death of one of his dear friends, a pilot, killed when his plane crashed into the Scots mountains. He was walking in a garden and came across a sundial with these words chiselled around the top:

I counte onlie ye sunnie houres. (1993, p. 33)

These words gave him solace at a time of great sadness, and he reflected on all the wonderful times they had shared together. These words have stayed with me too and 'I count only the happy hours' whenever possible.

References:

Goldney, F. (1993) *War Diaries & Memoirs of Flight Lieutenant Frank Hammond Goldney.* Hyde Park Press Pty Ltd, South Australia

Johnston, M. (1996) The Civilians Who Joined Up 1939–45. *Journal of the Australian War Memorial* Issue 29

RAF website (2012) History of 117 Squadron.

Robinson, B. (2012) Quakers Australia website

Winter, J., (no date), History of No 117 Squadron Royal Air Force – Ex 117 Squadron. Burma Star Association website

Frances Goldney Nilson

Frances is the oldest of five children all of whom attended Linden Park Primary School from year one through to Year 7. As the eldest child she tended to take her responsibilities a little too seriously and it wasn't until she left school, studied to be a registered nurse at the Royal Adelaide Hospital and headed overseas that she learnt to have fun – something she excelled in. She studied midwifery in London, nursed in Paris and travelled widely for three years before heading home. She completed a B.Ed. (Nursing) and has alternated between nursing and nurse education for more than 42 years. Her father was very proud that all three of his daughters did nursing, as did his beloved mother. Frances lives in Brisbane with her wonderful husband Ric and two beautiful sons, both of whom are employed in the finance industry, like their grandfather. History repeats itself.

Henry Stephen **HASSOLD**

(1914–1996)

by Elizabeth Anne Hassold Wake-Dyster

My father, Henry Stephen Hassold, was born in 1914 in New Zealand. He was a son of American Lutheran Missionary, Rev Dr Frederick Hassold and his New Zealand-born wife, Gertrude (nee Nitschke). In 1917, the Lutheran parsonage at Rongotea was destroyed by fire, and soon after the family transferred to Eudunda in South Australia. There my father attended the state school and then St John's Lutheran School after it reopened in 1925 following World War One. It is interesting to note that on Thursday 3 June 1926, Fred (my grandfather) wrote in his diary: 'Electric lights burning for first time in history of Eudunda.' An extract from 11 June 1926 edition of the *Eudunda Courier* confirmed this report. As a young man, Henry pursued several interests. He learnt the piano and the violin. He played social tennis. He was a member of the King's Rifles and took part in competitions around the state; being a good shot with a Lee-Enfield .303 rifle, he won several trophies.

In 1930, at the age of 16 years, my father began work at Weis and

Orrock's garage in Eudunda. He was an apprentice fitter and turner with Mr Colin Orrock. His weekly wage was 7/6. He learned oxy-welding and did mechanical work on many vehicles such as Model T Fords, Chevrolets, Pontiacs, Chryslers and trucks.

He had some difficult times while growing up. These included the death of his mother when he was nine years old, and the death of his older sister, when he was 20.

In the 1930s, my father moved to Adelaide in order to continue his education and to find employment; he lived at the home of Professor Winkler and family at Highgate. He married Alison (nee Harders). They lived at Unley before building the family home at the top end of Fifeshire Avenue, St Georges. They chose the site because it afforded unrestricted views of the city and hills.

Near the beginning of World War Two, Henry, together with his brother Eric Hassold and his brothers-in-law, Gordon and Clarrie Harders, sought to enlist in the AIF. However, due to his particular expertise, Henry was exempted from military service. AIF recruiters redirected him to specialist government contractors in whose employ he served throughout the war. He worked in the munitions and tool making factories from 1939 to 1945.

The *National Trust News* of South Australia reports in its May–July 2012 edition, that:

> The workshop buildings were first constructed in about 1881 and the factory became one of the largest wartime industry hubs in Australia along with General Motors-Holden's at Woodville. At the Regency Road end of the site, the now demolished, handsome red-brick and glass wartime tool-making factories, plus iron factories where the wings of Beaufort bombers, shell casings and armoured vehicles were once made, are being replaced with a retail precinct.

My father, Henry, was proud of the fact that other members of the family were recruited to serve King and country on the field of battle. Eric served in signals for the AIF; Gordon served with the AIF in Papua New Guinea; and Clarrie served as an AIF lawyer.

I want to add a further note about my Uncle Clarrie. My parents were delighted when he was honoured by the Queen and became Sir Clarrie Harders, and when in 1997, some former government ministers, whom Clarrie served, published a fine tribute in the *Sydney Morning Herald*. 'Australia recently lost one of its greatest public servants, Sir Clarrie Harders, who was head of the Attorney General's Department from 1970–1979.' The Hon Justice Michael Kirby AC CMG stated: 'Clarrie Harders was a man of great experience. From South Australia originally, he brought to Canberra like other distinguished officers of the Department from that State, a Germanic efficiency and a free-settler's open-mindedness.' My Uncle Clarrie stayed with us every year during the Christmas and New Year holiday season so that he could attend the test cricket at Adelaide Oval. During his visits, I recall many conversations in our home about the war years, and about losing loyal friends and relatives, also in bombing raids over Germany.

As the war in the Pacific was drawing to a close, my father received news concerning the death of his American cousin, Carl Hassold. He died of wounds received during the Battle of Luzon in the Philippines, just two weeks before the end of the war. About the same time, our family received news that another relative, Matron Olive Paschke, had been executed by the Japanese during the Banka Island massacre. I want to add that during the war, my father got to know Colonel Beevor, a veteran of the World War One Gallipoli campaign. Over the years, the Hassold and Beevor families became good friends.

My parents lived in the family home at St Georges for nearly 50 years. During this time they made many friends. Among their closest neighbours were the Children's Court Magistrate, Mr Les Wright, and the Ackland family. For several years, on Saturday afternoons during the summer, they spent many happy hours playing social tennis with the Acklands and the famous South Australian geologist Reg Sprigg and his wife Griselda who later developed Arkaroola Station in the Flinders Ranges.

In 1946, my father started work for Bonds Tours and worked

there for 26 years. He made very good friends there and I remember holidaying in the Flinders Ranges with a family from his workplace. In 1972, dad began work at Stateliner, which took over Bonds Tours. He worked there until his retirement. His work there initially involved doing general maintenance on the buses, then specialising in the repair of gearboxes, starter motors and alternators. He also worked on the general lathe machining and making stands for GMH V6 and V8 diesels. These stands were made from old bus chassis and enabled the mounting of a motor to turn in every direction. He also carried out a lot of welding repairs on broken chassis and rear-end suspensions. He really enjoyed his work at Stateliners.

My first memory of our home was standing on the slate terrace, which my father had built, and peering through the dining room window. I was about two-and-a-half years old at the time. I spent a lot of time in the expansive garden, while dad worked at his bench that was initially outside and later in his besser block garage with car pit. My father loved working in his shed and garden, which my parents had designed and constructed themselves. I used to enjoy playing in the garden that was divided into three main areas by stone retaining walls. The vegetable and fruit tree garden was a delight to walk through, as each year it took on a different perspective depending on what vegetables Dad decided to grow. The front garden was always a picture in spring with flowering annuals and prunus tree in blossom. The lawn area gave the family a place to enjoy games and barbecues with friends and relatives.

I remember my father as a quiet, gentle man, who always supported and encouraged me. Although he was a man of few words, he was always happy to talk to me about any project he might be doing and always listened to what others had to say. There was a strength in his quietness. Our family's Christian beliefs played a significant, positive role in our family life. Love and encouragement, I feel were the stronger elements together with the belief that God provided, no matter in what circumstances one might find oneself.

In conclusion, I should like to say that my older brother, Rev

Dr Michael Hassold, also attended Linden Park Primary School. He went on to study theology and to become a pastor, lecturer, and then principal of Luther Seminary in North Adelaide.

After graduating from Linden Park Primary School, I attended Unley High School and later went on to study medicine at Adelaide University with the help of a Commonwealth scholarship. My father did not influence my choice of career, but rather encouraged me in his own quiet way. I remember making a decision in kindergarten that I would like to become a doctor and this aspiration eventuated in 1974. I worked part time as a general practitioner, as family is an important part of my life. I recently discovered that my father's American cousin was also a GP. I married Colin who was also in Year Seven at Linden Park Primary School. We have three children and three grandchildren.

In my father's biography he mentions that: 'Despite many difficult times I thank God for so many blessings throughout my life.'

Elizabeth Anne Hassold Wake-Dyster

Elizabeth is the younger of two children, both of whom attended Linden Park Primary School and Unley High School. She studied medicine at Adelaide University and completed a MBBS in 1974. She married Colin and they have three children, two boys and a girl, all of whom have taken on very different careers. One of the boys is a police officer, the other an aircraft maintenance engineer, which is closely related to his grandfather's trade as motor engineer. Our daughter is a classical clarinetist involved in teaching and performing. Liz worked part-time most of her career as her children grew up and over the last 20 years, she worked in the southern suburbs of Adelaide as a GP. Travelling, photography, computing and more recently, archery, are some of the activities she enjoys doing, besides babysitting her three grandchildren.

Leonard Samuel HIGGINS

(1922–1995)

by Phil Higgins

My father's family history in Australia began in 1876 when William Higgins, then 36, a blacksmith and native of Cornwall, arrived in Melbourne on the SS *Durban*. With him was his wife Mary and their two daughters, Mabel and Anita. They would eventually settle in South Australia at Gawler where their third child, Dad's father Percy, was born in 1882. My father Leonard Samuel Higgins, born 28 June 1922 was the youngest of two children born to Percy and his wife Clare. They lived at 57 Kyle Street, Glenside (then known as Knoxville). Percy was a carpenter whose working life was cut short due to glaucoma and he would spend his latter years in almost total darkness.

Dad got to know Grandfather William rather well when he was in his 80s as he came to live with Percy, Clare and the two boys for 11 years following the death of Mary. He would tell the family of his experiences in Chile and Peru, but especially Mexico where he worked at his trade for six years in the 1860s, during what was a particularly lawless time following the execution of the Emperor Maximilian. He was unable to look at a pack of cards without recalling scenes of brutality and would tell of witnessing Mexican gamblers murder their companions, dump the body under the table and continue with the game.

This time spent in Mexico obviously had a long lasting effect on him. Dad told me of an incident when the whole family was woken up by a huge thump in the middle of the night. They went in and found him on the floor of his room with the blankets still covering him. He said that he had been dreaming that he was back in Mexico and had been captured by rebels who had tied him down across a railway line and left him there. When he heard a train approaching, he gave a mighty leap to get clear and woke up when he landed on the floor. He was then over 90 but survived the fall.

Most likely Dad would also have attended Linden Park Primary School had there been a school there then. Instead, he and his older brother Murray went to Rose Park School and then to Adelaide High School in Currie Street, which was then located on the site now occupied by the Remand Centre. Although Dad was a fair student, he left school early and commenced work as a clerk with AGE (Australian General Electric). In August 1942, he enlisted in the Army and was posted to Darwin where he witnessed the many Japanese air raids, which occurred until November 1943. He was still in Darwin and holding the rank of Staff Sergeant Supplies Section when he was discharged at the end of the war. In 1976 he made his only return visit to Darwin while I was living there and enjoyed showing me those places which had significance to him at the time, however he rarely spoke much about the war, perhaps because it had been largely uneventful for him and he never had any desire to march. It was during his time in the Army that he met Merle Smith through mutual friends while he was on leave and they began corresponding. As the saying goes 'romance blossomed' and they married in 1947.

In his youth Dad had been brought up in the local Congregational church but at around the age of 18 he had become a committed Christian and had commenced his association with the Brethren Assemblies, better known at the time as the Plymouth Brethren. In their early married life Dad and Mum lived in a house in Trimmer Terrace, Unley, right opposite the oval. Maybe those early days, perched on Dad's shoulders watching football matches, was the beginning of my life-long love of sports. On Sundays they would attend the local Brethren church, which at that time met in the banqueting room of the Unley Town Hall.

In 1951 Dad engaged the services of a builder friend and, armed with his War Service Home Loan, they began construction of a house in Collingwood Avenue, Hazelwood Park, which was to become our home throughout my childhood and theirs for the next 30 years. After the war Dad had resumed his employment with AGE but not long after they had moved into the new home, he decided that it was time to improve his career prospects and commenced an accountancy degree through the Adelaide School of Mines. In 1955 he successfully applied for a position in the accounts department of the Royal Automobile Association and would eventually advance to the role of chief accountant and later secretary.

It wasn't until I was in year six that Dad bought his first car. Up until then we used to go everywhere on the bus. His philosophy had always been never to borrow money for something that depreciated in value. A typical hot summer Saturday would see my sister and I pestering Dad to take us to the beach, which was always Semaphore as it was at the other end of our bus route. For several years January holidays would see us spend a couple of weeks at Port Elliot. This always seemed like a big adventure as getting there meant going by train.

These were also the days when everyone knew their neighbours up, down and both sides of the street. With a couple of exceptions Dad got on well with all of them especially those at our rear who were also a Brethren family. Dad had known them for a long time even before they moved into the area. On the other hand, however, there was the lady next door who was one of those people that made it her business to know everyone else's. She was also constantly 'on the borrow' for grocery and other household items. Often her head would appear over the fence, 'Are you there, Merle?' she would call. Dad, who was a bit of a stirrer would call back, 'We haven't got any!' even before he knew what she wanted. Eventually she took offence to Dad's regular banter and so we had our own version of the Cold War, which would go on for many years before they would finally reconcile.

On the other side lived the local mayor's daughter who was married to a rather taciturn chap. They owned a delightful black Labrador who was never restrained and would wander from house to house where he would always get food and attention. He was regularly at our back door of an evening after dinner hoping for some leftovers. Not only did Dad feed him but he also allowed him to come inside and lie in front of the open fire during winter. Inevitably the owner got wind of what was going on and one cold night there was a knock on the door. 'You got my dog in there?' he said abruptly. Dad's comment after he had gone was: 'At least I now know he can speak!'

Many of the families in our neighbourhood had young children who also went to Linden Park Primary School. In those days we made our own fun, which included marbles, tadpoles and billy carts (or 'bitsers' as we called them). At one stage it seemed everyone in the district had one. Our local billy cart course started at the top end of our side street and Dad was often called upon to act as a 'flag marshall' and indicate when it was all clear to commence the run. There was also footy and cricket in the park across the road where Dad would maintain a pitch for us with regular mowing over the summer. Saturday was always filled with this type of outdoor fun however all the local kids knew never to knock on our door on a Sunday.

Oh how I dreaded Sundays! Sunday was the exception to the bus when Dad would arrange for a taxi to get us from Hazelwood Park to the church at Unley in time for the 11 o'clock service. 'What's the damage?' Dad would say upon arrival at church. 'Five shillings and nine pence', would come the reply. The fare never seemed to change from one year to another. Was there no such thing as inflation in those days!

Dad's active service in the church commenced when he became a Sunday school teacher shortly after returning from the war. He had in his class a young lad named Robert Marshall, who would later go on to play league football for Sturt. They remained friends for many years and Bob and his wife would occasionally be visitors to our home and we to theirs. It was certainly often enough for me to remember that Bob had a finger missing on his right hand, the result of an earlier accident. As many South Australians would know, this is the same Bob Marshall who was killed in the Bali bombings. It was after the bombings that I read that the missing finger enabled Bob's sons to identify his body at the morgue in Bali.

By the late 50s Dad had become the superintendent of the Sunday school, which was held in the afternoon starting at three o'clock. This meant that Mum, who was also a Sunday school teacher, would pack sandwiches for lunch and we would be there all day until finally getting home not much before five o'clock. The only respite from this routine was during school holidays when the Sunday school was also in recess. On some occasions we would also go back for the seven o'clock evening service. As was the Brethren custom, visitors to the 11 o'clock service (or 'morning meeting' as it was known) would normally be expected to bring with them a 'letter of commendation' or, as Dad called it 'a letter of condemnation', from their regular assembly. However, the seven o'clock gospel service was open to all, with people invited in off the street. It was these people, usually referred to as 'outsiders' who would be the focus of the Billy Graham-style preaching which was very prevalent following the American evangelists crusades across the country in 1959. Dad was not a regular preacher then, although he had been in earlier years before determining that preaching was not his forte.

In the late 50s and early 60s, Dad seemed to suffer from his fair share of erroneous scuttlebutt involving someone else from the church. On one occasion, Dad had received a phone call from the senior elder at the church who told him that rumours were circulating that he was a member of the Freemasons Lodge. Not an acceptable pastime! Dad had no real idea how that rumour came about but believed it may have stemmed from him being regularly in the vicinity of the Freemasons building on North Terrace while studying at the nearby School of Mines.

Around the same time he also had to deal with a suggestion that he was operating as an SP bookmaker. No doubt this confusion came about as there was in fact a 'Les Higgins', living locally who was running such a service. Often the phone would ring, 'That you Les?' asked the voice at the end of the line, before Dad placed the handpiece firmly back on the receiver. Nobody in the Brethren either smoked or drank and involvement in any form of gambling would have been equally abhorrent.

Dad was also one of the supervisors of the Friday night boys club, which was held at the church during school terms. He would meet me in the city and we would often go to the old Savoy newsreel theatre in Rundle Street before catching a bus out to Unley. An issue arose after I had invited a few of my schoolmates to come along to the boys club. I can recall concerned parents phoning up and Dad spending considerable time doing his best to explain that the original Plymouth Brethren had split and that we were members of the Open Brethren and not the Exclusive Brethren. I was only ten or 11 at the time and my limited knowledge of the differences didn't extend much beyond the visual aspects, such as the extreme conservative dress standards, the plaited hair of the ladies and girls and the fact that the only family at school I knew to be of the Exclusive order, tended not to socialise with the other classmates. As I grew into my teens, I became aware of other, more significant contrasts. These included the Exclusive order having cultist overtones and rules for almost every aspect of life. Cinemas were banned, likewise television and radio as was eating and mixing with anyone not of the order. I was also aware of a family who had left the Exclusive order, which meant that those members of their immediate family who had remained within the order were given a church directive that they were to have no contact with them.

Although both the Open and Exclusive Brethren had retained some of the original Plymouth Brethren customs, such as the commendation letters and worship modes, these restrictions were never part of my upbringing. In fact, Dad and Mum encouraged my sister and I to invite our school friends home and in a few instances, they also came on holiday with us. But back to the boys club issue! Although Dad had done his best in trying to allay their fears, it was obvious that the concerns were still sufficient for the parents not to allow their sons to become involved. I can clearly remember Dad's words: 'I know you're disappointed but the main thing is you tried.'

In 1961 Dad decided it was finally time to learn to drive. He had no trouble finding people who were prepared to help him. There were relatives, RAA colleagues and church members who were all willing to let him drive their car. Not many sons have memories of their father learning to drive and one incident still remains quite vivid. It was a Friday night and as usual we had been at the boys club. One of the other leaders, who regularly took us home in his 1950-something Morris Minor, suggested that Dad do the driving. We came the short way through Frewville and Glenunga, then after coming up Windsor Road, he went straight over into Sturdee Street without even slowing down, let alone stopping. Just then, another car flew past behind us blaring its horn. Dad looked at his ashen faced passenger in the front seat and said, 'Was that Portrush Road we just crossed over?' Eventually he got his license!

About the same time an opportunity came to buy a four-year-old FE Holden sedan which had been owned by one of the RAA executives. So at 39 years of age, he became the owner of his first car, one which he would subsequently sell to me when I was learning to drive.

By the mid 1970s health problems emerged which would impact his life for the next 20 years. In 1975 when bypass surgery was still relatively new, he underwent a triple graft and required a repeat of the same procedure seven years later. There was also carotid artery surgery in between. It was following this second heart operation that he decided, on medical advice, to retire after 27 years at the

RAA. Until then Dad had lived almost all his life within a kilometre of the Burnside Town Hall so it came as a mild surprise to the rest of the family when he and Mum decided to sell up and move to a unit complex at Glenelg. Downsizing was understandable as his heart problem meant that simple routine tasks around the home had become rather difficult.

In retirement he continued doing voluntary administrative work for several church and Christian organisations and enjoyed reasonable health for many years, however in 1995 his heart condition deteriorated rapidly and he died on 27 July. Dad was well known for his natural wit and humour and I was told he provided much entertainment in the RAA tearoom with his repartee and in particular his mastery of a play on words which would have colleagues in fits of laughter.

His Christian principles determined how he lived his entire adult life both in the workplace, in the home and in his role as a husband and father. His family, work colleagues and church friends all knew him to be a humble and humane person who was also reliable, meticulous and efficient in everything he put his hand to. Thanks for your example, Dad.

Phil Higgins

At the end of 1964 his class teacher wrote: 'Philip has had a disappointing year. He has not found the work easy but with a bit more effort, he could have done much better.' After breezing through primary school around the top end of the class, Phil found high school a whole different challenge where his best efforts were always reserved for the sporting fields rather than the classroom. After leaving school in 1966, he commenced a 26-year career with the Coles organisation, which included store management and

regional management positions in two states. For the last 19 years he has worked as manager of an automotive parts and accessories store in Brisbane where he has lived since 1989. He has been married for 29 years to Nerida, a school teacher and they have two children, Catherine who is also a school teacher and Ben, a Fine Arts student.

His current interests include camping and four-wheel driving activities, which he plans to devote more time to in coming years.

Aussie Battlers

Reginald Joseph HARRISON

(1914–1997)

by Sandra Harrison Mikelsons

My father's story is not that of a famous man, but one of a typical Aussie battler.

Reginald ('Reg') Joseph Harrison was born on 22 June 1917, the seventh of nine children born to father Arthur William Minot Harrison and mother Hannah May Hill.

Arthur was a returned soldier from World War One where he had been a tunneller with the Royal Australian Engineers in France but contracted a disease (unknown) and returned to Australia to civilian life where he was employed as a carpenter, joiner and cabinetmaker until his death at the age of 51 when he was hit by a car at Keswick. Arthur attended Pulteney Grammar School but Hannah had to leave school at the age of 12! She had to help her crippled mother care for her siblings; this taught her homemaking skills which would come into play later in life.

Arthur and Hannah settled in St Peters, where they produced seven of their nine children. One child was tragically killed when a car hit her pram when she was only three years old. My father almost met a horrible fate when his sister put him on a chopping board and attempted to chop off his head with an axe! I'm sure she was most severely dealt with. Amazing that these things happened before anyone had the violent television and movies we have today!

Arthur was a very strict man with strong beliefs in a righteous family, always making meal times very formal occasions with seating on time. Grace was always said at the table and children were seen and not heard – a practice my dad tried to continue when I was a child, but he wasn't very successful! One interesting story Dad would tell from his early days was that when he was a little boy he heard and then saw a big aircraft flying low overhead with five or six escorts (an unusual occurrence for that time). This must have been quite a sight for those days! It turned out to be Sir Ross and Sir Keith Smith flying in from England at the end of their famous flight. Their plane is now in a memorial hangar at the Adelaide Airport.

The family moved to their next home at Clarence Park in 1922. Dad said it was a very eventful moving day as his brother was born in a taxi that night! Dad told of his outings to the cricket at the Adelaide Oval and he remembers the names A. Richardson and V. Richardson being on the teams. He told me that after a match they went to a pub and he was left in charge of the bike while his dad went inside the pub to 'see a man' – hours later his dad staggered out and they had to walk all the way home. Later his frantic mum sent Dad's eldest brother George out to retrieve the bike and his dad's shoes from near the pub. Unfortunately, similar events formed part of Hannah's struggle to raise her family.

Notwithstanding, Arthur always expected children to respect their mother; no forms of gambling were allowed and whenever he could, he would give a shilling or two to kids in the street, much to the detriment of the household budget. Unfortunately alcohol was a weakness and probably was involved in his death when he was hit by a car. It was 24 hours before the family received the news. Arthur tried to be a good father and provider; he took dad for long walks and often they went mushrooming. As a tradesman he did fine work such as parquetry floors in the Bank of NSW on King William Street and shopfront mouldings in various stores in Rundle Street. He also did freelance painting and decorating. These abilities I believe my dad inherited as he could turn his hand to most things at home – we never seemed to employ any outside 'tradies'.

His loss left Hannah with the task of raising eight children alone during the depression years. She struggled stoically and this made a huge impact on my dad who was only nine – he never forgot the lessons of the harsh frugal beginnings. Grandmother did receive some help from Legacy. Footwear and hand-me-down clothes were a normal part of life but they never starved. Food was plain but wholesome and I remember dad being proud of the fact that his teeth were perfect in his old age! The family became self-sufficient, growing their own vegetables and fruit, keeping chickens and ducks, and Dad and his brother George would trap rabbits and sell or exchange them for other household items. Dad even had to share a pair of shoes with his sisters!

A funny story Dad would tell was related to the chores done during the Depression, Uncle George was to procure and maintain the household firewood and each day he would cut some and set the fireplace. He started to become suspicious that someone was stealing their wood, so he set a trap – he drilled a hole in a log, filled it with explosives and plugged the hole again before placing it in a strategic position on the heap. Eventually the log disappeared and one night, a loud bang was heard from a couple of blocks away. It turned out that a house had lost part of its chimney – no more firewood went missing from the Harrison's!

Dad left school in 1931 from necessity and got a job carting shoes at Barlow's for 15 shillings a week! He worked at Barlow's for three years and one summer the English cricket team were in Adelaide playing the infamous bodyline test against Australia. Dad was given the task of periodically running from Barlow's up to the Beehive Corner to get the latest scores, which were displayed on a moving light bulb news display that ran along the facade of the shop veranda, then running back to his work with the news.

Apparently there was such a violent uproar against the Poms that they had to be given police protection when they left Adelaide Oval and were kept under guard at all times for the remainder of their tour here in Adelaide. He bought a bike in 1936 and paid it off at two bob a week. It took two years to repay Super Elliott's but he still had that bike until late in life. My brother Ian inherited it and modernised it with three-speed gears, lights, mudguards and a carrier, and I believe the bike is now in his daughter's possession.

Dad always wanted to do something in the electrical trade and he did some wiring work at the Camden Speedway and later at the Nairne Phillips Radio Engineers until World War Two. He was taught to drive by Jack Filsell who was then just a mechanic but went on to be an owner of Radio Rentals. Dad learnt in Jack's Pontiac but he had a secret longing for Harley Davidson motorbikes – he apparently had a couple of them! I only remember one, with a sidecar – they couldn't have been as pricey as they are today. He used to go rabbiting on the Harley on weekends.

Like so many young men of his day, he was keen to make his mark. The world had gone mad and he saw his chance to get out and see as much of it as he could without having to fund his travels himself, and probably without really contemplating the dangers ahead, so in 1939 he enlisted in the Army. He joined the Royal Australian Engineers as a field engineer (sapper) and served in the 2/3rd Field Company (9th Division), serving in Australia, Great Britain, Egypt, Syria and New Guinea. Dad was a desert rat of Tobruk. One of his experiences he told me about in the Middle East was when he and some of his mates who had been out on patrol laying or removing enemy mines, had to take refuge from a snow storm. They were in a cave along with some Arabs and a donkey and were stranded there for a few days. Unfortunately time and hunger resulted in the demise of the hapless donkey before they eventually managed to dig themselves out!

Another story was when they managed to relieve the British officer's mess (they had been assigned to re-supply labouring duties), of some cases of grog, which they smuggled back to their tent. They hid their booty in a hole under the duckboards of their tent but they never got to enjoy it because they had to break camp and move out before they could dig it up! It's probably there still.

After Tobruk, Dad came back to Australia and he loved to tell us kids that 'he travelled on the *Queen Mary* in convoy with the *Queen Elizabeth*'! He loved to tell us that he had to use his helmet as a pillow, that he had to sleep on the deck and that there were toilet paper rations – three pieces a day – how horrible! He never wanted to go 'cruising' later in life because after experiencing such privations during the war, he had the wrong idea about ship travel.

He was then sent to north Queensland for tropical climate training and amphibious landing training with the Americans. From there he was deployed to the north-east coast of New Guinea where he was to head for the Kokoda Track. As his landing craft was coming ashore at Finschhafen beachhead, Dad, who was carrying the radio on his back, was shot and fell back in to the landing craft. That Japanese soldier actually saved Dad's life because had he stepped out from the craft, he would have drowned due to the weight he was carrying and the fact that the craft was in far too deep water! He was not a strong swimmer and would not have made it to shore. Dad was evacuated back to Australia where he was sent to Daws Road Hospital and where he remained for the rest of World War Two. This turned out to be fortuitous as he met our mother Lorna, who was a nursing assistant there with the AMWAS. Romance blossomed and in June 1945 they were married in Mum's hometown of Sydney.

They settled in Adelaide, living with Dad's mother until dad was discharged from the Army in December 1946. They then moved to Sydney with their first born, Ian. Dad worked for a radio manufacturer, Stromberg Carlssen, but this wasn't going to last long as Dad found it difficult to settle in Sydney. So then the family returned to Adelaide where Dad was to join the Adelaide Electric Supply Company (ETSA). Dad worked at the Hilton workshops as an electrician, installing and maintaining Adelect appliances. In fact, my brother and I would sometimes go with him to the Yorke Peninsula on work trips when he had to follow up on appliances – we thought this was cool, travelling around South Australia 'helping' with his work! Then in the early 1950s he transferred to the consumer engineers branch in the Kelvin Building in North Terrace. Later his department relocated to the corner of Rundle and Pulteney streets – this area has since become a multi-level car park above Hungry Jacks and his department and ETSA moved to Greenhill Road, Eastwood. Dad retired from there in 1977. I have fond memories of the old site at Rundle Street, especially on Christmas Pageant day because the ETSA children were allowed to sit on part of the roof over the footpath and watch the parade. It was great! Also, when I started high school in the city at Adelaide Tech, I was able to hang out with Dad at his work and practice my typing before getting a ride home after school. Dad even organised a second-hand typewriter for me – I thought I was special! He was adept at finding excellent functioning second-hand electrical items – my first sewing machine was a beauty – I made my wedding gown with it! Also, when I got married he got me a perfectly running second-hand fridge, which I had for about ten years!

Over the years Dad tinkered with electrical appliances and made radios – I remember he could always fix our electrical issues and he liked a challenge. There was always a fridge, a stove, washing machine, radio, iron or other electrical appliances in his shed in various stages of repair! We lived in Camden until 1955 and then we moved to Glenunga as Dad had found this new home with a big garden and room for a big shed and he had less travel time to work. One thing I remember from Camden was the swing that Dad made and the gate in the back fence which he also made so our friends could visit easily. Mum wasn't as happy in Glenunga as she was in Camden, mainly because she had left many friends behind. The fact that she didn't drive and we never had a phone until many years later meant that she relied on ringing from telephone booths or taking buses to visit people. We often made our own fun but I remember Dad made us a spinning wheel on top of a dead tree stump, which we had a ball on. When we bugged him for an above-ground pool because he wouldn't take us to the beach often enough, he told us that the only pool we would ever consider having would be an in-ground pool, thinking that would be the end of it. How wrong he was! One day when he came home from work, we children and Mum were digging out the lawn out the back. He was furious but calmed down and with the help of our neighbour, who was a cementing contractor, dug out and made a pool, which we thoroughly enjoyed for many years.

Dad and Mum would sometimes take us on trips to the hills to get mushrooms or to pick blackberries, or to National Park for picnics and to catch tadpoles, and occasionally to the beach. Christmas was always special. Dad would take us to look at the lights beforehand and on the actual day he would cook the roast and Mum would do all the special treats for the table. Family holidays were often to Sydney to see our grandparents – we loved these times. On the surface our lives seemed to be idyllic.

My siblings and I all have memories of our Dad. I remember him as a man who wanted to provide a strong basis for survival. I think he taught us well as my siblings and I have been reasonably successful. We have all had good educations, and have all gone on and become self-sufficient. If we can pass on the lessons we have learnt from him to our children and loved ones then he can rest easy. He wasn't one to be demonstrative with feelings as I believe he found sentimentality to be impractical and he much preferred the practical side of life. Give him tasks and he was a satisfied man. I am not sure but I think he was a changed man after the war and possibly had a degree of post-traumatic stress disorder, which manifested itself more as he grew older. His relationship with Mum was thus affected and, as many people did in those days, the two of them just 'soldiered on', slowly destroying the love they originally had for each other. They did somehow manage to still bring up five children!

In latter years, they seemed to soften towards each other – probably once we were all gone and some of the financial pressures were lifted. They actually had some trips together and enjoyed parts of

Australia and also the United States of America. Unfortunately, once health issues got in the way of being fully able, Dad and Mum slipped back into their animosity towards each other. Dad died suddenly in December 1997 at the age of 80 due to a stroke. After this, Mum sold the house at Glenunga and moved to West Lakes. She always felt some guilt over her relationship with Dad and when she became ill in 1998, she believed she was being punished for his death. We lost Mum in November 2001 at the age of 78 due to multiple myeloma.

I find nowadays that I am more and more like my dad in the practical sense and I thank him for the skills I have learnt, apologise to him for not understanding him more in his life, and forgive him for his shortcomings. However, as I get older and wiser I have a much clearer view of life.

Goodbye Dad – see you one day in the future.

Sandra Harrison Mikelsons

Sandra is the second eldest of five children, all of whom attended Linden Park Primary School from year one to seven. After leaving high school, she followed a clerical path, working as a secretary and typist with the Commonwealth Bank for four years then with a secretarial agency for three years. She married Juris (bank officer) at the age of 18 and at 25 decided to have a complete change of working career and began her general nurse training at the Queen Elizabeth Hospital. This was to be one of the best decisions of her life. She finished her general training, then after a short time completed her Midwifery. After a short break to start a family, she completed her Neonatology Certificate and her Bachelor of Nursing studies. Her career fully focused on the care of sick and premature babies and she is

still working in this area today at the Women's and Children's Hospital in Adelaide. Her husband and her parents always fully supported her career. They were always there to help with her two children and were very proud of her achievements. A career in nursing was also followed by three of her siblings, and the other is an ambulance officer. Her children also have health-related careers, her daughter is a dietitian and her son is a laboratory technician. Her interests are travelling, gardening, theatre and walking for exercise.

Raymond Trevor HASSE

(1923–)

by Judith (Jules) Hasse

Dad was born on 2 September 1923 at St Peters, South Australia with a twin sister, Rita Lurline. Thus 'Jack and Jill' began their lives with their sisters Audrey and Joyce. 'Jack' as he was known, joined the Newstead Methodist Church where he sang twice every Sunday in the church choir. His Sunday school teacher was the father of Reg Roberts, a state table tennis champion. Hence it was he who organised table tennis nights, including a traditional pasty supper! During and after the Depression, the food and friendship offered by the church were not taken for granted. Jack was educated at St Morris Primary School and Adelaide Technical High School, which was then on North Terrace, situated on the third floor of the School of Mines Building. Alongside the school was the Open Air Chinese Gardens Film Theatre, situated beside the School of Arts and Crafts building where Bonython Hall now stands. So, from early on, for Dad, music, family, food, film and later travel and entertainment were important priorities.

Jack joined the Army at Wayville Showgrounds on 21 January 1942 in a batch of 60 of whom he knew 12. His schoolmates included John Hazeal, Brian Addicoat, and Bill Bristow, Keith Shand, Sam Walker, Royston Mayne, Peter Palmer, and Murray Stoddardt. Jack signed Hurtle Dahlenberg's papers for enlistment into the Army and Hurtle signed Jack's papers. This friendship begun at age 18 would remain for 70 years! Jack was posted to Fort Largs, built during World War One, participating in rookie training and gun drill for six weeks. In his words: 'On the beach we had no guns, so four three-inch guns were drawn in the sand to train with. Only two others guarded Adelaide at that time.' Then Jack was posted to Whyalla with the 26 Heavy Anti Aircraft Battery, the 'Whyalla Warriors'!

'Our rate of pay amounted to five shillings per day plus two shillings for the computer specialists,' Dad explained. These men worked with a gadget called The Predictor, which calculated where a plane's position would be, in order to attempt to shoot it down. An old monoplane 'Fairey Battle', hauling a drogue would fly out from Port Pirie for target practice. They managed to hit the drogue once, but were more likely to hit the plane! The British used The Predictor over London but had more chance of hitting the enemy with a barrage of explosions. The 'Whyalla Warriors', should have been renamed 'Dad's Army'!

The first computer-assisted technology arrived at this time. Given an estimate of the speed of the wind and a known speed of the projectile, a forerunner of the computer worked out the timing to trigger an explosion. This explosion had to be within 30 feet of the plane to have an impact. Dad handled the data input. He was always good with figures and later became an accountant, training at night school on his return to Australia.

In Whyalla four 3.7" guns were installed on top of Hummock Hill by BHP who owned the town and exported iron ore to Newcastle. BHP made steel in blast furnaces, manufactured munitions, and built merchant and naval ships like corvettes. Dad explained:

Our temporary camp consisting of tents was located near the Institute alongside the railway from Iron Knob. BHP carried water as ballast from Newcastle and the ships returned loaded with iron ore. When our permanent camp of six galvanized iron huts was completed, we were transported by trucks to the shipyards for each meal using the same menu as was used in the 'single men's quarters' of BHP.

Murray River water had not been connected at this time and recreation ovals were just red dirt and rocks. More guns were protecting Whyalla than Adelaide, showing the perceived importance of munitions and steel in South Australia.

During May 1943, Dad's anti-aircraft battery left Whyalla and travelled by troop train to places they had previously not visited such as Melbourne, Sydney and Brisbane where they stayed until they embarked on the HMAS *Katoomba*. They sailed via Whitsunday Passage and joined a convoy at Townsville eventually arriving at Port Moresby. The AHAA Battery consisting of 470 troop from Tasmania, and 471 troop from South Australia was formed to relieve the personnel of the battery known as the 'Mice of Moresby'. At that stage they were the only batteries to provide resistance to the Japanese bombing. Up to 5000 Allied aircraft were based in the Moresby area. Dad's group pitched tents around the airfield to defend up to 5000 Allied planes.

Living conditions left a lot to be desired. Showers consisted of lathering up and waiting for the tropical downpours to come. Dad's tent got washed away one night and they ended up fishing for their equipment in the dark. Friendships begun at this time were to continue later at home, families frequently meeting until recently. Jack, 'Maud', Brian, Hurtle and their wives laughed over their exploits for the next 70 years, the men marching together each Anzac Day. Jack was involved in an accident off Rona Road on the way up to Kokoda. After viewing an American film screening one night, his truck slipped off the road and flipped over. Dad landed underneath with the tray of the truck an inch from his nose. He ended up in Port Moresby Hospital. Consequently he was flown home to Townsville in an American DC3 with 30 Japanese prisoners of war. The American soldiers' facilities were far superior to those of the Aussies. Members of their unit returned on the *Boschfontein*.

After spending leave with his girlfriend, Joan, who later became his wife, he went back to the front. Dad was in another accident on the way down to Sydney, flung from a lorry, perilously hanging on for dear life with his wrist caught in strapping as the vehicle plunged on around the shoulder of the road. He went to Balkham Hills Hospital for a couple of weeks. Jack was in Adelaide for VP (Victory in the Pacific) Day, described by the Adelaide *Advertiser* on 14 August 1945 as 'a joyous occasion in Adelaide' with 'dancing in the city streets, concert parties and parades by bands'. He was discharged 28 May 1946.

Post war, Dad lost the 'Jack' label and became known as Ray or 'RT', except to his old mates, so I'll refer to Dad as Ray from 1946 onwards. Dad married Joan Bryan in June, with their first daughter Pamela arriving in September the following year. He loved Joan playing the piano and as she was classically trained, Dad was very proud of her. He began playing golf, and enjoyed tennis. Christmas and holidays were spent around friends and relatives and music like singsongs around the piano. Pam, my older sister, loved to play 'Fur Elise' and we enjoyed listening.

Ray and Joan travelled to the farm in the Riverina and beyond; a journey dad believed was worth the investment of time. 'Don't leave for tomorrow what you can do today', was Dad's philosophy. We headed off in 1954 on this journey. I got carsick and the floods in the Murrumbidgee that year were record-breaking. We passed 12 trucks that were bogged and had to decide whether to turn back or row across the river at dusk. The family was wedged into an old utility. We managed to get to Griffith after dusk but couldn't find the farm. Fortuitously word got to Sam and Glad who came in to pick us up and take us to their new farm, which didn't ever live up to their previous farm. This disappointment meant that Sam and

Glad followed the sun and the rivers eventually up to Queensland. The Riverina family became my extended family and our cousins provided experiences Pam and I still treasure.

At home later in Adelaide, television was the new technical miracle. I used to go next door to see my favourite Western at 5.00 pm daily. Mum was exasperated with me in her kitchen. Neatness was next to Godliness in her view. I used to wash my hair over the laundry sink where the soft rainwater tap was. A little lemon juice added to the water kept my hair blonde. It hurt my back and I needed Mum to pour the rinse water through my hair with no hairdryer afterwards to style it.

Mum ruled the kitchen and cooked loin lamb chops, potato and greens frequently. A washing machine reduced the load especially when Mum got tired, having a bad back for years after Pam was born. Dad helped Mum get her driver's licence. Mum made all our clothes and Dad had organised a great deal on the loan he got from War Service to build the house. After many years, they were still to pay off the principle, even with an interest rate of one per cent from the broker, Ewen Waterman (in those days you were friends with the broker!). Ewan had also given them a night's accommodation for their honeymoon at The Australia Hotel in Melbourne.

Prior to the Army, Dad's working life started at Ozone Theatres the day after he left school, aged 16 years. The secretary of Ozone Theatres had requested 'a suitable boy' from Adelaide Technical High School to be a junior clerk. Ray's course had included book-keeping, shorthand and typing and he had a conscientious attitude, so he qualified. He claims he had a company vehicle all his working life – even though in the beginning it was a bicycle on which he scooted round Adelaide delivering cheques. His wage was 25 shillings per week.

Ozone offices were in the CML building, formerly in the Enfield Theatre, Nailsworth. His duties consisted of relieving on the switchboard, filing, and reconciliations. This continued until he joined the Army in January 1942. Ozone was a private company owned by seven brothers namely Sir Ewen, Clyde, Donald, Laurie,

Gordon, Douglas and Keith. They operated theatres in various locations in South Australia. The 'hardtop' sites included Port Adelaide, Semaphore, Alberton, Enfield, Prospect, Goodwood, Murray Bridge, Victor Bridge, Port Pirie, Whyalla and Mt Gambier. In Victoria the Ozone theatres were in Mildura, Redcliffe, Merbein and, Midland (Ararat). In New South Wales they were at Broken Hill, Hillside, Wentworth. The city cinemas were the York, Civic, Majestic, Royal and Tivoli. The Chinese Gardens on North Terrace, alongside The School of Mines, was an open air theatre with deck chairs and Chinese lanterns. It closed about 1938. Jack had used the iron stairs each school recess time leaving from the third floor to play by the Torrens, passing this unique theatre of the Watermans. The Majestic Theatre was committed to live shows prior to 1941. Some of the old performers included Gladys Moncrief, George Wallace, Moe Rene, Will Mahoney, Evie Hayes and Jenny Howard. Zabados and Kellen, Hungarian professional table tennis players, performed on stage at suburban theatres in front of the screens with phosphorous balls, which replaced one of the two nightly films. The Symphony Orchestras and all manner of shows were replaced by organists like Knight Burnett after the war. Many weekly newsletters and the social scene created by a large exciting employer, Ewan Waterman in South Australia, were also to decline.

When Ray came home from war, he went to work at the York, then the Regent Theatre in Rundle Street. Live theatre was subsumed by the cinema, and Hollywood's big stars made entertainment big business. Twentieth Century Fox bought out the Watermans who had installed Cinemascope to attract bigger audiences. The business became Hoyts Ozone. The distribution Australia-wide of American movies saw eventually contracts whereby Australian buyers had a choice of nine out of ten American movies made by Twentieth Century Fox.

Dad became a pioneer in the theatre industry taking a service ethic in catering into the new era, engaging and keeping staff through their loyalty. These included trayboys, manageresses, fundraising personnel, concessionaires, accountants and suppliers, all part of one happy family around the regional circuits including drive-ins and event locations. Generosity and energy were required so my father could be said to have definitely won the peace. I grew up around candy bars and screens and romantic stories fed with chocolates and liquorice all sorts.

My political independence I date from this period but I couldn't voice concerns at home where girls were supposed to be 'seen and not heard'. The Cold War was not a theme discussed in the movies, and when I stumbled upon broadsheets being distributed in front of the Regent Theatre one day, I spoke with the volunteer of this Democratic Socialist paper who told me about the Marshall Islands and French nuclear tests. I went away assuming this revelation was fantasy, but my curiosity shocked me into thinking it through. I later discovered Science Fiction was the only legitimate method to explore the dangerous notion of nuclear tests. School readings from *The Lord of the Flies* made me keen to disappear into my room with a book, reserving Saturdays for tennis and netball with Dad's enthusiastic joy. We'd end the day with fish and chips and I'd sneak a Coke as well. I don't remember talking about sex, politics or religion at home. I was to learn that in earlier years during the Cold War it had been literally against the law to register political dissent.

Dad was to learn the overall operations in Hoyts Ozone. Sir Ewen Waterman asked him what he wanted and Dad replied, 'It seems to me I'm being groomed to become a theatre manager and that's not what I want. I am studying accountancy and that is what I want.' Ewen appointed Dad the accountant of Hoyts in 1946 on a wage of five pounds a week overseeing the catering at 30 theatres from 9 am to 5 pm. Then he supervised concessionaire staff four nights a week, driving to every location and getting behind the counter if need be at intervals if staff were sick or too busy. Chicken Maryland dinners were served in double quick time as I remember. This regime included holidays. Mum resented the isolation and Dad's new passion – golf – which regularly took him away with his male companions!

Dad invented The Ice Cream King. I know. I was the guinea pig with my sister, Pam, seeing the third movie for the night, trying to eat an ice-cream dipped in syrup in a cone in the dark. It ended up with chocolate in our laps every time. It thus got modified and frozen and dipped in nuts, a great idea by Dad. Pamela Joan was born at Enfield and was the eldest by three years. I came in 1950 and social changes were rapid so that there was almost a generation between us as we later came to realise, in priorities and politics. Ironically, our reading and priorities in families and friends have reversed and she's now setting the pace, with far more of an eye for organisation and travel.

There were good days at school and our bunch of friends playing Stonehenge in the bitumen playground at Linden Park was the highlight of uneventful weekdays. I did manage some celebrity by daydreaming on a swing one lunchtime, and some boy for a lark jumped on the end of the seesaw, rocking it high up. I fell off pronto and saw my thigh bone protruding through the skin with a bad break. The teacher lifted me and I remember being out of the sight of other kids, the first priority for all emergencies. Mum saw the ambulance. She was entering the school and someone thrust her into the back with me. Pam was forgotten by everyone and she remembers being upset because she was ignored.

I spent three months swinging with my leg in traction in a vast ward at the Women's and Children's Hospital. Mum fed me, the Italian boy next door got spaghetti and the Aboriginal boy in the next bed with soft bones and no one to visit from the northern Pitjatjantjara lands got visits from Mum as well as a share of our treats. When his broken leg repaired itself, he went out to play – and broke it again! The day Mum and Dad did not visit with a salad for me to eat was the afternoon they ripped off the plaster cast, but the surgeon had forgotten to insulate the skin from the hot plaster. It left my whole leg with raw, painful skin. In addition I suffered a curved spine that an X-ray showed had permanently lifted one hip. Dancing and gymnastics have been lopsided ever since.

I loved exercise but I was never in a sports team at Linden Park Primary School, preferring instead to play tennis at Beaumont

Tennis Club where Dad, in summer, spent a lot of time encouraging me so I felt strong and quietly confident.

In America, television had arrived. In Australia it came in 1956. This resonated and hit the movie industry necessitating the closure of some theatres and staff reductions. Ray was offered the opportunity to move interstate but declined on the basis of his daughters' secondary education. Mum and Dad were to move to Melbourne in 1969 (after Pam was married) and I had a scholarship on $45 a week go to Monash to train as a secondary teacher. Ray accepted a transfer to manage Victorian, South Australian and Tasmanian concessionaires, with his offices at MidCity Cinema in Bourke Street. The big time! I would attend premieres and meet stars that were at events that Ray catered for. On these occasions we dined with new executives who valued real estate, not always the movie families and audiences that lived and breathed the industry and the making of films. Later in Melbourne I marketed Australian films like 'Dot and the Kangaroo' to school groups and saw the life of a bigger cosmopolitan city. Ray was the secretary of the Motion Picture Industry Provident Fund, which was formed to assist all the employees of the industry with any financial problems. It ran the Movie Ball each year and was a grand affair with the ladies in their element in glamorous gowns and fashion parades down the mall, beauty queens and royal visitors such as the Duke and Duchess of Bedford, escorted by Ray and Joan! During the Korean War, Watermans arranged collections from theatre patrons who donated for the troops. Ray was responsible for this.

In retirement Dad was treasurer of the Friends of the Aldinga Scrub, pioneers in vegetation management south of Adelaide and reinvented himself at this time, having built his third house above the esplanade of the Aldinga Beach. Preservation of the environment became my parent's passion with Mum's paintings of natural landscapes and colours occupying her time. Mum and Dad propagated and repaired plants, hosting dedicated neighbours at their home always with a smile and a laugh. Mum was part of the artists group who put the crown on Willunga Hill for the Tour Down

Under. Frequent gatherings had my parents camping out in the Flinders, visiting and receiving knowledge from environmentalists like Aboriginal representatives from the Coorong and the Tiwi Islands of the Northern Territory. They were intrepid travellers into Arnhem Land, The Twin River Gorge and Dad had his first close encounter with a freshwater crocodile sharing their camp one morning along the creek while he was 'relieving himself'. 'I don't know who got more of a shock! The croc or me?' Dad said.

Stories still exist and will persist of a legendary good guy, a stalwart of good grace and good manners, my father. Simple but heartfelt gestures and consistent loving tributes to those he befriends are attributes he maintains every single day. Dad has emotional generosity to spare. I recall my days at his side in the numerous picture theatres he frequented. Now his Pioneer Gold Pass enables him and Mum to go to the pictures and this keeps them abreast of the times. Such is the recognition of Dad's services to the film industry, and his many mates around Adelaide and Australia.

Judith (Jules) Hasse

I seem to be returning to my 12-year-old mindset of Year Seven vintage. My identity, values and thinking I can remember beginning at this age, knowing self-consciously I'm me. Life in Adelaide in 1962 was expanding and so was I. No preconceived ideas … I could quietly just try it on. Socially naive we headed for high school ill prepared for competition but I was curious and felt that I had to get to Matriculation, and maths and science should be included. My role models were girls in sport and my heroes came from books … all male. Then, in addition, girls in theatre and in music and with academic ambitions appeared at our all-girls school.

So it led to my evolution to be the best I could be: to teach at the best school system for adolescents developed in Darwin; a producer of one of the best original theatre companies that was brave and local in Adelaide; with themes of historical significance and the environment and politics and the personal power of the imagination. I learnt to be in a team focused on clear deadlines and trust. Then finances and real fears surfaced overseas. I was vulnerable and I could have disappeared in a blink of an eye. I returned to Australia sick and needed to refocus, once again retiring to Mum and Dad's home for care and recuperation. The Northern Territory beckoned. Back to teaching and I fell into a relationship of a lifetime, two children and a creative, scary but adventurous audiovisual business following my partner's ethic of excellence and dedication.

I now return to my roots and find what my intuition and research had shown all along: that security is a mirage; that our endeavours towards a nurturing and new green economy have been sabotaged, and it's back to the drawing board. We need help in this and my multicultural insights and music give me energy and personal hope for the renewal of our physical world. However, it's wonderful that people emerge once again to help resurrect my optimism, that and my love for my family. It's back to the beginning to create a long-term lifestyle that is sustainable. History is one technique to continue looking back in order to open paths to the future.

Wakefield Press is an independent publishing and
distribution company based in Adelaide, South Australia.
We love good stories and publish beautiful books.
To see our full range of books, please visit our website at
www.wakefieldpress.com.au
where all titles are available for purchase.

Find us!

Twitter: www.twitter.com/wakefieldpress
Facebook: www.facebook.com/wakefield.press
Instagram: instagram.com/wakefieldpress